ESTHER

ALSO BY JULIE WHEELWRIGHT

Amazons and Military Maids:
Women Who Dressed as Men in Pursuit of Life, Liberty and Happiness

The Fatal Lover: Mata Hari and the Myth of Women in Espionage

Esther

THE REMARKABLE TRUE STORY OF
ESTHER WHEELWRIGHT
PURITAN CHILD, NATIVE DAUGHTER, MOTHER SUPERIOR

JULIE WHEELWRIGHT

HarperCollins*PublishersLtd*

Esther
Copyright © 2011 by Julie Wheelwright.
All rights reserved.

Published by HarperCollins Publishers Ltd

First Edition

HarperCollins books may be purchased for educational, business, or sales promotional use through our Special Markets Department.

HarperCollins Publishers Ltd
2 Bloor Street East, 20th Floor
Toronto, Ontario, Canada
M4W 1A8

www.harpercollins.ca

Library and Archives Canada Cataloguing in Publication information is available upon request

ISBN 978-0-00-200723-8

Printed and bound in the United States
9 8 7 6 5 4 3 2 1

For Thames and Isis Menteth Wheelwright
And for my parents, David and Tish Wheelwright

CONTENTS

*T*HROUGHOUT THIS BOOK, I HAVE USED THE TERMS that most accurately describe the peoples to which I am referring without being anachronistic. Wherever possible, I have referred to the Abenakis of Maine and Québec, members of the Wabanaki Confederacy, by their tribal name. "Abenaki" is a linguistic and geographic grouping. However, when referring to larger groups of aboriginal peoples, I have used the term "Indian," since this was in common use in the period when the book is set.

Several places that are relevant to Esther's story have been known by more than one name. The city from which Reverend John Wheelwright was exiled was Boston, the capital of the Commonwealth of Massachusetts and historical centre of the colony of New England. Esther was born in Wells, the farthest outpost of Maine, which became a state in 1820. On the other side of the unpatrolled border lay New France, also known as Canada, a colony extending from the St. Lawrence River to the Great Lakes and down into what is now the American Midwest. In 1759, the British conquered

New France, using the name Québec for the colony north of the St. Lawrence and the name Canada for the rest of the territory. I have referred to the city throughout as Québec, since Esther Wheelwright inhabited it long before the founding of the province, or Lower Canada, in 1791.

There is documentary evidence that Esther lived in at least two Jesuit missions within the territory of New France. The first was at Norridgewock, located on the Kennebec River and known to the French as Nanrantsouak. The second was at St. François, or Odanak, and is referred to by a variety of other names, including Seigneurie de la Rivière Saint-François, Seigneurie de Joseph Crevier, Mission Saint-François, Saint-François-de-Sales, and Municipalité de Saint-François-du-Lac. For the sake of clarity, I have always called this mission either St. François or Odanak.

ESTHER

As MY SYRIAN CABBIE, AHMED, WEAVES HIS WAY through the molasses of Friday afternoon traffic, his radio hisses out, "*Cinquante-trois, cinquante-trois*" (Fifty-three, fifty three). He pulls into Belmont Cemetery for an impromptu detour on the way to Québec City's Jean Lesage International Airport. My plane leaves for Montréal in just over an hour, and if I miss my connection to Heathrow, I'm sunk. But Ahmed has assured me I have time for this diversion.

I check my watch. In the distance, a mower thrashes across the bright green lawn, sending up a perfume of freshly cut grass and raw petrol. I look down at the rough pencil-drawn map of the cemetery moistening between my fingers. When we arrive at the gates, I see the vast expanse and realize that this sketch is the thinnest of guides; there are thousands of headstones to search, a daunting task.

I climb out of my seat and ask a woman walking her dog for directions to the plot I'm looking for. She furrows her brow and gives an indifferent heave of her shoulders. "*C'est fermez aujourd'hui,*" she says, gesturing at the cemetery gates. I call myself an idiot under my breath, cursing myself for not having looked up the opening hours.

But Ahmed isn't so easily dissuaded. He flags down the young man on the insanely loud mower and, after a lot of hand gestures, convinces him to allow us inside even though it's past the four o'clock closing time. The cemetery's big enough that I need to climb back into the taxi. I check my watch: sixty-five minutes to check-in.

Once inside, we crawl down several small streets as I tick off the family names on the headstones we pass—Richard, Berger, Le Clerk, Vincent, Lesande. No sign of the Ursulines.

Ahmed leans over to me. "What exactly was the name again?"

"Wheelwright." I spell it out, since it's a hard one for non-English-speakers. "But she's buried with the other Ursuline nuns. The sister at the convent who told me about this said she was buried near a big cross." I suddenly realize how absurd this sounds. It's a cemetery, and of course it's full of crosses. I consult the map yet again. "Maybe she meant a mausoleum?"

Ahmed catches me looking at my watch. He waves a hand languidly, smiling. "Don't worry, we have time." I'm not convinced and have visions of spending the night at Jean Lesage. I feel a pang, missing my two daughters, now fast asleep across the globe in their London beds.

I sound off more names, hoping this will be worth it. "Soldat Tanguay."

"Tanguay?" Now Ahmed's doing it too. "It should be here."

But it's not. "Simone, Vaudrie. Shit." Fifty-five minutes to check-in.

Then, "Ah, there? Where it says 'Soeur'?" This is only a hunch, since senior Ursuline nuns like the one I was seeking were called *mère*, not *soeur*.

Ahmed stops the car, walks and then sprints towards a little signpost with directions pointing in black lettering to rue Navarre, the one we need. "*C'est ici,*" he says. Joy and relief flood over me.

But when we reach the end of the road, the Ursulines' collective resting place is nowhere to be found. My relief evaporates in an instant. It's another false lead. I can't help glancing at my watch: forty-five minutes to check-in. The remains of my ancestor Esther Wheelwright, originally laid in the convent's crypt, were transferred to this city cemetery when the nuns were asked to reinter their dead in 1996. Health and safety extending even beyond the grave.

I'm now stalking through the cemetery, my fine linen dress clinging to my back as sweat forms a rivulet down my spine. I'm weary of searching for this relative of mine, who remains elusive even when I feel I am within touching distance of her very bones. I'd pray, but I'm too long out of practice.

Ahmed approaches me with his own scrap of paper and a pen. "Can you write her name here?" he asks.

I spell out the words: La Mère de l'Enfant Jésus. And then: Esther Wheelwright. And finally: Mère Esther Marie-Joseph de l'Enfant Jésus. Take your pick.

More scrambling with no results. I sigh loudly and rest my hands on my hips. "We're really going to have to give up now." I am close to tears, my cheeks hot with sun and frustration, the linen dress shot to buggery.

But Ahmed stops wandering through the remains of Québec's dead and holds up a hand. If he really has found it, I will kiss him, my moustachioed knight of the cemetery. He makes one last foray among the headstones.

I turn on my tape recorder, intent on capturing the moment. I begin musing on the complexities of historical research: "The thing about trying to recover someone's biographical details is that it can turn into an obsession . . ."

❦

The story of Esther Wheelwright, a girl taken captive by Indians in 1703, when she was only seven years old, had always been a puzzling and maddeningly vague one in my family. Esther was the great-granddaughter of the larger-than-life John Wheelwright, a fire-and-brimstone Puritan preacher who was immortalized by the novelist John Irving in *A Prayer for Owen Meany*. But I fell in love with Esther's story because it spoke to me more directly. There was just enough flesh on the bones to let me imagine her character, her adventurous early life in a wigwam deep in the forest and her parents' repeated attempts to bring her back home. Her rebel's will of iron was something I admired.

The story also resonated with my mother, who was severed from her own family in 1940, after the fall of France. My mother's father, Major Charles Ball, thought the German military could successfully invade Britain, and as a precaution, he sent his daughter, Tish, then aged seven, and his son, my uncle Peter, on a passenger ship across the Atlantic to live with business contacts in Toronto. Once there, my mother, who in England had been sent to weekly boarding school at the age of five, at last experienced full-time family life. She attended a local school, where she was feted as a "war guest," and loved her adopted family. At the age of twelve, she was sent back to England. But her mother seemed a stranger after such a long separation, and she never settled there.

I was always haunted by my mother's story of that terrible rupture and its powerful echoes of Esther's life. My mother's experience was fused with my fascination for my eighteenth-century ancestor. Her story gave me insight into Esther's motivations, her character and her ability to survive. When I grew up to become a writer and historian, I knew where to look for documents and how to piece together the scraps of Esther's life, and my appetite was whetted further when my uncle Peter died and left my parents a file of family trees and other bits and pieces of family history. But always, the emotional thread belonged to my mother.

My search for Esther would take me several years, through the birth of my own two children, but it all began in earnest with a trip to Boston.

PART I
Life on the Borderland

CHAPTER I

The Impetus

*I*T IS FEBRUARY IN BOSTON AND THE SIDEWALKS along Boylston Street are streaky with sun-warmed slush, the air sharp. I arrive at the Massachusetts Historical Society, housed in a building designed by my relative Edmund "Ned" March Wheelwright, to trawl through the Wheelwright Family Papers. Once I've shed my heavy winter coat and boots, a young woman ushers me down a corridor hung with portraits of tight-lipped Boston patriarchs and their demure wives to the deep green calm of the reading room.

There's a file box from the collection already waiting for me. Ned was a direct descendant of the family rebel, Reverend John Wheelwright, a Puritan preacher who fled Lincolnshire with his wife, children and followers for the colonial settlement of Boston in 1636. Ned was best known as Boston's first city architect, the designer of the Longfellow Bridge, the Boston Police Station and the Boston Fire Department. He was also a keen family historian, a collector of what he termed "Wheelwrightisms" and the author of

A Frontier Family, published by the Colonial Society of Massachusetts in 1894.

I get a shiver of connection as I open the first box of papers compiled by Ned more than a century ago. His fascination with the Wheelwrights began when, as a young man, he made a trip to England, where he met several relatives and later corresponded with them about their shared ancestry. This first box contains his carefully written notes on all the births, deaths and marriages of several generations of Wheelwrights, including Esther, my childhood heroine.

I read through Ned's yellowing letters, full of antiquated turns of phrase and random thoughts on our mutual ancestors. I've left my laptop in London but make do scribbling notes on anything related to Esther and probably a lot that is not. In the hushed room, readers shuffle up the aisles with their boxes. A giant clock slices off the minutes.

Then I realize from the society's catalogue of its holdings that a portrait of Esther is hanging just upstairs. I inquire at the desk, and with brisk American efficiency, I'm soon guided up a grand cascade of stairs into a turreted room to meet Anne Bentley, the curator of art. Her hands encased in pristine white gloves, she lifts the gilt-framed portrait of Esther Wheelwright onto an enormous oak table for my inspection. Anne tells me that it once hung in the hallway here, and that she would glance up at Esther's warm but solemn face as she arrived at and left her office each day.

I look at a small oval face framed so tightly within a bright wimple that everything else, even her eyebrows, is obscured. Across her midriff is a black space where her hands would meet if they weren't tucked modestly into her voluminous black robes. The resemblance to my father is unmistakable: the long, straight nose; the high, smooth cheekbones; the pert chin; and a serene expression that only hints at a smile on the corners of her mouth. Despite the Mona Lisa quality of her gaze, I like to think that she was warm, that she would approve of my quest to find out who she was. I spend a long few moments lingering, and I sense Anne smiling in a shared appreciation.

I continue to study the face of this powerful, maternal presence who survived abduction, war, near-starvation, epidemics, sieges and estrangement and still rose to the highest position available to an eighteenth-century woman. Esther was exceptional, one of the few Wheelwright women who left behind a record of her life, and now I'm more determined than ever to make use of this rare birthright.

CHAPTER 2

The Wheelwrights of Wells

*I*N EVERY FAMILY, THE GREATEST LEGACY IS ITS HISTORY. Even if every silver spoon, photograph and property deed has vanished, the narratives remain. For Esther Wheelwright, the enduring family story—and the one that casts the longest shadow over her life—was that of her great-grandfather, Reverend John Wheelwright. This man, who died at the age of eighty-seven, less than two decades before Esther's birth, was the Wheelwrights' founding father, a patriarch who passed down to his great-granddaughter his unwavering self-belief, his deep religious conviction and his sense of clear moral purpose. Reverend Wheelwright was our crossing ancestor; he fled religious persecution in Lincolnshire for Boston, where he and his followers hoped to realize a true reformation.

Esther would inherit what one Wheelwright historian has described as Reverend John's tendency towards "contrariness and independent thinking."[1] Born in Lincolnshire in 1592 to a prosperous yeoman and his wife, John was raised in a family sympathetic to the new Puritan ideas. After his father's death, he attended that "nursery of Puritanism" that was Sidney Sussex College, Cambridge, graduating in 1618.[2] Studying for his divinity degree, he gained a reputation as a talented but ruthless athlete. Among those he outscored at football, where opponents regularly kicked and punched each other bloody, was the young Oliver Cromwell, who entered the college in 1616. The future military leader confessed to being "more afraid of meeting Wheelwright at football than of meeting any army since in the field for I was infallibly sure of being tripped up by him."[3]

But if John dominated as an athlete, he failed as a diplomat. He was banned from preaching in public in 1632 after rejecting the orthodox services at his church in Bilsby, Lincolnshire. He had refused to take part in any liturgical ritual that smacked of Catholicism, such as wearing a surplice, using altar rails or displaying crosses at baptisms.[4] This reputation as a firebrand followed him to Boston, where he moved in 1636 with his wife, Mary Hutchinson, his son Samuel and four other children. Mary's brother William—with his wife, Anne Hutchinson, and their children—had immigrated two years earlier. The Wheelwright brood moved into the Hutchinsons' recently built home to begin their new life.

Boston should have been for the Wheelwrights that "city on a hill" envisioned by Governor John Winthrop. But within months, Reverend John was being accused of heresy and threatened with expulsion from the Massachusetts Bay Colony. He had intemperately preached to his congregation at Mount Wollaston (now Quincy, on the outskirts of Boston) that their religious leaders were in league with the devil. Any true believer, he railed from the pulpit, could interpret the Bible and form his own "covenant of grace," or contract with God. Who needed ministers? On that Sunday, John insulted Boston's council of elders and single-handedly divided opinion so deeply that the warring camps of new and old Puritans threatened to tear the colony apart.[5]

Reverend John and his fellow believer, his sister-in-law Anne Hutchinson (an early advocate of women's rights to free speech and public office), were tried in 1637. When both refused to repent their beliefs, they were exiled. The Hutchinsons left for Rhode Island, while Reverend John sailed north from Boston to the Piscataqua Falls, in New Hampshire, with his family and a handful of followers. He seems to have established good relations with the aboriginal people there, purchasing land from the local sagamores, or sachems, the Abenaki leaders. He founded the town of Exeter on "tracts of natural meadow" and "marshes bordering upon the tidewater."[6]

The families worked hard to clear farms from the wilderness and build a new meetinghouse, where Reverend John served as pastor. But four years later, in 1641, the Massachusetts Bay Colony took over New Hampshire, and once again, John Wheelwright and his family were forced into exile. The New Puritans repacked their humble belongings and sailed up the Atlantic coast. They landed in Maine, then regarded as *terra incognita* and populated by dubious characters described by the nineteenth-century historian Edward Bourne as "adventurers coming hither to take advantage of what might turn up . . . Some of them were, perhaps, outlaws, driven from the mother country for their crimes."[7]

The Wheelwrights were part of a new breed of "gentleman adventurers," who brought law and order to the frontier. John purchased four hundred acres of land that extended from east of what became the town of Wells to the Ogunquit River and then down to the sea.[8] Although John would remain for only four years, Esther's grandfather Samuel and her great-uncles, Thomas and William, settled here, becoming politicians, merchants, farmers and officers;

they built sawmills, traded with the Indians, opened a public house, ran the courts, were given the best pews in the new church, had large families and prospered.

As the Wheelwrights uprooted trees and rocks to build their new northern home, Reverend John's political star rose again. His expulsion was revoked (after he apologized for insulting the Boston elders), and in late 1655 or 1656, he was made commissioner to England for the colonies. In London he met with his old friend Oliver Cromwell and lobbied for the colonies' interests before the Lord Protector's death in 1658. John returned to New England in 1662 to take up a position as pastor in Salisbury, New Hampshire. He died there in 1679 and was buried in King's Chapel, Boston.[9]

Although Esther Wheelwright's grandfather Samuel fled Boston with his parents as a young child, Reverend John insisted that his son be educated in the family homeland. Indeed, Esther might have been raised an English child if the civil war had not forced her grandfather to flee back to Maine in. Once back in Wells, Samuel began clearing the two hundred acres of land John had deeded to him. His elder half-brother, Thomas, was already serving as the local magistrate, and Samuel would soon follow him into law. In 1663 Samuel married Esther Houchin, and Esther's father, John, was born a year later. Samuel was eventually appointed a magistrate of Wells, then represented the town and York at the General Court. In 1681, he was named the provincial councillor (equivalent to governor of the state) and made responsible for defending the settlement against its enemies.[10]

This proved all-consuming. As the English settlers encroached farther into Indian lands during the late seventeenth century, the Native peoples began to fight back, often forming alliances with the French colonial government. The Natives, largely Algonquin people, were mostly Catholic converts who had been driven to New France from their ancestral homelands through war and European diseases such as smallpox, to which they had no immunity. Because fewer white people died from these epidemics, the French Jesuit missionaries seemed to offer a spiritual protection that was welcomed by many Algonquins. These charismatic French priests were effective missionaries who, as one Jesuit brother explained, would endure any privation to spread God's word among the "savages":

> To make a Christian out of a Barbarian is not the work of a day . . . A great step is gained when one has learned to know those with whom he has to deal; has penetrated their thoughts; has adapted himself to their language, their customs and their manner of living; and when necessary, has been a Barbarian with them, in order to win them over to Jesus Christ.[11]

The Puritan ministers, by contrast, expected their converts to settle in towns and turn from hunters into farmers, animists into Protestants. They were no competition for the French missionaries, who prayed with their Indian converts; translated the Bible from Latin into indigenous languages (which they spoke fluently); built churches and schools; shared their food, medicines and knowledge. When war between England and France erupted in the late seventeenth century, the French were already allied to several powerful Indian nations with hundreds of expert warriors.

If Reverend John had envisioned New England as a haven where Puritanism would flourish, that dream for his heirs was shattered by almost continuous warfare. Tensions between the colonists and the Natives erupted in 1675, when the Wampanoag leader Metacom—King Philip to the English—took revenge for a series of murders by conducting raids along the New England border; the English retaliated, burning villages and killing warriors, women and children. The war, according to the American historian Alan Taylor, was the bloodiest conflict in New England's history.[12]

Esther's father was only eleven years old during King Philip's War, but he lived through its terrible aftermath. The death toll among the Native peoples was huge: about three thousand, a quarter of the population, were killed in southern New England. The survivors took refuge with the Abenakis along the borderlands between the colonies and New France. In a long series of conflicts between 1688 and 1763, the refugees and their descendants guided French raids, repeatedly reducing the English frontier settlements to heaps of smouldering ruins.[13] Wells was attacked in 1691, one incident among dozens that marked the beginning of Reverend Cotton Mather's *Decennium Luctuosum*—decade of grief. In a summer raid on Wells, French and Indian warriors killed two men and took another captive before torching houses and barns; this coastal outpost became the absolute frontier and the final buffer against New France.

As the eldest Wheelwright son, John followed his father into the local militia. Samuel was a colonel, and John was commissioned as a lieutenant "in early manhood." The younger Wheelwright was remembered locally, according to the historian Edward Bourne, as "the bulwark of Maine against the attacks of its enemies," both a "man of war and a host . . . sent into the world by Providence to assist in protecting the new settlement against the assaults of the French and Indians."[14] In 1688, he married Mary Snell, the daughter of a local sea captain, and began his own family, applying his military vigour to both his community service and his religious devotion. He rose in the militia's ranks to captain, then major and finally colonel.

Having inherited his famous grandfather's piety and strong Puritan values, John served for four decades as a judge, a town clerk and a councillor of the province (equivalent to a senator), living up to the family motto, "*Spectemur Agendo*," or "Let us be judged by our actions."[15] But however justified the actions of the Wheelwrights *père et fils*, they faced formidable enemies who were expertly trained, with a superior knowledge of the wilderness and a powerful desire for revenge. After the January attack on Wells, nearby York was struck in early 1692, adding another terrible story to the growing volume of cautionary tales Esther would learn as a child.

Just seven miles to the south, a day's ride along the shoreline, York was the site of the Candlemas Raid in late January. As a blizzard descended on the twenty-fifth, the hard-pressed sachem Madockawando led his warriors to seize a garrison and then attack ten houses lying on the outskirts of town. Within hours, forty-eight settlers had been killed, a handful wounded and many more marched through the driving snow and freezing temperatures into captivity. Reverend Shubael Dummer, a friend of the Wheelwrights, was shot from his horse, then "barbarously murthered, stript naked, cut & mangled."[16] Three of John Wheelwright's female relations were among the captives.

That day, Esther's parents had most likely been visiting John's cousin Mary Plaisted. On the Wheelwrights' homeward journey, they learned from a passing traveller that warriors had carried Mary Plaisted, along with her daughters from a previous marriage, eleven-year-old Mary and seven-year-old Esther, away from their farmhouse at Cider Hill.[17] That night, two Abenaki warriors arrived in Wells bearing a white flag of truce and offering to ransom the prisoners, who were being marched to the settlement of Sagadahoc (now Portland), almost ninety miles north. When a sum was negotiated in mid-February, however, James Plaisted, Mary's husband, was unable to pay it, so his wife and stepdaughters joined other captives in a long, perilous march to New France, where they would be sold into domestic service. The raid was a warning to the people of Wells, who had repeatedly broken their treaties with the Natives, that they were not immune to attack.[18]

In early June of 1692, the war struck right at the very heart of the Wheelwrights' home when Abenaki and French forces led a seaborne raid on Wells. After three days of exchanging gunfire with the local militia, the French commander, named La Brognière, assumed the villagers were prepared to surrender. In victory he shouted across to Lieutenant Joseph Storer at the garrison, the settlement's main defence post, that his men would return to enslave Captain Wheelwright and his wife for the Abenakis. La Brognière was killed soon afterwards, but neither side forgot the threat. After the raid, John Wheelwright served with Major James Converse, the commander-in-chief of Maine's forces, to prevent the prophecy coming true, scouring the woods for warriors on a trip that lasted several weeks.[19] But rather than seeking their revenge, the leaders—Madockawando and his fellow sachem Edgeremet—urged their allies to sue for peace with the English.[20] Without a truce, everyone faced starvation because crops were routinely burned during raids and the fear of capture or death prevented settlers from gathering the harvest during late summer.

These border wars rumbled on for the following decade, but the Wheelwrights nevertheless put down ever-deeper roots in Wells. During a period of relative peace, Esther's grandfather Samuel died from "dropsy and black jaundice" (usually carried by rats), and was buried in the town cemetery on May 13, 1700. Although English-born, Samuel had risen to become a member of the Massachusetts

Assembly and a friend of many influential founders of Boston, including the diarist and judge Samuel Sewall, who noted on May 15, 1700, that "most gentlemen" were out of town to attend the funeral of this long-serving and popular councillor.[21] There was no meetinghouse in which to hold the funeral, however, because the First Church of Christ (Congregational) was still being rebuilt after the last raid.

⚜

When it was finished, the first order of business for the new church, a tiny space of only thirty square feet with no doors or windows, was a baptism. On November 9, 1701, Esther Wheelwright was admitted into the community, along with her siblings, Samuel, Hannah, Jeremiah and Elizabeth.[22] Esther was a middle child, born on March 31, 1696, less than two years after her sister Hannah and a year before her brother Jeremiah. At Esther's baptism, the Wheelwright clan included her father and her pregnant mother, Mary Snell; her recently widowed grandmother, Esther Houchin Wheelwright; her aunts and uncles; her siblings; and two servants, Thomas Wormwood and Elizabeth Goodale. There were other relatives in the close-knit congregation, including the Storers, who had been among Reverend John Wheelwright's original followers from Lincolnshire.[23]

By the time of her baptism, Esther had a delicate oval face, a small snubbed nose, hooded eyes and full lips, perhaps leading her parents to hope that she was destined for a good marriage among the local merchants. From an early age, she displayed a keen intelligence and a stubborn streak born from standing her ground against her siblings.

But Esther's lively spirit, growing body and quick mind were forced into submission during the long weekly church services.

Under John's watchful eye, religion dominated the Wheelwrights' lives. The Sabbath stretched from Saturday evening, when John would lead a family service from the Bay Bible, to Sunday night. On Sunday mornings, the family walked to the meetinghouse in a procession with John at the head, the servants and children trailing behind.

Even on the Sabbath, the men were armed against possible attacks from the enemy or wild animals. Once inside the meeting-house, they left their weapons at the door, and each family took its designated pew (chosen by committee and paid for in cash), with women and young children on one side and men on the other.

In the plain, unheated building, the villagers would gather for an all-day service led by the Harvard-educated Reverend Samuel Emery, who timed his two-hour sermon with an hourglass. The congregation would sing psalms and read from orthodox biblical texts while young children such as Esther and Jeremiah attempted to suppress their boredom. If the girls itched at their stays (an early corset) or the boys blew spitballs, a tithingman "equipped with a long staff, heavily knobbed at one end" would punish them. He would also pitilessly rap the heads of "too sleepy men and too wide-awake boys."[24] Young children were regarded as animals to be domesticated, especially on the Sabbath.

Even after the service, Sabbath rules were still in force. Esther's mother was forbidden to kiss or cuddle the children, her father remained unshaven, games were banned, the beds were left unmade and the supper was cold. On Sabbath night, the family would review the sermon they had heard that day; a pious girl like Esther might even have taken notes. Children were also encouraged to develop their own private habits of prayer and mediation.[25] Since Wells had no school, skills such as reading, writing and simple arithmetic—so vital in a small community—were passed on by parents and older children.

Puritan children like Esther were raised to be vigilant for signs of their own sinfulness and could never forget that whatever befell them, God ordered the universe and his will must be obeyed. Around the hearth and dinner table, Esther would have heard stories of Reverend John's fight against the Anglican Church and the notorious Star Chamber (a secret English law court with no right of appeal, where cases of political libel and treason were heard). In Boston, her great-grandfather had demanded the right to free speech and preached the radical idea that ordinary citizens could commune directly with God. He had been forced into exile after supporting Esther's great-aunt Anne Hutchinson, who believed passionately in a woman's right to interpret the Bible, to act as a religious prophet and to participate in the Church.

All these stories were Esther's heady legacy. In the tiny frontier settlement where she grew up, the Wheelwright men were local power-brokers—leaders in the meetinghouse, the militia and the local government. In her blood flowed Reverend John's strength of character and his blind ambition. These were the gifts that would, in the greatest and most terrible irony, lead Esther away from her parents and into Catholic hands.

CHAPTER 3

Esther's Beginnings

*G*REG AND HIS PARTNER, MIKE, ARE MY CHARMING
hosts at the Ogunquit Beach Inn, a stone's throw from
Wells in the resort community of Ogunquit. It's taken me a year
to carve out another few weeks to continue my search for Esther
Wheelwright, and this time I've enlisted the support of my friend
George and his partner, William, both historians from New Jersey.
To accommodate them, I searched online for "gay bed and break-
fasts," and that's how I found the Ogunquit Beach Inn. I'm sure my
Puritan relatives would be rolling in their collective graves at the
inn's listing for the Naughty Pine Room or the town's annual Miss
Gay Ogunquit Pageant, not to mention the free HIV testing at the
Frannie Peabody Center.

But I am delighted with my accommodation in the Green
Room, where I can hear the ocean. The other guests (I'm the only
woman) smile politely as they pass me on the stairs on the way down
to breakfast. I am charmed by the 1920s Craftsman cottage, and by
Mike's freshly baked blueberry muffins and herbal teas.

Slumped in an overstuffed armchair one night after a long run, Greg, a local policeman who patrols the town's streets on a mountain bike, asks why I've chosen to write about Esther and spend my vacation from single-motherhood across the Atlantic in the local archives in Wells, tracing this long-dead ancestor.

This is not an easy question. But biographers often feel this inexpressible need to do what the British biographer Alison Weir has described as "ocular history," literally retracing their subject's footsteps hoping to find some vestige of his or her essence en route. In Wells, there are remnants of buildings that date from the eighteenth century, as well as plenty of Wheelwright headstones in the Ocean View Cemetery, and much of the landscape is unchanged.

The Puritans are not easy to grasp for modern atheists who crave rational psychological explanations for human behaviour, but I explain to Greg that I want to uncover whatever has survived of their legacy since Esther's abduction in 1703. In this way, I can learn about the people she came from and what she lost.

Finally, I tell him in the gathering twilight, "I wanted to see Wells for myself, even a twenty-first-century version of it."

"Did you find what you were looking for?" asks Greg, leaning forward, expecting an answer. "Is there really any trace of her left?"

❧

Jetlagged, I spend the early morning down at the beach. I brace myself for a swim but then, shocked at how cold the Atlantic can be in summer, turn back. I look across to the marshlands that kept Esther's family fed on waterfowl in the autumn and provided cattails for their bedding. I feel a shiver wandering down streets that once bordered farmland near Eldridge Road that the Wheelwrights had hacked from the forest to keep starvation at bay. It's a tiny shred of shared history.

Then I visit the First Church of Christ (Congregational), a whitewashed building with bright green shutters. A national landmark since 1862, the church was built on the site of the town's original meetinghouse, where Esther was baptized in 1701. Up a steep wooden staircase above the church, I find the Historical Society of Wells and Ogunquit, where I meet a local historian who tells me that since she is a Moody and I am a Wheelwright, we are cousins. (Esther's sister married Samuel Moody in 1724.)

I pore over a file marked "Wheelwright Family Papers" and pull from it a handwritten chart titled "Relatives and Neighbors Killed or Captured by Indians." And there is Esther's name with an asterisk beside it and, below, the words "Captured 1703, Wells, ME." Esther was luckier than those with a double asterisk, which signified they'd been killed.

When I'm done, I make my way down to the church below. In a display along the walls there are examples of the metal foot-warmers that kept parishioners from freezing in the depths of their bitter winters (the mini ice age had yet to retreat in the early eighteenth century) and a small stool "made from wood of the first pulpit in the meetinghouse." Inside the meetinghouse itself, I slide into a hard wooden pew. Everything suggests austerity and an ardent focus on God in the abstract; there is no colour, no warming gilt or statues to relieve the expanses of glaring white plaster and dark wood. The only scents would have been of pine resin, wood smoke, wet wool, unwashed bodies, and perhaps gunpowder from the weapons lined up at the entrance. There was no altar—only a stark pulpit on a raised platform underneath a high, flat ceiling.

Walking back along a highway crowded with SUVs filled with

parents hauling their kids back from a busy day at the beach, I look deep into the dense forest that had represented the worst kind of danger to Esther. I try to see it as a dark, despairing place, and after pushing away the noisy present, I do.

Thinking back to Greg's question about whether I've found any trace of her, I reply, "Yes, but she wasn't where I was expecting her to be."

CHAPTER 4

Taken Captive

*D*URING ESTHER'S SHORT CHILDHOOD IN WELLS, she lived with her siblings, parents, grandparents and family servants in a noisy, crowded household on the northern edge of the town. Esther's father had built a garrison (a wooden fortress) for his ever-growing family after her sixth birthday. By then, John was licensed to "keep a house of public entertainment," serving wine, rum, cider and spruce beer—all Puritan essentials for a healthy body and efficient mind. Ten-pin bowls were available in the garden, as were illegal games of skittles, an archaic form of bowling the Puritans brought with them from England. The garrison attracted "governors, judges, ministers, generals and lords"—men of influence who would stop on journeys between Boston and the colonial frontier.[1] John gained a reputation as a thoughtful, cheerful and sensitive host who, despite his piety, ensured the garrison always had "an air of life and activity."[2]

Even though Mary Snell was constantly pregnant or breast-feeding throughout Esther's childhood, she helped run the public house, where her tasks ranged from taking in guests' washing to providing nursing services.[3] John also had a share of a sawmill on the nearby Mousam River; the mill produced tar and rosin, which supplemented the family's income. The Wheelwrights' large farm grew from Samuel's original two hundred deeded acres to support their expanding household, which now included indentured servants who worked alongside mixed-race and African slaves. (Devout families like the Wheelwrights believed slavery was justifiable because it delivered these heathens into a Christian life.[4]) At times of crisis, the garrison swelled with local militia members, colonial soldiers and families from outlying farms seeking shelter).[5]

While everyone worked on the harvest, the rest of the time there was a strict division between men's work—hunting, plowing, chopping timber, clearing fields, raising new buildings, animal husbandry—and women's work. At age seven, Esther was expected to help her mother and the female servants with small, simple chores in the kitchen. Her family lived close to rich fishing grounds, so there were cod, alewives and shad to gut, as well as lobsters, crabs and oysters to prepare. Corn, grown in nearby fields, was boiled, then pounded with a mortar into coarse meal, sifted and pounded again. Girls were taught how to make bread and churn fresh milk into butter and cream. They also searched the forest for wild beans, peas, parsnips, turnips, whortleberries, blackberries, strawberries and grapes, as well as collecting sap from the sugar maples. A kitchen garden supplied pumpkins, squash and yams, and all required watering, weeding and picking.[6] Black tea and coffee were unknown, so the women made spruce beer and ale for family meals and for their guests.[7]

When Hannah and Esther had finished their chores in the kitchen and garden, they were expected to mind their younger siblings, Jeremiah and Elizabeth. The hands of Puritan girls were never idle, and before they were taught the more difficult craft of spinning, they learned to knit stockings and mittens for the family.[8] Wells had yet to hire a teacher, so girls like Hannah and Esther would learn their letters from an older sibling or their mother. Just a generation earlier, these same skills had been denied to Esther's grandmother and namesake.[9] But despite her grandfather's reservations about the value of women's education, Esther was raised in a family with "a distinguished intellectual history," as reflected in the published sermons of Reverend Wheelwright and in the set of books that his grandson John had inherited from Samuel.[10] If Esther wanted to practise her reading, however, there was little quiet or comfortable space to do so in this bustling household. The kitchen in the garrison doubled as a parlour and sitting room; several family members shared each bed, and individual privacy was rare.

Like any child growing up on a frontier post in the eighteenth century, Esther had never travelled beyond her family's home and would have had little contact with the world outside its boundaries. Sermons by the local preachers denounced Roman Catholics and their military allies, the Indians. The Puritans were united in their struggle against a feminized Catholic Church, a clash epitomized by Elizabeth I's battles with Mary, Queen of Scots, for the English throne, more than a century earlier. Protestant propagandists, according to the historian Ann M. Little, effectively linked Catholicism with femininity, then claimed that political and spiritual corruption sprang from this toxic combination.[11] Unlike the mysterious French Catholics, who lived far away in settlements across the border, the Indians were ubiquitous; indeed, there was a summer camp of about a dozen wigwams near Wells. The Abenakis would likely have been familiar to Esther, since they sold their beaver, otter and bear skins to English traders like her father for essentials such as bread, cloth and tobacco or for imported European goods.[12]

The Abenakis, however, had a bad reputation with John Wheelwright, perhaps because of the Sayward girls' capture or his experiences with Major Converse's military expedition against them in 1692. When John discovered that Governor Joseph Dudley was holding peace talks with Abenaki sachems in Casco, on the Kennebec River, in June 1702, he saddled a horse and rode "with a party of friends" to intervene.[13] He feared that an English–Abenaki alliance could only be in the Indians' interests, and that the French were hatching a conspiracy against the settlers. John believed that the Indians were incapable of making their own decisions, and that the Jesuit missionaries had manipulated them into raiding the borderlands under French military command.[14] The distrust and animosity were mutual and unmitigated by ties of family or religion. The Abenakis, many of whom were Catholic converts, regarded the English as heretics and enemies of their symbolic father, King Louis XIV.

When Dudley refused to meet Wheelwright and signed the peace treaty anyway, John wrote to him on August 4, warning that Wells was now in "great danger" of attack. "I cannot have charity for [the Abenakis]," he explained, "I having Experienced so much of their deceitfulness in the Last war." The villagers had no choice, however, but to harvest their corn and hay or starve during the coming winter, so John asked that Boston supply his town with an armed guard of twenty or thirty soldiers.[15] But Dudley failed to send the troops, and John hastily expanded his garrison to shelter up to sixty people if and when the raids came.

Throughout the late summer and early fall of 1702, the garrisons in Wells were alive with talk of imminent attack. Esther's own cousins had been taken in the last war, and every family in this hamlet of roughly 250 people had stories of a relative killed or taken captive. Just before Esther was born, Mary Plaisted had returned home in a prisoner exchange, but her daughters were sold as domestic servants to households in Montréal, and both were probably educated at the Congrégation de Notre Dame school and baptized as Catholics.[16] Mary Sayward was doubly lost once she took her vows as a nun and later became a missionary, converting Indians at Sault-au-Récollet on the St. Lawrence River.

Grace Higiman, who was a captive with the Abenakis before Esther was born, provided terrifying details of her ordeal to the Massachusetts Assembly. For three years, she said, she was "remov[ed] from place to place as the Indians occasionally went, and was very hardly treated by them, both in respect of provisions and cloathing, having nothing but a torn blanket to cover [her] during the winter season and oftentimes cruelly beaten." Then she was sold "for Forty Crowns" in Québec, where she lived for another two and a half years and gave birth to a daughter, the father unidentified.[17]

Before and after the raid of 1703, John Wheelwright saw several employees, slaves and soldiers either shot or captured after venturing from the garrison.[18] The tales—of warriors who would materialize from the forest silently, like apparitions, to seize innocent citizens— sometimes grew in the telling. There were reports of "savages" who killed pregnant women, ripping infants from their wombs or mercilessly battering the brains from a babe's head. Others were said to have eaten children, roasting them like game over an open fire in the woods.[19]

When Esther was seven, in July 1703, travellers to Wells brought to the garrison the disturbing news that enemy forces had been sighted along the border with New France. Esther and her siblings knew these were dangerous times, and they had been warned to stick close to the safe confines of the family's home. War had broken out again between England and France after King Louis XIV supported his grandson's claim to the Spanish throne and recognized the Catholic James II as the English king, violating the Treaty of Ryswick. By 1702, the war of Spanish Succession had spread across the countries of Europe and into the North American theatre, where it was known as Queen Anne's war. Across the border in New France, meanwhile, the French were shoring up their Indian allies, and peace along the frontier threatened to collapse at any moment, fulfilling John's prophecy. As he explained in a letter to the authorities in Boston, this summer terror of an enemy attack kept his family "in close garrison," a condition by which "we are brought very low."[20]

By 1703, the garrison had become a place where families were "thrust and Heaped together" without "Common Comforts."[21] Being confined there during the brief weeks of summer was a tedious business for the Wheelwright children. Despite the inevitable parental warnings, Esther's longing to escape its wooden walls must have been great. To the north was a vast forest known as the Commons; the ocean was a short distance from the garrison, and the town was full of meadows bursting with wildflowers and fields thick with corn and grazing animals. Immediately outside the garrison was the mill, which had been built on an inlet that supplied the water to the huge wooden wheel that turned the saws.[22] The temptations for Esther, an inquisitive child with preoccupied parents and a household full of siblings and strangers, were many.

As the children grew restless in their garrison confinement, more than a hundred miles northwest Indian warriors were already gathering for an extensive raid of the English settlements along the borderlands. That spring, some two hundred Mohawks, Iroquois and Abenakis from Odanak (a settlement south of Québec on the Saint François River), along with thirty Frenchmen and officers, had ridden south through the Chaudière Valley under the orders of Philippe de Rigaud, Marquis de Vaudreuil, the governor of New France. These warriors were charged with conducting the raids that would ensure "the Abenakis and the English would be irreconcilable enemies."[23]

·⁂·

Early that summer, Abenaki sagamores from settlements spanning the borderlands of New England and New France met to discuss the coming conflict. They agreed to Vaudreuil's request for help in defeating the English militias and driving the land-hungry settlers and their domestic animals from their ever-expanding communities. Officer Jean-Baptiste Hertel de Rouville and Captain Alexandre Leneuf de la Vallière de Beaubassin rode to Norridgewock, the Jesuit mission on the Kennebec River and the largest Abenaki village in New France.[24] When Hertel de Rouville and de Beaubassin arrived, the young men killed several dogs and served them as dishes at a war feast. John Gyles, who lived with the Abenakis as a captive from Maine in 1689, described the ceremony:

> They kill a number of their Dogs, burn off their Hair, and cut them into Pieces, leaving only one Dog's Head whole; the rest of the Flesh they boil, and make a fine Feast of it: after which, the Dog's Head that was left whole is scorch'd, till the Nose and Lips have shrunk from the Teeth, and left them bare and grinning; this done, they fasten it to a Stick and the Indian who is proposed to be Chief of the Expedition takes the Head

into his Hands and sings a Warlike Song: in which he men-
tions the Town they design to Attack, and the Principal Man
in it, threatening that in a few Days he will carry that Man's
Head and Scalp in his Hand, in the same manner.[25]

While the dog meat boiled in an iron kettle, guests watched the ceremonial dances. Afterwards, a pipe filled with *odamo*—tobacco, a sacred herb that would lift their prayers to heaven on its smoke— was passed round. Before the warriors left, the mission priest, Father Sébastien Rale, heard their confession at the Norridgewock chapel.[26]

The next day, the party swept west, taking several days to reach the coastal settlements of Casco, Saco and Wells. The warriors usually broke camp a few days before a raid, sending scouts into the village to establish when the men left for the fields and noting who was sleeping in which house or garrison.[27] The raids allowed clans to avenge relatives who had been killed during these decades of cross-border fighting. When the Abenaki sachem Toxus and Madockawando descended, they knew who they were looking for—and the Wheelwrights were prime targets. John was the captain of a large local militia; he had evaded capture during earlier raids and had tried to intercede with Governor Dudley during the peace talks at Casco. All of these were powerful motives for eliminating John and his family.[28]

Before dawn, the French and Indian forces scattered into six or seven smaller groups, with the sachems giving their warriors last-minute instructions on the impending attack with the words "To you is given this hamlet to eat."[29] Over the next two days, they would cover an area of fifty miles in coordinated attacks, killing those who escaped capture, then looting homes and barns before torching the buildings and slaughtering those hated symbols of English colonialism, the cattle and sheep that consumed the grasslands.

The warriors followed a pattern, attacking the outlying farms first and then moving towards the farmhouses and garrisons in the town's centre.[30] That morning, Esther may have simply slipped past the watchful eyes of her parents, grandmother, elder brothers and sister, even avoiding soldiers or travellers at the inn, to walk out of the garrison's heavy gates. She was the only member of the extended Wheelwright clan to be taken captive that day, and there are no reports of an attack on the family's garrison. One possible explanation is that Esther was across town, visiting John's sister Hannah Parsons, who lived with her husband, William, and their children in a two-storey house near the town centre. To make this journey, Esther would have crossed the pastures where sheep, horses and cows grazed, walking south over Break Neck Hill to the bridge of the Webhannet River and across the fields to the farmhouse.

If Esther was playing with her young cousins, William, Hannah, Abigail and Samuel, she might not have noticed the first sign of attack: gunshots reverberating through the still morning. The sound of the shots would have reached the Parsons' neighbour Thomas Wells, who had just fetched the midwife to tend to his wife's third child. As Goody Wells recovered in bed with her newborn infant, the first warriors reached the village, breaking open windows and doors with hatchets. Goody Wells and her baby, too weak to make the arduous 120-mile journey north into French territory, were killed, along with four-year-old Sarah and Joshua, aged two. The warriors searched the house for booty—kettles, blankets, tools and dried food—before setting alight its wooden walls. As flames appeared in the summer sky, the warriors moved into the town centre and attacked Joseph Sayer's place, only a few feet from the Parsons'. Joseph was assaulted but lived, while his daughter, Mary, was taken captive and their house torched.

The unusual noise of gunshots and the smell of the burning house would have alerted the children that something was very wrong. Smoke, musket fire and anguished screams spread through the village, pierced by the unearthly tremolo war cries the Indians used to unnerve their enemies. If Esther had glanced across the fields, she would have seen racing towards her dozens of Mohawk, Iroquois and Abenaki warriors brandishing clubs, hatchets, swords and axes. As the men reached the Parsons' farmhouse, she would have seen faces obscured by masks of vermilion, ochre, white clay and soot, rendering them unrecognizable. The men wore silver and beads across their muscular chests, their loins draped in breechcloths and their long black hair tied into a stiff ruffle along the top of their shaven heads.

There are only a handful of eyewitness accounts of the raid on Wells. Esther herself left with a Jesuit priest her only recorded memory of "that treacherous day" and a host of unanswered questions. But if the Abenaki warriors were intent on avenging their kin by taking John Wheelwright as "their Principal Man," something went badly wrong. No Wheelwrights perished in an attack that saw twenty-two murdered and seven kidnapped, affecting more than a third of the hamlet's families.[31]

Esther would later tell Father Vincent Bigot, the Jesuit superior of New France, about her panic at the "terrifying commands conveyed . . . by an arrogant band of warriors whose ferocious looks froze the blood in [her] veins."[32] There was no escape—even if Esther had been capable of moving her numbed limbs, she could not hope to outrun these swift, superbly trained warriors. Young William and Samuel Parsons, like Goody Wells and her children, were killed quickly, likely with a swift blow to the head from a hatchet or war club. Somehow Aunt Hannah, her two daughters, and her husband were spared by their captors.

If Esther and the children had managed to reach the imagined safety of the Parsons' home, they soon found it offered little protection. A warrior dragged Esther across the rough floor, where she stood frozen with fear, and out the door. The warrior urged her to stop resisting and accept her fate. "You are your father and mother's happiness but you must cut yourself off from their caresses," he said. In her testimony to Father Bigot, Esther suggested that in that moment she understood this man was now her master, commanding her to leave.[33] Esther lashed out against her attacker but was powerless to stop him. He slung her over his shoulder as easily as he would a sack of corn or the limp carcass of a freshly slaughtered deer. The warriors then set alight the Parsons' home and outlying buildings, sending up waves of glistening heat into the summer sky. The cattle screamed as the blood poured down their cindered sides, and women knelt over their dead or dying kin. Esther hung her head while tears burned tracks down her flushed cheeks. Looking over her captor's shoulder, she caught her last glimpse of Wells and her family home. She would never return.

As Esther and the other captives were carried away, more killing followed. On their way out of the village, the warriors broke into the Old Berwick Road house of James and Catherine Adams, stabbing three-year-old Mary, plunging a hatchet into their son James, eighteen months, and taking the adults as captives. Catherine, who had given birth eight days earlier, was dragged from her bed and tied to a wooden post while the warriors rifled through the house. (Her newborn infant was killed.) Later, they unbound her hands, loosened her stays and provided her with a stick for the long march north.[34]

William Larrabee, who had been at Storer's garrison when the raid began, returned home to hide in the bushes and wait until the warriors left. When he thought it was safe, he opened the front door to find the corpses of his wife and children. Samuel Hill, a thirty-five-year-old sea captain whose ship provided the outlying settlements with a lifeline to Boston, was taken captive, along with his wife, Elizabeth, and their sixteen-month-old son, Aston, considered "old enough to travel." Their home was then torched. Aaron Littlefield, aged eight, was taken with his younger sisters, Tabitha and Josephine, from a garrison in the south end of the settlement.[35]

All along the borderlands of New England, colonists were murdered or captured, many joining Esther on the captive trail that led through the dense pine forests to the Abenaki village of Norridgewock. Musket fire from the attack was loud enough that two farmers, Benjamin Preble and Lewis Bean, heard it in nearby York. They estimated that about fifty Indian warriors had fallen upon Wells that day.

In the chaos left by the attack, where corpses lay along the rough roads and wounded neighbours languished in their homes, John and Mary Wheelwright feared for their daughter. The garrison had been spared, but John, the local militia captain, was charged with rounding up the "four score of men" equipped by Governor Dudley to chase the enemy as they swept west along the Old Berwick Road. This was the most dangerous time for the warriors. Physically drained, they were slowed and distracted by their captives and loaded down with their plundered goods. They had only a narrow window in which to make their escape and melt away into the vast forest. After that, it would be impossible to find these experts at wilderness camouflage.

If the colonial soldiers took chase, however, they proved ineffectual in tracking down the raiding party and recovering the captives. While the governor of New York, Lord Cornbury, would later report that all his foot soldiers in Maine had survived the raid—"we lost nothing there, scarce a man at each garrison," he recounted— this was most likely because they took little action.[36]

Wells was one of seven Maine settlements—Casco, Blackpoint, Cape Elizabeth, Kennebunk, Saco and Winter Harbour were the others—attacked that day. According to Thomas Hornabrook, a farmer,

> *At [Kennebunkport] they ript up one Goody Webber that was big with child, and laid her child to her breast, and so left her. At Sparwink River they knockt one Jordan's sucking child's brains out against a tree. The Father of said child seeing the Indians approach went in a friendly manner to meet them, thinking of no danger, and shook hands with them, and as he was so doing they knocked out his brains and scalp'd him, and took several families and carried them away captives.[37]*

In their terror, farmers left fifteen hundred bushels of corn and other grain standing in fields east of Wells, "nobody venturing to destroy it or take it away." Villagers were too frightened to gather both this precious winter food and the corpses of their loved ones. In Boston two nights later, Judge Samuel Sewall received a dispatch from Wells with news that while fifteen people had been buried, the villagers were too frightened to inter the other seven victims. "[They] durst not go to bury their outermost. Lost as they fear 60. Enemy numerous."[38] By the time these dispatches were written, Esther was among that numberless enemy, and she had already been marched dozens of miles away from home.

Despite the Wheelwrights' belief that it was part of God's mysterious plan to have their daughter taken from them, the guilt must have been profound. Esther's father, captain of the local militia, had failed to rescue his daughter or any of the six other captives from Wells. Although the rest of his children had all escaped injury and death that day, Esther had been singled out as the most tangible proof that his prophecy was right. Now began the time, stretching into years, when the Wheelwrights would live without news of their daughter.

CHAPTER 5

Return to Norridgewock

LUCILLE GREER, A LOCAL HISTORIAN IN NOR-
ridgewock, Maine, has bundled me into her oceanliner
of a car and we are floating down Highway 201A towards Old Point,
the original site of the Abenaki village where Esther was taken in
1703. "It's easier with my leg if I drive," she tells me in a voice grav-
elled with age and cigarette smoke. Lucille may be verging on her
ninth decade, but she has a firm grip to her handshake, a passion for
local history and the energy of a woman half her age.

As Lucille revs the engine, she tells me that our historical
connections run deep. Esther's nephew Nathaniel Wheelwright
was sent to Québec on a mission to rescue a relative of hers, Fanny
Noble, from her Abenaki captors in 1754. I know Nathaniel failed,
but I hope Lucille won't hold it against me.

We head across gently rolling hills towards Old Point, now
a public picnic and camping site beside the wide, clear Kennebec
River, roughly a hundred miles north of Portland, Maine. Above the
smooth hum of the engine, Lucille tells me that the Abenakis used

to call the river at Norridgewock "smooth water above the rapids," a reference to the waterfall near Madison now called Bombazee Rips. Farther north the river was known as Orantsouak; to the south it was called the Canabais and the Sagadahoc.

About half an hour later Lucille pulls the cruiser up beside a field of sweetgrass where a large boulder has been emblazoned with a bronze plaque, paid for by the local chapter of the Daughters of the American Revolution, "to mark the road built by Colonel Benedict Arnold for carrying past this place on his march to Québec." Near the river is a stone spire several feet high, built on the place where the English killed Father Sébastien Rale and massacred the Abenaki villagers in a raid. I wonder about the connection between the English colonial army's murder of a Jesuit and an organization of women who celebrate their revolutionary heritage.

I notice a small leather pouch, decorated with feathers and bright beads, attached to a birch near the boulder. "What's this?" I ask Lucille, touching the bag, which fits neatly into my palm.

"The Indians from Canada come down and leave those tobacco pouches here. They're a memorial to their dead too," she tells me. Tobacco is a sacred herb that the Algonquins used to mediate between the earthly and spiritual realms. The bag looks as new as a freshly laid bouquet of flowers on a headstone.

This very piece of broad, flat land was Esther's first home with the Abenakis after she was taken captive. Although the tall grass has gone to seed, dried spires of foxgloves poke up through the undergrowth and marsh wrens fly overhead, skimming the silver birch that bow gently in the warm wind. I wander through the deserted picnic grounds, wishing away the rusting BBQs and trash cans so I can more easily imagine a village of birchbark wigwams, campfires, Father Rale's mission church, a school.

Lucille has given me directions to a sacred spring just on the edge of the riverbank, so I head through the birch, the long grass prickling my bare legs, and down a muddy slope. The spring bubbles up just as she described it. I bend my head and splash the freezing water over my face, feeling that same stirring connection I felt in Wells as it touches my skin. A current runs through me. Three hundred years earlier, Esther squatted here among the birch trees and beside this fast-flowing river.

Spiritual connection doesn't have a place in biography—or history, for that matter. Writers of such accounts are meant to deal with evidence, with facts and their interpretation. But I can't help it. Sitting here with my hands in the spring, fighting off the mosquitoes and wondering whether Lucille's growing impatient by her car, I feel something I cannot rationalize.

Later that evening, my friends George and William arrive back from Wells with tales of successful antique hunting and present me with a magazine produced for the town's three-hundredth anniversary. It has a passing mention of "the Reverend John Wheelwright . . . and a mere handful of settlers" who founded Wells in 1653.

Tonight we're staying at an inn with several rooms whose walls are lined with dolls in period and ethnic costume. George pulls me into their upstairs suite and points at the landlady's collection, assembled neatly along the shelves. "Look! The eyes follow you. I don't know how I'm going to sleep tonight." He's right—there is something unsettling about these waxen faces all staring blankly into the middle distance, their outfits and hair unnaturally pristine.

I bid him goodnight, struggling to make sense of my own spooky moment in Norridgewock, when I dipped my hand in the sacred spring. Here at least I feel one step closer to Esther, who left behind so little information about the people who would change her life and my family's history.

I close my eyes in a room without dolls and dream of my own blonde children.

CHAPTER 6

The Captive Trail

O<small>N THE HURRIED RETREAT FROM THE COAST, THE</small> warriors force-marched their hostages across almost 125 miles of rough ground. Esther and the sixty-eight other captives were keenly aware that if they resisted or slowed down the group, they would be killed. On the captive trail, warriors needed all their cunning to evade the English militia. Campfires were banned; they moved swiftly through the forests and staked their captives to the ground at night to prevent escape. Among the adult captives was poor, post-natal Catherine Adams, who later recounted her tale in Cotton Mather's *A Memorial of the Present Deplorable State of New England*. The captives had hurried through dense spruce forests, she said, stopping half a dozen times to forge swift-flowing rivers or dank swamps, up to their necks in icy water. Catherine was so weak that she fell into a slough after sunset and "was hardly got out alive."[1]

Over the week or so it took the war party to reach Norridgewock, the warriors usually divided their captives into smaller groups. With Esther were many of her relations and neighbours: Samuel and Elizabeth Hill and their child; Aaron, Ruth, Tabitha and Josephine Littlefield; Mary Sawyer; Mary, Priscilla and Rachel Storer; and Titus Jones, a slave.[2] Some of the captives, including the Hill family, were sold to the French and taken north to Montréal or Québec to work as domestic servants. They were stripped of their valuable silver buckles, buttons and whatever serviceable clothing they owned.[3] The fate of the remaining captives would be decided in Norridgewock.

For Esther, the journey was physically arduous and psychologically harrowing. The unnamed warrior who had grabbed her was now her master and had total control over his charge, a right that was respected by the other warriors.[4] He alone could decide if she should be sold or killed, or if she was suitable for adoption into an Abenaki family. Father Bigot described Esther's terror and the punishing demands of this trek, which marked her "violent separation from all that [was] dearest to [her] in the world." She was, he reported, "obliged to follow new masters who paid little heed that [her] steps [could not] keep up with the speed of theirs."[5] Esther quickly learned to keep pace with her master, though, and once the Abenakis were beyond the range of the English militia, she was relatively secure. Women and girl captives in Algonquin culture were respected as potential sisters or cousins, and were therefore safe from sexual harassment or attack. There was a strong taboo against rape, which was considered a capital offence.[6]

As Esther would later tell Father Bigot, she memorized the painful details of the journey, comforting herself that one day she would "tell them to a father who would take a boundless interest." In those first few days, she regarded her captors as members of "a brutish race" who forced her to endure "the discomforts of a harsh life." The Jesuit superior recounted conversations with Esther in which she described, "so vividly and eloquently," the Abenaki life as full of "awful miseries" and "beyond anything imaginable to those who have not experienced such hardship."[7]

Once the immediate danger had passed, however, the attitude of Esther and the other children towards their captors began to change. Early on, the warriors replaced the children's "straight" shoes—made of leather, hard-heeled, with no left or right—with soft deer- or moose-skin moccasins. The men shared whatever food they had: nuts, wild berries or Canada plums, as well as staples such as dried corn that could be boiled as porridge when they were far enough from the English militia and it was safe to light a fire again. Over those long days, the captives were encouraged to learn a song or a few words of Abenaki. If the children grew tired, they were hoisted onto shoulders or carried in their captors' arms.[8] Over days blasted by weariness, Esther would observe her captors' skills at negotiating the wilderness, measuring the points of a compass from a tree or calculating time by the position of spires against the sky. The Abenaki warriors moved quickly, expertly and silently through the forest, imitating a wolf's howl to communicate with their brothers and conceal their position from the enemy.[9]

While Esther marched northwest towards Norridgewock, her family members back in Wells were helping to bury the dead, hastily rebuilding burned-out homes and asking Boston for help after the "sudden and secret falling upon the whole province of Mayn."[10] The raid had been a severe blow. Captain Wheelwright and others later reported to the Massachusetts Assembly that "more than a third of our number are, one way or another, gone from us: & a great part of us being left, are destitute."[11]

By August 11, news of the disaster had reached the colony's capital. Judge Samuel Sewall spoke with a "little youth that narrowly escaped the enemies [*sic*] hands" during the raid, and two days later, the Massachusetts Assembly gathered to hear "the sad Letter from Capts. Willard and Wheelwright," although the latter seems to have made no special plea for his missing daughter.[12] Into the autumn the attacks continued, and John's sister Hannah Parsons and her daughter, also named Hannah, were taken from York in October. Boston responded smartly, with Governor Dudley ordering weapons and dispatching to Wells half a company of dragoons, about one hundred men "under proper officers."[13]

Within two weeks of the raid, on August 16, 1703, the colonial government began negotiations for the return of Esther and the other captives. Captain Cyprian Southack sailed north along the coast to Sagadahoc, where the French and Indians were holding some of "the prisoners in their hands."[14] Despite these talks, the Massachusetts government declared war on the Abenakis, arming another thousand men. The French had struck hard against their enemy by shoring up their Native allies. As Father Pierre-François-Xavier de Charlevoix, the eighteenth-century French historian, observed, "[The warriors] committed some trifling ravages, and killed about three hundred men, but the essential point was to engage the Abenakis in such a matter that to retract would be impossible."[15]

The captives arrived, likely a week after the raid, at Norridgewock, a village built on roughly 250 acres of broad, flat land. Here, at a large bend in the river, the water flowed smoothly past three sides of the village.[16] Esther would join a community of some two hundred people—roughly the equivalent of the thirty households in Wells—living in twenty-six large birchbark wigwams inside a circular stockade of round logs nine feet high and 160 feet long. Two streets ran down from the four gates, intersecting neatly at the village centre, which was shaped to symbolize a womb. The villagers (known to the English as "French Indians") were Catholic converts under the ministry of Father Sébastien Rale, who was born near the French–Swiss border in Pontarlier and landed in Québec in 1689. He had worked alongside Father Jacques Bigot[*] on the Chaudière River in New France, where he quickly learned the Abenaki language and earned a reputation as a zealous missionary. At Norridgewock, he built a church "adorned with many Pictures and Toys" and a mission school that lay outside the stockade, about twenty paces from the east gate.[17]

As the party of returning warriors and captives approached the village, Chief Hopehood, the sagamore, issued the security signal, "*kwey*" (rhymes with "day"), before the warriors echoed back with "*kwey-kwey*." The masters escorted their captives into Norridgewock, where excited children and women dressed in embroidered buckskin, their ears and necks laced with heavy bronze and silver rings, crowded round them. Since children were the most prized captives, hands would have eagerly reached out to touch Esther, scoring her chin, cheeks and forehead with dashes of vermilion. Esther's master washed off his war paint in a birchbark basin while the women made the final preparations for a feast to honour the fallen warriors and for the adoption ceremony that night.[18]

Since initiation into Abenaki society was the women's responsibility, they often gave the warriors specific orders for the types of captives they wanted. Women, older men and children usually stayed behind in the village while the men were away hunting, and therefore they were acutely aware of lost clan members. If a dead relative's honour was not avenged, they believed, the lost one would return to

---

[*]To avoid confusion, Father Vincent Bigot is hereafter referred to as Father Bigot, and his younger brother Jacques as Father Jacques Bigot.

haunt the village. Known as the "crying blood," these spectres would wail outside the wigwams, crying mournfully into the night until a replacement was found or a scalp brought to avenge their death. Only when the crying blood continued their journey into the next world would the wailing cease.[19]

Although Esther did not describe her first night at Norridgewock to Father Bigot, other captives have left records that enable us to imagine her experience. A woman would have led Esther to the riverbank to wash her, perhaps shocking the English child with her uncovered hair worn in braids, loose broadcloth dress without stays and elk-skin moccasins. Esther's homespun clothes would have been stripped away and, after a quick wash with freezing spring water (another new sensation, since the English feared water and rarely bathed outside in the ocean or a river), her skin smeared with golden yellow bear grease to protect her from insects. After pulling on a plain cotton dress and wool skirt, Esther would have returned to the village, where her soft, pale skin and light hair, now clean of grime, would attract attention. The women would have decorated it with feathers and hung her with necklaces made of shells, long tubes of dark blue glass, and silver, copper and multicoloured beads.[20]

There is no record of how many captives were sold to the French, or of how many survived the journey. But at Norridgewock, the English survivors were privy to rumours about the brutal treatment that awaited them. To join this community, they had to be transformed from Europeans, "people coming from yonder" or "white eyes," into "the Algonquin people of the dawn"—Abenakis.[21] The adult English men endured an initiation known as "running the gauntlet," where they were stripped naked and made to run along lines that stretched from the east gate to the centre of the community. With axe handles, tomahawks, hoop poles, clubs and switches, the villagers flogged the racing captives as if their weapons and instruments possessed the power to rid them of their whiteness.[22] The corridor represented a birth canal, and the idea was that through their pain, like the agony of childbirth, these English colonists would be reborn as Abenakis.[23] As the blows fell upon the captives, the villagers wept, sang and shouted, a noisy, vociferous purging of rage for losses the enemies had inflicted upon them.

Running the gauntlet was a test of masculinity that was rough and humiliating but far from lethal. Once they had passed through this ritualized beating, the English colonists were invited to begin a new life that many experienced as being "as full of love, challenge, and satisfaction as any they had known."[24] The captives who passed this test of their manhood were led into a circle, where a fire burned long into the night. Their old identity was now destroyed and they were symbolically purified. They were given Abenaki clothes and ceased to be recognizable as European. During an adoption ceremony, the captives were distributed among families who had lost loved ones or were owed favours.

At the end of the ceremony, the villagers would fall momentarily silent, contemplating their dead. The captives now belonged to a patriarchal community organized along clan lines.[25] Each captive received a new clan name, and the women urged the child captives into the circle, which vibrated with the music of drums, rattles, chanting and singing. A celebratory war dance began.

If Esther's master had taught her to sing on the captive trail, she would have been encouraged to show it off before the villagers and to join the dancing, however awkward her steps.[26] Then she and the other captives would have been led towards their new homes, the wigwams spread throughout the stockade. She would have entered the tent through a deerskin flap to an overpowering smell of woodsmoke, animal hides, stale tobacco, cooking odours, sweating bodies and dogs. Once inside, Esther would have been instructed by the elder women on the correct way for a girl to sit—with her legs stretched out in front. Opposite the entrance, near the fire, her master would sit cross-legged while his wife tucked her feet underneath her. The elders huddled down with the children while above them dangled bark containers of dried meat, bunches of herbs and ears of corn. The wigwam's outer edges were lined with storage bags, blankets, tools, food stores and toys.[27]

Although Esther was likely given an Abenaki name, the only record that survives, from a Catholic baptism, is that of Marie-Joseph. She was expected to mould her personality to that of the clan's lost member, assuming her memories and role within her adoptive family. As a governor of New France would later explain, "There is nothing so difficult as to get [the Abenakis'] slaves from them, especially when they have distributed them among their Wigwams to make up for their Dead."[28] Once the crying blood had been avenged through the captive's presence in the wigwam, the dead girl or boy could make the journey into the Land of the Souls and leave the clan in peace.[29] As an adopted daughter, Esther would enjoy all the duties, rights and responsibilities of the missing child.[30] In this strange home, as she would tell Father Bigot, she fell asleep wrapped in "an impenetrable gloom," while outside the tremolo of singers accompanying the war dance carried on into the night.[31]

Marie-Joseph—probably shortened to the more popular "Molly," since the Abenakis found the vowels in "Marie" difficult to pronounce—was treated as an equal to her new siblings, who shared their possessions, food and clothes.[32] But her first lesson in adjusting to Abenaki family life was learning how to eat. The Wheelwrights, like other English colonists, had regular family meal times, when food was prepared by servants and served on a dining table that may even have been covered with linen. Drinking cups and wooden trenchers, or serving dishes, were used communally, and there were strict rules governing eating. The historian Alice Morse Earle describes what was expected of colonial children:

> [*They*] *were never to ask for anything on the table; never to speak unless spoken to; always to break the bread, not to bite into a whole slice; never to take salt except with a clean knife; not to throw bones under the table . . . If they were "moderately satisfied," they were told to leave at once the table and the room.*[33]

Like many Europeans, Esther was disgusted by the alien-tasting stews of strong meat or strange vegetables eaten communally at any time of day from a giant turtle shell or from birchbark bowls. A meal might consist of a hawk's head, beaver entrails or squirrel generously passed to her on a skewer of wood. Instead of ale (a staple for English adults and children), the only beverage was the stock left over from the boiled meat or corn. As she would later tell Father Bigot, Esther found the eating habits of her Abenaki family "gross and infinitely contrary [to my own and] very revolting."[34] But like other English captives, she would soon grow to appreciate Indian cuisine and the generosity with which it was shared.[35] She helped to find and prepare these meals as she worked alongside her sisters and female elders. Although Esther was used to assisting her mother in the family home, she now found herself performing chores that were normally done by the Wheelwrights' servants. As she learned the values of mutual reciprocity, her Abenaki family "became attached to this child with an extraordinary affection."[36]

With the older women and younger children, Esther laboured in the fields outside the stockade to harvest corn, peas, squash, beans, pumpkins and tobacco. Once the corn was harvested, Esther observed how the women ground it with a mortar and pestle and then boiled it with maple sugar. Mothers worked while their babies slept on carved wooden cradleboards, swaddled in cloth and covered with a small bearskin. Women's work also included making canoes. The younger boys played at hunting with miniature bows, aiming arrows with surprising accuracy at birds or small animals.[37] Esther's work was usually outdoors, drawing water from the river, fishing, skinning animals, lighting fires and carrying supplies to and from the wigwam.[38]

Unlike the English, who had a terror of the wilderness, the Abenakis viewed the forest as a spiritual place. Esther would observe that when they gathered herbs and plants, the women offered tobacco to mythical little people (the Manogemassek), and promised to take only what they needed.[39] Offerings were made at a chapel to the Virgin Mary and another to a guardian angel on the paths leading into the forest and fields. Working alongside the village women, Esther was taught how to collect the sacred sweetgrass (burned to waft prayers to heaven) and firewood, harvest bark and pick wild fruits such as sour grapes, thorn plums or the bayberries used in making Father Rale's votive candles.[40]

Adult captives reported that children usually lost most of their English words within six months, a sign that they had become "wholly swallowed up with the Indians."[41] Esther, however, appeared to demonstrate an exceptional "facility in understanding a barbarian tongue," even helping younger children learn to read their lessons at the mission school.[42] As Esther learned to speak Abenaki, she understood more about the spiritual world that lay behind many daily rituals. The elders explained the seasons to children as myths, with each representing a cycle of spawning, birth, flowering and death. August was "seals fattening" moon, September "reddening of leaves" moon, and October "ice forms on rock" moon. To the Abenakis, the natural world was inhabited by spirits like the sun Kisuhs, the ultimate spirit-power in a cosmos where everything possessed a sacred force was Manitou, or the Great Spirit, which could live within bears, moose, the morning and evening stars, trees, rivers and rocks.[43]

Despite her Puritan background, Esther was expected to regularly attend Father Rale's splendidly decorated mission church. In sharp contrast to the austerity of the First Church of Christ, the mission church was ablaze with colour and lit with dozens of candles. The altar was hung with an embroidered cloth and decorated with wampum belts of different designs, tubular beads, strings of porcelain beads and other articles stitched with glass beads and porcupine quills. "I thought it my duty to spare nothing," said Father Rale, describing his place of worship, "either for its decoration or for the beauty of the vestments that were used for our holy ceremonies; altar-cloths, chasubles, copes [vestments], sacred vessels, everything is suitable, and would be esteemed in the churches of Europe."[44]

Just as the decor was equal to that of any parish church in France, Father Rale's service was as traditional as any other. While the Mass was said, he placed small wafers on a salver and covered them with a glass. After consecration, the bread and wine were offered as Christ's body, his flesh and blood, then the altar boys kissed Father Rale's hand and rang a brass bell to signal communion. Psalms, translated by the father from Latin into Abenaki, might be sung for hours. The villagers had learned part-singing and were especially talented in harmonies, with the men taking the bass and the women the high notes.

Father Rale explained his Bible reading as words "not written like the words of men, upon a [wampum] belt [made of cowrie shells], on which a person can say everything that he wishes; but they are written in the book of the Great Spirit, to which falsehood cannot have access."[45] The priest spoke fluent Abenaki, equating God and the Great Spirit, and giving equal weight to wampum belts and the Bible in his sermons. Whether it was Father Rale's hybrid theology, the decor or the villagers' reputation for exquisite singing, the church attracted worshippers from distant places throughout the territory.

At the core of Catholicism was a search for communal well-being that appealed to the Abenakis and harmonized with their spiritual beliefs. Catholic liturgy supplemented their traditional song-and-dance cycles, while its symbolism pervaded all Abenaki culture. A Christian God was easily understood as "He-Who-Made-All," and was believed to ensure a successful harvest, a bountiful hunt and victory in warfare. Father Rale introduced the idea of patron saints, used medals and crucifixes as personal power objects, and encouraged the Abenakis to place chapels in fields, all of which elaborated on ancestral beliefs.[46] The sachems at Norridgewock might have found meaning in these spiritual rituals, but they likely also participated in the church to forge stronger military ties with the French and gain access to their firearms and trade goods.[47]

Esther attended Sunday Mass and was given instruction in the catechism at the mission school to prepare for her baptism. Among the other children who attended these classes was Dorothy Jordan, also known as Dorothée Jeryan, who had been taken from her family home in Spurwink, Maine (near Portland), in the 1703 raid. Just four when she was captured, she grew to love her adoptive family and "refused all offers to be taken away" from them. Like Esther, she learned the catechism from Father Râle and was also known as Marie.⁴⁸ The Jesuits would exert an enormous influence over the lives of both girls.

Through her first Catholic teacher, Esther observed the privations and joys of a monastic life. Unlike Esther's English relations, who traded but did not pray with the Indians, Father Râle was immersed in Abenaki society.⁴⁹ A rhetorician and intellectual, he spent years compiling a French–Abenaki dictionary, having learned his parishioners' language by paying rapt attention to the shape and movement of their lips.⁵⁰ He lived in a cabin alone, tended his own garden, cooked his own meals and chopped his own firewood—for which he was deeply respected by the community. He attended the sachems' councils and feasts, claiming that his "advice always determines their decisions." A skilled artist, he spent hours making furniture and decorations for the church and gathering bayberries or wax myrtle to make the light green votive candles. "My days are so full," he once wrote, "that I am obliged to shut myself up, that I may find time to attend to prayer and recite my Office."⁵¹

After only a few months with the Abenakis, Esther would have been barely recognizable to her English family; she wore a broadcloth dress, walked and ran, free of her stays, spoke Abenaki with ease, attended Mass on Sundays and may even have learned to swim. As the winter began and the family was confined to its wigwam, her intimacy with her clan deepened. Now Esther learned a different set of skills from the elders, who were experts at weaving baskets, pouches, boxes, bowls and dishes from birch bark. She watched her sisters dip porcupine quills in brightly coloured inks made from berries and roots to decorate boxes for the church altar. During these short, dark days, women also worked on wampum belts made of cowrie shells and sewn with vegetable fibres into complex symbolic messages.

To protect her from the snow and icy winds, Esther would have needed a new wardrobe of lined elk-skin leggings, a woollen blanket and a hood made from black or navy wool and lined with red cloth. Abenaki women often stitched cone-shaped beads to their pouches, and copper pendants completed these winter outfits. Under their hoods and blankets, the women dressed their hair with beads and earrings, and wore necklaces, garters and feathers. During stormy weather, there were games of dice made from moose bones and the telling and retelling of stories while hungry wolves howled outside the stockade.[52]

By January, known as "the moon that provides little food grudgingly," Esther was probably remembering with longing the gristly stews that had revolted her that summer. It was a lean month with little in the way of fish, vegetables or fresh meat. When the hunters did return home with a caribou or a moose, the women, children and captives were grateful. According to one captive, John Gyles, they stood outside their wigwams shaking their hands and bodies, singing with gratitude and joy at the prospect of tasting meat again.[53] The women then quickly skinned the carcasses, curing and drying the meat in birchbark containers within the wigwam; the skins were used for moccasins, dresses and leggings. When the weather was fine, the children usually played on wooden sleds that slid at break-neck speed across the snow or used teardrop-shaped snowshoes to navigate the fields. Adults and children alike skipped large, flat pieces of snow across frozen ponds like stones across water. There were feasts at Christmas, or the "birthday time," and evenings of singing, dancing and storytelling to hold families spellbound before the fire.[54]

Esther's life in the village changed in the spring, when the snow melted and the rivers became navigable again. Her family would load their canoes and paddle up the Kennebec River past churning waterfalls thick with fish. Men, women and children would scoop up shad or alewives to use for fertilizer, while the men speared salmon running upstream. The fish were smoked and dried for the winter in bark cabins. At the coastal camp, tantalizingly close to Wells, they lived on fish, seals, clams, oysters and fowl—all foods familiar to Esther. Father Rale would set up a crude chapel here with a temporary altar made from silk, a rush mat and a bearskin that doubled as his bed. Prayers were said every morning and evening.[55] Everything caught or picked was carried back by canoe to Norridgewock, where it was hung or stored in bark-lined pits.[56]

After the spring thaw, which marked almost a year of captivity, Esther might have begun to wonder if the Wheelwrights would ever arrive to take her home to Wells. But however much her parents agonized over the loss of their daughter, John Wheelwright was painfully aware of how dangerous it was to travel into Abenaki territory. On May 11, 1704, four soldiers who were being billeted at the Wheelwright garrison in Wells were attacked when they went out to help John round up his cattle. Two of the soldiers were killed, one taken captive and another escaped.[57] That spring, Abenaki attacks had escalated, so that by July 12 all colonists living within two hundred miles of the New England border had been confined to garrisons while the militias sought out "those Bloody Rebels in their obscure recesses under cover of a vast, hideous wilderness."[58]

It is impossible to know what news, if any, reached Norridgewock about these sporadic attacks, or whether the Abenakis were the "Bloody Rebels" the colonists so feared. But as the months passed, Esther's misery at missing her "well-to-do family" turned to equanimity. Along with her instruction in the catechism, she was learning a new narrative, one in which she was no longer the great-granddaughter of a Puritan founder but one of God's chosen, a Catholic rescued from heresy. The story presented to Esther, now Marie/Molly, told of how God's "invisible hand" had helped her to survive the captive trail and discover the Wheelwrights' lost faith. Alone among her family, Esther could, by returning to the Catholic faith, right the terrible mistake made by her forefathers. According to Father Bigot, Esther became "boundlessly content" with her Abenaki family, and her initial horror of Norridgewock was transformed into "an earnest desire to stay there."[59]

The conceptual leap, even for a child, was fantastic. Esther was living among the people who had snatched her from her parents' home, murdering her cousins, and whose religion she had been raised to fear. To survive, however, she needed to believe this new story, which Father Rale and, later, Father Bigot were eager to supply.

CHAPTER 7

Among the Artifacts in the
Musée des Åbenakis

I'M STARING AT MASON JARS FILLED WITH GOLDEN bear grease on a scrubbed pine tabletop. I'm longing to dig my hand into that slippery-looking pile, to know what it feels like to rub the grease along my arms and legs. But while I'm dithering—has my obsession reached a new stage?—the *ah-ha, hey-yey* of the Ojibwa jingle dancers drifts down from an outdoor stage. I turn towards the sound of the throaty singing and snare drums, mesmerized.

Today I have driven from Québec City to the Odanak Abenaki Reserve through Trois-Rivières, a town founded in 1634 by the fur trader Laviolette, where the farms are still pressed into shapes dictated by the eighteenth-century seigneuries of New France. The reserve, just south of the St. François mission, is at the northern end of the Kennebec–Chaudière Corridor, a major tourist route that runs along the old captive trail northwest from Casco Bay to Québec City. This was the site of Esther's second home with her Abenaki clan members, who fled Norridgewock in 1705.

The stallholders for the annual pow-wow were just setting up along the riverbank when I pulled my rental car into the parking lot. You can buy anything here, from silver bracelets engraved with traditional clan icons to dream catchers and moccasins and Father Joseph Aubrey's Abenaki–French dictionary. Off stage, a Montréal rock band is rehearsing for this evening's performance. Along the grass, a group of jugglers dressed in Indian print trousers, their faces covered with oily paints, are tossing hacky sacks in the air while a group of children dance round them. Hippy pastoral.

I make my way into the spanking new space of the refurbished Musée des Abénakis to meet my guide, Patrick Côte. Founded in 1962 as Québec's first Amerindian museum, it has recently undergone a major renovation, and today its vast collections of baskets, trade silver, lacrosse sticks and ceremonial clothes are housed in cool, floodlit rooms.

As I wait for Patrick, a couple with midwestern American accents are being shown round by a floppy-haired museum worker, a boy so young I wonder if he's a student working at a summer job.

"And this," he says, waving a hand at a display, "was used by the women for their time of the month."

"Time of the month?" asks the male of the couple, his features crinkling underneath his baseball cap, a hand straying into baggy beige shorts. His wife nudges him and rolls her eyes skywards.

The floppy-haired student grins. "For their menstrual cycles."

"Oh," says Beige Shorts, and they move swiftly to safer ground, a display of war clubs and tomahawks.

As soon as Patrick arrives, he leads me down to a temperature-controlled storage room lined with dozens of snowshoes racked up like dried fish skeletons. It's like being in the shoe warehouse of a department store; there are hundreds, of varying shapes and sizes.

Patrick passes a hand through his thick dark hair and looks across at the collection lining the far wall.

Patrick explains how the snowshoes that Esther wore at Odanak were of an ingenious design that enabled the Abenakis to cross even the harshest winter landscape. "It was all about survival," he says, "because in the wintertime, that's when you're at your most vulnerable." He brings a beaver's tail snowshoe down from the rack, his hand tracing its edges of bent wood. These were made for navigating forests and frozen ponds, and Esther would have worn them on her journey from Norridgewock in early 1705. "If you don't have snowshoes in the winter," Patrick tells me, "you don't get very far."

Upstairs is a room that recreates the dark blue interior of a wigwam. On the walls are painted life-sized figures of children and elders, mostly women; they sit round a campfire inside a lodge while outside winter deepens. This visit is proving to be much better than my previous attempts at "ocular history." It doesn't take much imagination to call up Esther, despite the power tools and plastic sheeting along the floor in this almost-finished display.

Patrick explains why the Abenaki lifestyle was so attractive to the English captive children. "If you were a girl, you were nothing in English society," he says. "The Abenakis never hit their children; they were never spanked or scolded." The children experienced warmth and affection from their captor-parents, upon whom they were utterly dependent for their survival. I wonder how the parents so easily accepted this unknown child into their family. Since the Abenakis left no written record of her time with them, I can't even recover the names of Esther's adoptive parents, let alone their feelings towards her.

I thank Patrick for the tour and head outside into the afternoon sun, where the jingle dancers are doing a second show, stomping boots decorated with trade silver while a rich smoke drifts up from a stall where tonight's dinner is being prepared. I decide to stroll down the road to the site of the original Odanak church, where Esther celebrated Mass after she and her family relocated from Norridgewock, and where she learned to pray, to count her rosary and to genuflect.

Although the original church was burned down in 1759 by Rogers Rangers, an English militia, it was rebuilt and this second-generation version dates from the eighteenth century. It is nestled among birch trees near the riverbank, and I enter it through a bright vestibule. The interior is exquisitely decorated with gilt, stained glass and an elaborate altar; the scent of pine sap mingles with incense. It was here that another captive, Reverend John Williams of Deerfield, watched in horror as the English children went "native" and the Abenakis celebrated Mass, singing, praying and listening to a Latin sermon all at once. Forced by his captors to attend church in 1704, Reverend Williams clung to his sense of English superiority, humiliated in his subservient role as a captive.

With so little information available about Esther's experience during these crucial years of her childhood, I'm finding that my journey is becoming one of imagining. Despite the clean, warm images of the wigwam and Patrick's assurances about the humane treatment of English girls by their adoptive families, I can't shrug off Esther's status as a captive and the image of the grieving Wheelwrights, whose lost daughter was their very own "crying blood."

But the past really is another country—one where you are forced to look beyond an individual story to understand the actors' options and choices within a given context. My ancestors were colonists who drove the Abenakis from their land, broke treaties and carried epidemics. Their children paid the price for their religious mission in the New World.

Earlier this afternoon, Patrick had explained that during the imperial wars of the eighteenth century, the Abenakis, the French and the English all took women, children and men as captives. This ensured the survival of their own captured people and enabled them to organize exchanges. There was a hierarchy among the captives, and a member of the English nobility, as the Wheelwrights were presumed to be, was worth three or four Native prisoners.

No one's hands were clean during these bitter cross-border conflicts. Even as Esther was growing closer to her Abenaki family, the Wheelwrights were doing whatever they could to get her back. They had yet to play their trump card in this story: they had acquired their own captive, a nameless Abenaki boy.

CHAPTER 8

The Crying Blood

*I*N THE DEPTHS OF WINTER, LIEUTENANT COLONEL Winthrop Hilton led a force of three hundred "hail and lusty" English volunteers to Norridgewock to capture the dangerous Father Sébastien Rale and sack his mission. The English believed Rale had urged the Abenakis to join French forces in raiding their borderland settlements; as John Wheelwright had warned Governor Dudley, "Their teachers instruct them that there is no faith to be kept with Hereticks, such as they account us to be."[1] Exactly a year after the Wells raid, the English took their revenge by sailing a fleet of ships north from Boston through eastern Acadia and Nova Scotia, burning and destroying French settlements, killing their cattle, breaking their dams and taking "about 100 Prisoners and a good Plunder."[2]

But as Hilton's soldiers were soon to discover, there was little "good plunder" to be had in the Abenaki village of Norridgewock. Despite the absence of enemy tracks en route, the men approached Old Point on February 16, 1705, with caution. As they passed through

71

the walls of the eastern gate, Hilton noted about one hundred wig-wams, all abandoned. As the wind cut sharply through the stands of birch and white pine, whirling up eddies of powdered snow, the soldiers lifted the deerskin covers of the wigwams, but they found only "a few household utensils of little value." Disappointed at such poor booty, they pressed on.

Inside Father Rale's mission church, the altar and walls had been stripped bare except for "a few popish relicks," and everywhere there were eerie signs of a swift departure. Ears of corn were scat-tered around the barns, as if Father Rale and the villagers had fled "upon some alarm," leaving behind their precious winter stores. The soldiers deduced from old snowshoe tracks that the inhabitants had decamped at least six weeks earlier. Any chance of redeeming the captives at Norridgewock was lost. In revenge, they lit their torches to the few scattered buildings and watched as they burned to the frozen earth.[3] There would be no news to give the Wheelwright family and others anxiously awaiting the return of their relations.

Only weeks before, the people of Norridgewock had, as the soldiers guessed, quickly packed up their belongings and fled north into New France. Acting on intelligence gathered from among his Indian contacts, Father Rale had decided it was time to leave. A wise decision, it allowed him to both evade capture by the English and respond to pressure from King Louis XIV to move the mission deeper into French territory.[4] During Esther's second autumn with her captors, Father Rale had been singled out for royal criticism. The king was convinced that the mission priest had done a poor job of rallying the Indians in the fight to drive the English colonists from their territory. Father Rale and the villagers were encour-aged to move nearer to Québec, where the Norridgewock warriors could help protect the important settlement of Trois-Rivières from

Iroquois attacks.[5] For the Abenakis, however, moving to Canada meant losing their independence. In the forests along the Kennebec River, they were farther from Québec's influence; they could remain neutral in the ongoing battles between the French and the English. But once they were within Québec's political sphere, their neutrality was in danger of being lost.

Esther and her Abenaki clan were among those who made the dangerous winter journey, following their priest to a newly built palisade on the Saint-François River, south of Trois-Rivières. The villagers strapped on their snowshoes and carried their cargo up the steep portage over the Bombazee Rips, rapids about a mile away. When they reached the Kennebec River on the other side, the canoes were packed tight with bags, food stores and passengers and laid in the icy water, forming a flotilla of twenty or more. Before they reached the highlands, they paddled their canoes through the southernmost chain of ponds that began at Dead River, a tributary of the Kennebec.[6] Esther was old enough to paddle, canoeing with her family downriver before crossing to the headwaters of the Chaudière River. From Moosehead Lake, the villagers portaged on snowshoes, carrying the canoes and all their baggage on their shoulders through the dense forests. This was hard travelling through deep snow in sub-zero temperatures. The travellers slept in the snow—ignoring the cold and the powdered flakes falling round them—and subsisted on a diet of frozen hare and suet. The young men raced ahead of the others across the icy, windswept landscape in their snowshoes, carrying their baggage trains and using their provisions only in extreme emergency.[7]

After more than a week, they arrived at the St. François (now Odanak) mission. Built by the Jesuits on land donated from the local seigneur—it housed refugees driven north because of the border wars and successive outbreaks of smallpox—Esther's second Abenaki home was along a major route for fur traders and merchants.[8] A palisade fort, the settlement consisted of a bastion at each corner, the Jesuit mission church at its north entrance and, in the centre, eighteen houses and the home of Joseph Hertel de Saint-François, the brother of Hertel de Rouville, who had led the Wells raid.[9] Once again, Esther was living inside a military camp, and Father Rale worried about the corrupting influences of the French and the mixed-race traders from nearby Trois-Rivières and Québec. "We are truly out in the country here," he wrote, "but too close to French towns where the Indians go drink and bring ruin upon their bodies and souls."[10]

Proximity to Québec also meant, however, that St. François was within easy reach for Father Bigot, arguably the most powerful priest in New France. Born into an aristocratic French family in Bourges in 1649, Father Bigot entered the Society of Jesus at Paris in 1664 and took up his first Canadian mission in 1680. Accompanied by Father Rale and a delegation of Abenakis, he was credited with establishing, in 1695, the settlement on the Kennebec originally known as Naurakamig.[11] Father Bigot shared with Father Rale a mission to convert both the Indians and the English Protestant captives. As superior general of the Jesuit missions in Canada from 1704 to 1710, Father Bigot often travelled out from Québec to visit missions along the St. Lawrence and down the Kennebec.[12]

An emotionally demonstrative man with a lively humour and a strong sense of his New World mission, Father Bigot was credited with converting hundreds of Abenakis and many English captives, including children, during his long career. As his younger brother, Father Jacques Bigot, reported from the mission of St. François-de-Sales on October 26, 1699, "Our [Abenakis] have begun during the last few days to restore by exchange the English prisoners whom they had taken in war; and in this way . . . the Catholic religion has triumphed over heresy in the very persons of its children." Esther's age, keen intellect and family background made her a prime candidate for a Catholic education.

The historical record offers conflicting evidence on whether Father Bigot stumbled upon Esther after her move to St. François or had "known her from the time of her capture."[13] He may have met her at Norridgewock as well; he mentions encountering her "in those villages," which suggests they met at more than one location. But if he met the Wheelwrights' daughter soon after her capture, it could only have been fleetingly, since he was elected the Jesuits' superior general in 1704 and had moved to Québec by late autumn. Father Rale, then, was Esther's most important Catholic influence once she arrived in Norridgewock.[14] But neither Jesuit priest had the sole authority to negotiate with the Abenakis for Esther's release from her adoptive family.

From Father Bigot's account, it seems that he had ambitions for Esther, who had, in a few short months, become "unwittingly familiar with the holy exercises of a Christian life which were practiced in those wild solitudes."[15] How "unwittingly" captive English children were exposed to Catholicism is questionable, since they were expected to attend Mass with their adoptive parents and were actively encouraged to convert. There were numerous reports of grief-stricken English children being forcibly returned to their Protestant families, terrified at spending the afterlife in hell. Father Jacques Bigot saw one adolescent boy sob when an English officer arrived at his Indian village to take him home. "I shall be lost," he cried, begging his captors to "keep me with you, so that I may not be damned." Another contemporary report described four English girls who "positively refused to return to Boston, and preferred to live with our Savages rather than run the risk, they said, of being perverted by the ministers." A group of seven English boys, hearing that they were to be sent home, hid in the forest "through fear of being taken away."[16]

While the Jesuits suggested that the captives' conversion was based on pious insight and loving persuasion, English observers were convinced that abuse and coercion were at work. Reverend John Williams believed the English children at St. François were under constant pressure to change their beliefs. Reverend Williams, a fervent anti-Catholic and Puritan minister, and later the author of a bestselling book about his captive experiences, was taken with his children, Stephen, Esther and Eunice. "A sight very affecting," he noted in his diary of the child captives at St. François, "they being in habit very much like Indians, and in manners, very much symbolising with them."[17]

Reverend Williams described how the Abenakis separated the children from the adult captives to encourage their assimilation. At St. François, the Abenakis would not allow the captives to miss Mass and compelled them "by force and violence to bring us to church if we would not go." The children quickly learned to please their captors and adoptive parents, Williams claimed, by refusing to speak English and scorning those who did. As his son, Stephen, recalled, "Some English children would scoff at me, and . . . [were] worse than the Indians' children but when alone they would talk familiarly with me in English about their own country, etc., whereas when before the Indians they would pretend that they could not speak English."[18]

Whatever their methods of conversion, Esther was increasingly dependent on her adoptive family once they had moved deeper into

French territory and thus farther away from Wells and the prospect of rescue. On their first meeting, the influential Father Bigot cast an approving eye over this pale-faced English girl, in whose veins, he imagined, ran aristocratic blue blood like his own. Father Bigot saw immediately Esther's potential as a candidate for Québec's convent schools. As he later wrote in a sermon about her, "I shall always remember . . . the sorry guise in which you presented yourself to me the first time that I saw you in those villages—a guise so little in keeping with the frailty and delicacy of your age, which moved me deeply."[19]

The sight of Esther's tattered clothes and thin face moved Father Bigot to tears, but he held back his emotions so as not to upset her adoptive family.[20] Esther had arrived at St. François with her family in 1705, a year when New France was plunged into an economic crisis by the drawn-out war in Europe.[21] Esther's fate was no different—she shared her family's privations, which included exposure to deadly epidemics. Her time with the Abenakis began and ended with outbreaks of smallpox, where the pestilence "entered every wigwam."[22]

Still, it pained Father Bigot to see the white daughter of an important English family so dirty, underfed and poorly clothed, and living among "savages." He believed that Esther remained "an outsider," despite her adoption, because she lacked the physical and psychological toughness to survive the hard mission life.[23] But if Father Bigot was appalled by her physical state, he was deeply impressed by her intellect, since she spoke "the Indian dialect at the end of three years as well as if it had been her own."[24]

Father Bigot listened to Esther, empathizing with her difficult journey along the captive trail, committing her story to memory. Since he had acquaintances in New England, he understood something of her former life and how to turn her experience from a tragedy into a glorious triumph.[25] "An invisible hand," Father Bigot would later explain to Esther, "guided by a sovereign providence was helping you in those rude villages, and indeed it had to keep you there as it did until a more advanced age rendered you capable of making a sound choice of your religion."[26]

Father Bigot realized that the conversion of John Wheelwright's daughter—proof that even a staunch Puritan could be turned—had the potential to attract attention among the French nobility. Among the Abenakis, Esther might prove an able translator and go-between, helping to proselytize about her new religion. A European girl was also more likely to undergo a cultural as well as a religious conversion. The majority of Abenaki converts hoped to tap into the power of Christ and the saints but were less willing to change their lives and customs. Chronically understaffed, Father Rale and the Bigot brothers struggled to persuade their followers to stop eating to engorgement, taking revenge on enemies, torturing captives, and engaging in sexual promiscuity and excessive drinking.[27]

While God's "invisible hand" waited patiently for Esther, Father Bigot set in motion his earthly plans for her future. First, the Jesuits needed to persuade Esther's Abenaki family to release her into their care. Father Bigot offered cash, goods and even another prisoner in exchange for Esther, and when that failed, he tried using "prayers, threats, advantageous promises"—all "without effect." He even considered arranging a kidnapping, but he realized that if Esther were forcibly removed, it would alienate not just her adoptive kin but all Abenakis, who remained vital French allies.

Even if the family had agreed to Esther's release, her politically influential father had already contacted Governor Dudley to demand that the Marquis de Vaudreuil, the governor of New France, return his daughter. The Wheelwrights had probably received news of Esther's move to St. François from one of the English captives already returned to New England, and they were eager to bring her home. As Father Bigot recalled, "If [your parents] are desolated at being deprived of their dear daughter, they are all the more so by the frightful harshness of a savage life to which they see you reduced. There is nothing they are not resolved to do to free you from this harsh slavery."[28]

There were wild rumours circulating in the English colony of the terrible fate of these child captives. Cotton Mather reported in his popular and hysterical pamphlet *Good Fetch'd Out of Evil* how the daughter of Hannah Parsons, Esther's cousin, also named Hannah, narrowly escaped being eaten alive. After three days without food, Mather wrote, Hannah's Indian captors had decided to roast her over a fire, and she was saved from cannibalism only when another Indian fortuitously arrived at the camp. The horrified stranger offered to trade his dog for the English child and took her away from them. "The Child is yet living," wrote Mather. "Her name is Hannah Parsons." Another version of this story had the Indians so intent on eating the girl that they insisted on having a gun *and* the dog before they completed the exchange.[29]

This particular report must have affected the Wheelwrights deeply, as John and Mary had taken in Hannah's surviving sister, Abigail, after William Parsons was killed and his wife captured during a raid on York in October 1703. Taking in Abigail was an act of great charity, since John as a selectman was responsible for rebuilding and feeding the village. As he explained to the government in Boston, the settlers were so fearful of being attacked in their fields during harvest that they faced starvation; the crops they were able to harvest would "come far short of finding us Bread corn." About a third of Maine's population was "either murthered or taken captives, their houses burnt and goods spoiled" during the raids, and the sheer business of survival took precedence over bringing home lost relatives.

But a few English adults and children were redeemed and made the long journey back to New England, including Abigail Parsons' mother, Hannah, who was among forty-four captives released in January 1707.[30] Mrs. Parsons, however, brought back to Maine the distressing news that while living in Montréal, her younger daughter, Hannah, had been baptized a Catholic. With this revelation fresh in their minds, the Wheelwrights must have realized that Esther, living with a Catholic Abenaki family in a Jesuit mission, would be under great pressure to convert. The mother of John Gyles, who was taken captive at age nine from nearby Pemaquid, Maine, described her fears in this way: "I had rather follow you to your grave, or never see you more in this world, than you should be sold to a Jesuit; for a Jesuit will ruin you, body and soul."[31] This terror was another powerful impetus to get Esther back to Wells as quickly as possible.

The Wheelwrights waited a long time for news. The first faint hope that Esther had even survived the raid came in two letters from the Hill family, who were taken captive from Wells in the same raid as Esther. The historian Edward Bourne describes "a day of rejoicing to many, long-waiting hearts" when a letter from Samuel and Elizabeth Hill arrived in October 1704. "The news spread from house to house that a letter had been received," finally confirming that there were survivors of the raid. The Hills reported that the French had treated them well, but they said that the colonial government could be more proactive in helping to gain the release of the other English prisoners. "If the Governor of Massachusetts had only sent one man for me, I and all my family would have been restored," complained Hill. "We are not likely to come here until next summer, when there will be a general exchange of prisoners." A second letter, dated March 1705, from Elizabeth Hill confirmed that Joseph Sayer's daughter and Mary Storer were still alive. Neither letter contained a report of Esther's death, offering hope that she might be among that first batch of prisoners brought home.[32]

The Indians had taken eighty-seven adults and about seventy children captive during the Maine raids, while another one hundred New England colonists remained with the French in Québec.[33] There were half a dozen meetings between French and British officials to discuss these captives' fate, but no agreements were ever signed. Instead, the prisoners were released back to their families at an agonizingly slow pace in a series of "good faith" gestures. Although John Wheelwright had the political connections to maintain pressure on Dudley to act on his behalf, this did nothing to speed the process. While Esther's parents waited for her return, they were keenly aware of just how vulnerable the English children were to acculturation within the Abenaki nation. The longer Esther lived among these foreigners, the more likely she would be lost to an English identity.

The Wheelwrights had much to fear, as Father Bigot was clearly a charismatic and persuasive priest who had successfully converted several English girls, even finding sponsors for their education at the excellent convent schools of Montréal and Québec. His brother Jacques had brought many Abenaki girls from his missions to be schooled by the Ursulines, who took a fourth vow (along with chastity, obedience and poverty) to educate Amerindian girls. Among Father Bigot's protegés was Marie-Anne Davis, who was taken during a raid on Oyster River (now Durham), New Hampshire, in 1693. "Half-dead with terror" after witnessing her parents' murder, she was adopted into an Abenaki family at St. François-du-Lac and soon had "no wish to break her captive bonds." Father Bigot was her spiritual confessor, and he praised her enthusiasm for prayer while teaching her French and "the elements of science." On visits to Québec, Father Bigot often spoke to the St. Augustine sisters at the Hôtel-Dieu about his *petite sauvage*, whose "angelic virtues" stretched to gathering lakeshore flowers to decorate the church altar and spending long hours in prayer.[34]

Brilliant students like Marie-Anne and Esther demonstrated the importance of Father Bigot's mission work and were useful in attracting financial support in France. There was a vogue among wealthy Catholic women to contribute to a dowry, or *dot*, when these former heretic girls entered a religious order. Father Bigot introduced Marie-Anne to the Mother Superior at the Hôtel-Dieu in 1707 and later found a sponsor to fund her admission to the novitiate. "This fair daughter of England, in her picturesque costume with her hair falling over her shoulders," met the Mother Superior wearing beaded moccasins and a white hide robe decorated in quillwork. After Marie-Anne's pleading, she was granted permission to enter the St. Augustine order, and after two years as a novice, she became Sister Davis de Sainte-Cécile, a hospital sister.[35]

Father Bigot had similar plans for Esther Wheelwright, and he gently encouraged her to understand her physical and emotional suffering as a spiritual test. He exposed her to the virtues and rewards of a monastic life that, for the Jesuit missionaries, had its greatest fulfilment in martyrdom. The missions in New France were risky enterprises that could end in torture, murder or death through any number of misadventures. The Jesuits sought out the most isolated and dangerous places in North America, hoping to find there a good death. A Jesuit would salute his brother by saying, "Go, we are delighted you are going to such an abandoned place. God grant somebody splits your head with an axe." And the retort? "No, that's not enough. You must be skinned and burned and suffer all the barbarous ferocity, the cruelest that can be invented. We suffer all that willingly for the love of God and the salvation of the Indians. If it happens, we'll sing the [hymn] *Te Deum*."[36]

Father Bigot's education of Esther was, however, a private affair and contrasted sharply with the grand public displays of the Abenaki boys chosen by Father Rale as his "soldiers of Jesus." On Sundays and feast days, Esther would watch the boys parade through the fortified mission grounds dressed in red gowns with matching caps, supporting a magnificent canopy. Two boys would follow swinging a censer, while a third carried a large set of candlesticks. Another pair held Father Rale's flowing cape aloft, while a second group, dressed in white albs or calico robes, bore a standard of multi-coloured taffeta with St. Xavier's name stitched in gold lettering. Heading the procession was the sachem's son holding a flag of St. Xavier, and behind him followed a line of fifty or sixty "soldiers" dressed for church and armed with pikes. All wore crowns of freshly picked flowers in their hair. Once at the church, the congregation sat before a ten-foot-high painting of St. Xavier while Father Rale sang the Mass in Latin, which he had taught his parishioners to pronounce "as well as the French do." The villagers filled the pews on both sides, with the men at the south end, the women at the north and the children crowded together near the front. In the middle sat the choirboys, all of whom were taught to read so they could follow the words set before them on a lectern.[37]

While Father Bigot quietly lobbied Esther's adoptive parents and kept abreast of negotiations for her return, he maintained a watchful eye over "her practice of Christian virtues" in this heady atmosphere. But religious instruction in the missions was not the sole responsibility of the busy Jesuit priests. Many Abenaki women were respected as spiritual advisers and even followed the practices of the religious communities in Québec and Montréal. Relatives and friends of newcomers to Roman Catholicism often taught them important rituals in preparation for baptism. Then the Jesuit fathers carefully examined the neophytes over an extended period of time. Esther's conversion was neither quick nor superficial.[38]

Esther may even have witnessed women practising self-inflicted mortification, a trend that Father Bigot's brother, Jacques, found disturbing. As the long-serving missionary described it in a letter, "They treat their bodies so harshly I have been surprised by it and have often been alarmed by the blows of their discipline that I have heard when they have withdrawn secretly to some spot removed from their cabins."[39] Father Jacques Bigot described women who, like their European sisters in the colonial convents, attracted their own followers and rejected marriage to lead a monastic life of spiritual contemplation.

One young widow who received her First Communion following her husband's death vowed never to remarry, praying, "I now belong wholly to you, my divine Jesus, and I have no other spouse but you." Another enlisted Father Jacques to explain to her parents that she had promised God to remain celibate to follow a spiritual life.[40] Other women fused Abenaki and Catholic beliefs, and tried to educate their priests about the significance of their prophetic visions; a woman from St. François-de-Sales explained to Father Jacques that her daughter had predicted a serious illness in a dream. "This appears extraordinary to you, my father," she explained, "[but] for us who are accustomed to it, all her dreams are but prayers."[41] What Esther learned from these women is lost, but from her family, siblings and elders she learned to speak Abenaki and her survival was dependent on those qualities of quick learning that Father Bigot so admired in his protegé.

While the negotiations for Esther's redemption continued at a great distance across the two colonies, Father Bigot decided that she was ready for a provisional baptism. Godparents were chosen and she was welcomed into the Catholic Church as Marie-Joseph. Esther was asked to "abjure and renounce" her Protestant faith as "false and full of error" before promising to live and die in her new religion.[42] By renouncing her Protestant faith, Esther was making a devastating break with her English parents. Their passionate adherence to their Puritan beliefs had forced Reverend Wheelwright to be exiled into Maine and had kept three generations of her family clinging to the frontier at Wells. But it was impossible for Esther to resist the subtle persuasion of the Abenakis and the Jesuits; they had determined her identity, while her English parents had failed to keep her safe and then failed again to rescue her.

Father Bigot faced one more obstacle before Esther could leave for Québec to enter the Ursuline convent school. The Marquis de Vaudreuil was under increasing pressure from Governor Dudley to return all captives in exchange for those held by the English. Vaudreuil had to balance these exchanges with his need to maintain the Abenakis as military and political allies while the war in Europe dragged on. The English, meanwhile, failed to understand that the Native peoples acted autonomously and could not be forced to give up their captives. Vaudreuil told the English governor that his ability to redeem captives living among the Natives "was limited." Each prisoner's release must be negotiated individually. Without the co-operation of Esther's adoptive family, it was impossible.

What further complicated prospects for Esther's release was a growing trade in Indian captives. English colonists were offered a cash reward from the government for "any Male Indian Enemy or Rebel capable of bearing Arms, or above the age of 12 years," and this created a demand for Native prisoners in New England. John Wheelwright, realizing that by offering to release an Indian child he might finally persuade the Abenakis to redeem Esther, began his search. Lieutenant Josiah Littlefield, taken from Wells in April 1708, suggested in a letter from Montréal that summer that John had found two Indian men or boys to use as hostages for exchange:

> *Now I have liberty to write . . . for my redemption and for Wheelrite's child [Esther] to be redeemed by two Indian prisoners that are with the English now, and I have been with the governor [Vaudreuil] this morning and he has promised that if our governor will send them that we shall be redeemed, for the governor have sent a man to redeem Wheelrite's child and do lookes for him now every day with the child to Moriel [Montréal] where I am, and I would pray whilrite [Wheelwright] to be very brief in the matter, that we may come home before winter, for we must come by Albany, and I have also acquainted our Governor dedly [Dudley] with the same.*[43]

The man sent to "redeem Wheelrite's child" was most likely Father Bigot, since he was the only known party involved in the negotiations for her release. When there was no sign of either the Jesuit or Esther, Littlefield grew impatient and wrote a second letter, urging "Wheelright to be mindful . . . consearning our redemption."[44] John responded by hiring an agent named Mr. Belcher to accompany "an Indian boy sent from Wells by Mr. Wheelwright, to Albany, by way of New York, or otherwise in the best manner he can, to be exchanged for Mr. Wheelwright's daughter, now Prisoner at Canada."[45]

The Abenakis believed that proper moral conduct rested overwhelmingly on reciprocal relations between people and spirits, and so they took the utmost care in negotiating such arrangements. According to their custom, a family member could not be exchanged for a ransom, so this unnamed captive boy was offered as another crying blood to take Esther's place. There may have been other "small presents" offered, such as a new birchbark roof for their wigwam, and finally Esther was free to accompany Father Bigot to Québec.[46]

The Jesuit superior was convinced that his protegé's "love of our holy religion" was so profound that she already possessed a religious calling. The Wheelwright family, eagerly awaiting the return of their redeemed child, remained the final obstacle to his plans. Father Bigot seemed convinced that if Esther could be sent to a convent school, her vocation would be carried out. The Marquis de Vaudreuil's wife, Louise-Élisabeth de Joybert, a graduate of the prestigious Ursuline school and a friend of Father Bigot's, obliged and provided a home for Esther at the Château St. Louis. The "invisible hand," it would seem, was working in Bigot's favour. With her departure up the St. Lawrence River to Québec, Esther was about to undergo yet another profound transformation in her young life.[47]

CHAPTER 9

At the Ursuline Monastery

*T*HE CHOCOLATE-BOX SCENERY OF QUÉBEC CITY, with its pale green copper roofs, winding cobblestone streets and the Château Frontenac hanging over the Terrasse Dufferin like a cartoon gothic castle, still dazzles. I know the British flattened the city's French architecture in 1759, but the eighteenth-century buildings constructed by Normandy craftsmen feel as European as Calais, Dinan or even Edinburgh. Charles Dickens understood this when in 1842 he described Québec as "the Gibraltar of America . . . a place not to be forgotten or mixed up in the mind with other places, or altered for a moment in the crowd of scenes."

I try to imagine Esther's arrival here in a birchbark canoe with her Jesuit mentor, but the toned muscles of the competitors of the World Police and Fire Games distract me. The emergency workers mingle with Chinese, Dutch and German tourists fresh off the luxury liners docked in the city harbour and packing into the designer shops along the rue du Petit Champlain to buy hand-stitched toques and tins of maple syrup.

A bagpipe's flinty note floats across the street as I check my watch and decide to head up the Rue de la Montagne for my appointment at the Ursuline convent archive. The street where the convent, the school and a museum are housed is mercifully hidden from the heaviest tourist traffic. In the small front garden is a large bronze statue of Marie de l'Incarnation, the Ursulines' founder in Québec. In a bed of pink and white annuals, she stands flanked by two of her pupils; one is dressed à la française and holds an open book, the other wears mocassins, braids and buckskin and holds a pinecone.

It's a romantic, idealized maternal image, even though by today's standards Marie de l'Incarnation might be judged a negligent mother for abandoning her twelve-year-old son to enter the Ursuline monastery in Tours in 1631. It still induces a spasm of guilt that I have left my own daughters at home.

I take a deep breath and push at the convent's heavy oak door and step into the flagstone interior. I fear trespassing in this tranquil place where Esther arrived at the age of twelve, her deerskins smelling of the river, and where she died in October 1780. Have I come halfway round the globe only to find that Esther is just a name on a series of documents, anonymous in her spiritual life hidden behind these cloister walls?

An elderly woman with a wreath of carefully coiffed white hair sits behind the reception desk watching a dubbed episode of *Desperate Housewives* on a tiny television. I reluctantly interrupt the antics on Wisteria Lane to announce my appointment at the archive, where I hope that the convent's extensive collection of letters, diaries and annual histories will provide a record of Esther's life here.

The receptionist picks up the phone and motions for me to wait on a wooden bench worn smooth by generations of nuns and schoolgirls. Within a few minutes, I can hear the click of footsteps down the long interior corridor. As I wait, I notice that the nuns of this ancient community dress in trouser suits and dresses, having long ago ditched their heavy black habits. These days, as one nun tells me, their dress is simple, decent, modest and compatible with their religious character. I wonder what they make of the "wives'" rooms full of shoes, ever-coiffed locks and boob jobs. A guide soon takes me briskly down a maze of lengthy corridors to the tiny archive that holds the convent's institutional history from its founding in the seventeenth century.

The archive is in the St. Augustine wing, built in 1642 on the foundations of the original convent and renovated in 1946. The archivist-curator here is the custodian of the community's heritage, overseeing not only the collections of documents but also the family keepsakes. On a large table, there are already laid out a vellum-clad volume entitled *Registre des entrées et sorties des petites filles française et sauvages de 1641*, a meticulous list of every French and Indian girl who attended the boarding school until 1718. To handle the books I must wear a pair of too-small white cotton gloves. I slip them on awkwardly before opening the volume to search the columns of names.

On a far wall is a niche that houses an altar to the patron saint of mothers, St. Anne. On either side of her flutter two small angels made of cotton and jute, a splendid pair of wings sprouting from their backs. The room is decorated with richly bound leather books in polished wooden cases, paintings of former Mother Superiors and heavy candelabras. The archive is open five days a week, and an appointment is usual. It closes between noon and one p.m.

I open the first register, running my finger down the list of entries. I pull off the gloves and turn to my laptop, typing the names and dates of all the entries for *"angloises,"* English girls who were bought from the Indians by the French and then brought here to be educated as a gesture of piety. I'm surprised by the number and pleased that when Esther arrived, she was not alone.

Gloves back on, my finger stops at the entry for 18 janvier 1709: *une petite Angloise nommée Esther.*

As I read this, the world drops away and I am transported, absorbed, overtaken by an intense curiosity and thrilled at this tiny scrap of physical evidence. Here, in the place that was Esther's home for her entire adult life, I feel her stirring. The slightly sour smell of the paper, the silent slide of cotton on vellum, the fragile scratch of her English name—all contain minute traces of her.

I turn the heavy pages, feeling a shock of recognition every time Esther's name leaps out from the list of girls identified as *"angloises,"* their English names corrupted by a rough translation.

There are astonishing connections with the Wheelwright family and the other captive girls here, and my unsheathed fingers type feverishly, oblivious to time passing, until the archivist politely indicates that the archive will close for lunch. I stumble into the bright summer light.

Esther's parents never saw the school where their daughter was educated, the home where she would live and be buried. As the Jesuit founder, St. Ignatius Loyola, once said, "Give me the child until seven and I will give you the man." Father Bigot, whose prize converts were all girls, understood this to the marrow of his bones.

If there was such a thing as individual choice for Esther, an eighteenth-century captive English girl living among the most powerful and charismatic Catholics in New France, I need to know if she exercised it.

CHAPTER 10

Daughter of Albion

*E*STHER WAS TWELVE YEARS OLD WHEN SHE FIRST glimpsed the jumble of copper gables, slate roofs and brick chimney tops of this rocky outcrop between the Saint-Charles and the St. Lawrence rivers. In the early eighteenth century it was a thriving imperial port; in the ice-free months ships from France, the West Indies, and the Maritime settlements of Louisbourg and Île Royale jostled for space along its wooden docks. There were more buildings and goods than Esther had ever seen before, either at the Jesuit missions or back in Wells. Here Huron and Iroquois traders swapped pelts of beaver, elk, caribou, fox and wildcats for the hard currency of kettles, fish hooks, sewing thread, Venice beads, fuses, powder lead, linens and woollen cloth.[1] The vast square near the docks was a noisy blur of cosmopolitan human traffic: French merchants, domestic servants, seamen, aboriginal traders, African slaves, French *desmoiselles*, housewives and stableboys, as well as nuns from the Hôtel-Dieu and schoolchildren.

If Esther was to resist the sensual temptations of urban life to pursue a spiritual one, then Father Bigot needed to enrol her as swiftly as possible in the Ursuline convent school. Meanwhile, the Marquis and Marquise de Vaudreuil were awaiting their new charge at the Château St. Louis in the city's Upper Town. Originally the site of Samuel de Champlain's defensive fort, the château was still being renovated as the governor's residence when Esther arrived. Their carriage passed by a troop of royal guards in pale grey waistcoats, breeches, cravats and tricornes while a ceremonial drum roll announced their arrival to Philippe de Rigaud, the Marquis de Vaudreuil.[2]

After five years of living at Jesuit missions and in Abenaki hunting camps, the girl who stood before the marquis was barely recognizable as an English child. The first order of business at the château was to wash and dress this Abenaki girl *à la française*. The marquis' young wife, Louise-Élisabeth de Joybert, daughter of a French officer once imprisoned by the English, had the job of supervising the transformation. The marquise was well acquainted with the bewilderment a girl like Esther would be feeling. She herself had lived at the Ursuline boarding school with six Abenaki girls, all but one brought by Father Jacques Bigot, and would have seen these pupils being stripped of their blankets, buckskin, bear grease and silver decorations. She knew well the nuns' expectations of a new pupil fresh from the wilderness of a Jesuit mission. In an eerie reversal of her adoption ceremony at Norridgewock, Esther was washed with perfumed towels, her braids untied and their ornaments discarded. The household would provide her with new linens, silk stockings, a petticoat, a boned bodice, a second-hand sack gown and a linen cap for her freshly washed hair. Esther would be given the first pair of hard leather shoes she'd had since her captivity began.[3]

The marquise would play a more important role in Esther's future than mere guardian with an impressive chest of extra clothes. A fervent Catholic, Louise-Élisabeth was criticized for her close ties to the Jesuits and for being the power behind her husband's throne. "At present everything is in a wretched state," said one of the marquis' opponents, describing her influence. "[A] mere woman is in control, to the same extent when she is absent as when she is here."[4] Father Bigot had delivered Esther into the hands of the most powerful woman in the colony, a woman whose husband would ensure that the English captive was enrolled with the Ursulines and set on the path towards the monastic life the Jesuit envisioned for her.

For the first few weeks after her arrival in Québec, Esther lived in the colony's most resplendent building. The weak winter sunlight drifted through stained-glass windows in the great hall and played on exquisitely handcrafted furniture that rested on flagstone floors. This may have been a residence in a far-flung French colony, but everywhere were reminders of the Marquis de Vaudreuil's powerful royal and religious connections. The wainscotting was lined with portraits of Louis XIV, colonial bishops, intendants (Crown appointees responsible for colonial law and finance) and generals. Above the governor's seat in the dining hall hung a shield engraved with the royal arms and framed by a cluster of white flags that sparkled with golden fleurs-de-lys. Walking through the château, Esther would have passed armouries, walls draped in elegant tapestries, huge stone fireplaces, a shelf with leather-bound books and even a chess set.[5]

If the luxurious furnishings were a surprise for a girl from the forest, so was Esther's new family. In sharp contrast to the fuggy intimacy of the wigwam and the Abenakis' close and affectionate ties to their kin, French families employed wet nurses and sent their children off to school at a young age.[6] The Vaudreuil daughters,

Marie-Louise, aged seven, and her younger sister, Marie-Joseph, would soon be sent to boarding school. Their brothers were destined to become officers serving the French king or to run the colony, like their father. The eldest son, Louis-Philippe Antoine, entered the army when he was just seven, while his younger brother, François-Pierre, was made a gentleman midshipman at five. When Esther arrived, the Vaudreuils were still mourning the loss of eight-year-old Hector and five-year-old François, who had died the previous year, probably from one of the smallpox epidemics that decimated the city's population throughout the century.[7]

Although Esther had to quickly adjust to a new family, this life had its compensations. At the Récollet Cathedral, where the family worshipped, she heard a familiar Latin liturgy read to the exquisite accompaniment of violas, harps and cellos. The meals at the château were served on china plates with silver cutlery and included the unknown luxuries of coffee, imported cheeses and even chocolate. She slept in a soft feather bed between clean linen sheets and was helped to dress by a governess. In the evenings, she attended lavish banquets and all-night balls in the château's brilliantly illuminated hall, where guests spent hours dancing to minuets.[8] The Vaudreuils' houseguests included envoys who stayed so long suspicions arose among staff and townspeople that they were spies; the children's boarding-school friends also stayed, as did visitors from France and the colonies.[9] The household also accommodated many servants, including a cook, a carpenter and a wine steward. Sometimes there were upwards of forty people sitting down to breakfast and dinner.

This interlude at the château, however, was short lived, as the marquis enrolled Esther at the Ursuline boarding school on January 18, 1709. For Father Bigot to see his mission through, timing was becoming critical. Madame de Vaudreuil would sail that spring for France, and without her influence, Bigot may have feared the marquis would take the easy option and send Esther back to her parents, who were pressing hard for her return now that she had been released by the Abenakis. Father Bigot's health was failing too, and his long mission in Canada would come to an end in 1713. While ambassadors travelled between Boston and Québec, carrying letters concerning the protracted negotiations over the many captives held in New France, Esther took her place in the convent school with the Vaudreuils' elder daughter, Marie-Louise.[10] Already Esther was being looked upon not as an Abenaki child but as a European. She was allowed to enter the school reserved for French and English girls under her given name, while aboriginal children were educated separately and expected to go by their baptismal names.

Esther was welcomed into the school with the backing of the Ursulines' most prestigious former pupil, Louise-Élisabeth de Joybert. The marquise had enrolled as a refugee on February 20, 1688, after her mother fled Acadia following the death of her husband, a French officer and fur trader. Two years later, Louise-Élisabeth married the much-older Marquis de Vaudreuil, and the nuns prepared their pupil to move straight from the boarding school into the château—all of which was duly noted in the register.[12] Although such connections were important to the Ursulines for future patronage, every European student, whatever her family background, was treated equally upon entering the school.[13] The *maîtresse des pensionnaires,* or boarding school principal, comforted each new "trembling child" before leading her to be blessed in the Ursuline chapel. The head teacher, Mother Marie-Anne Migeon de Branssat, would decide if Esther lived up to Father Bigot's assessment of her spiritual and intellectual potential.[14]

The physical proximity of the Ursuline convent and school to the colony's centres of power was proof of its importance; the Château St. Louis was opposite and the Intendant's Palace just a short walk away. When Vaudreuil escorted his charge here, she reverted to her English name in the register. As a boarder, she was charged forty *écus* (the large silver coins then used as French currency) for the first term, a fee that Father Bigot paid.[15]

Esther was entering a convent school that had educated French, Indian and captive English girls for more than half a century. It was founded by Marie de l'Incarnation, a young French widow from Tours who left behind her young son to enter an Ursuline convent in 1632. After reading *The Jesuit Relations,* she was inspired to establish a mission in Canada, arriving in 1639 with two Ursuline sisters and a wealthy patron, Madame Madeleine de la Peltrie. She worked ceaselessly to build and fund North America's first school for girls and the Ursuline monastery, proving her business acumen in dealing with local merchants and in drawing up contracts. Aside from running the convent, she found time to write spiritual and historical tracts, an Iroquois catechism, Algonquin and Iroquois dictionaries and hundreds of letters, and she was actively involved in colonial politics.

The Québec Ursulines had a long tradition of educating Algonquin, Huron and Iroquois girls brought to them by the Jesuits. The missionaries, according to the Ursuline historian, "would send the most intelligent of their young neophytes, knowing the immense benefit it would have for the whole tribe."[16] But Marie de l'Incarnation would admit that the school struggled to keep the Native pupils. Esther, who had the special protection of Father Bigot, could sympathize with the difficulty these girls had in adjusting to such an alien environment. As Marie de l'Incarnation wrote,

When they come to us they are as naked as worms and must be washed from head to foot on account of the grease their parents put on their skin, and no matter what care we take or how often we change their linen and dresses, it takes a long time to get rid of the vermin.[17]

These girls were expected to welcome the process known as "Frenchifying," which included being washed with wine or vinegar and dressed in white linen, changed daily. They were to become advocates for and teachers of their new religion and lifestyle. But no Native girl ever took her vows as a nun, and most stayed for only short periods.[18] Some, like Agnes Reskeek, who was brought from Odanak by Father Jacques Bigot on January 19, 1687, quickly died from European diseases to which they had little or no immunity. Nine Native girls were registered as pupils at the Ursuline school before Esther arrived in 1709. These "birds of passage" often found the convent's physical confines depressing—some even scaled the walls to escape or built wigwams in the convent grounds.[19] Marie de l'Incarnation recognized that the free and independent lifestyle these girls were used to was so appealing "that it requires almost a miracle to detach them from it." Even European girls like Esther could succumb to its charms, since "it is far easier for a Frenchman to become a savage than for a savage to adopt the customs of civilized nations." Still, the Ursulines worked to steep the Indian girls in the domestic arts while their brothers remained in the Jesuit missions to learn the catechism and become altar boys or "soldiers of Christ."[20]

When Esther arrived at the convent school, she could speak and read some French and Latin, and was considered ready for classes with the other French girls.[21] Although the Ursulines took pupils from all social classes, the Native students were educated separately.

The *séminaristes* boarded for only four or five months and were set apart by their long-sleeved serge tunics in poppy red, "to satisfy the *sauvagesses'* obvious taste for this colour." To the aboriginal people, red was a colour of animation, emotion, intense experience—of fire, heat and blood. The girls had matching red belts and at night wore bright red bonnets.[22] Their education was limited to reading in their own language, religious studies and housework. If they remained longer, as *séminaristes sedentaires,* they were dressed *à la française* in a simple wool or cotton tunic and black leather shoes made by the monastery's shoemaker. The *séminaristes* who were considered more promising students learned to read, write and sing in Latin, French and their mother tongue. They were trained in "good manners, in the art of needlework and . . . in a thousand other little skills."[23]

Just as Father Bigot had hoped, Esther was educated with girls "formed in virtue." For an intelligent girl who had already endured the traumas of living in the war zone that was Wells, a separation from her family and life as a captive, the convent was a sanctuary. Here there was order: well-cooked food was served at regular meal-times, and there were routines and schedules for washing, for les-sons, for prayer and for play. Esther's interest in monastic virtues would blossom in this clean, ordered school, where the nuns were charged with treating the pupils "like true and loving mothers, car-ing tenderly for their bodies, nurturing their hearts and souls."[24]

In the school dormitory, Esther was woken at 5 a.m. for Mass and an early morning examination of her conscience before breakfast. There were fixed hours for recreation, for class and for study. There were also rules about clothing; the students' necks must be covered, and they were forbidden from having their hair either "frizzed or powdered." While walking in the cloister, even in the garden, they were expected to behave with modesty. They were allowed to play only games that were considered decent and proper. "Comedies, cards, dances, and vulgar songs" were forbidden according to the rules set down in Paris, but battledore and shuttlecock (an early form of badminton), bowls and chess were encouraged.[25]

The standard of education was high. Esther improved her French and Latin, and she learned penmanship, history, science, all in addition to her religious instruction. The sisters taught mathematics using round, flat pieces of ivory or metal called *jetons*. The girls would arrange these in a vertical scale on a box or table, like an abacus, beginning with one at the bottom and moving up in ascending numbers. They were taught the multiplication tables and given simple mathematical problems to solve.[26] The girls recited prose and verse to encourage reading, to improve their memories and to challenge their intellect. On special occasions, the girls acted out dialogues on moral or pious subjects, to learn graceful manners and modesty. As future noble wives, they spent hours over their embroidery, needlework and spinning.[27]

The girls formed strong bonds with their classmates and with the convent's seven lay sisters, who were addressed as "*ma tante*" (my aunt). Class mistresses supervised the girls in their dormitories, even nursing them through illnesses and washing their soiled underwear. The beds, all enclosed with linen curtains for privacy, were lined up in large dormitories, allowing for twenty-four-hour supervision. The girls rose early for Mass in an unheated room before washing and eating a simple breakfast.[28]

In the boarding school, which operated separately from the much larger day school, Esther received the maternal affection of both a class mistress and a supervisor, the *maîtresse générale*. Her teachers followed the direction of Angela Merici, the Ursulines' Italian founder, who felt that nuns should "hold the place of a mother."

The class mistress supervised the girls' life in the dormitory, as well as their religious life through their prayers, and she taught them a range of subjects. After each meal, the nuns watched as the girls washed their "mouth and hands" and brushed their hair (to prevent the spread of head lice). The girls bathed in vinegar or wine, as hot water was believed to spread disease and was used only on the face and hands. Their minds were carefully trained towards religious thought, and they learned to control their emotions and studied in an atmosphere of silence and order.[29]

Father Bigot was proud to learn that Esther was showing promise in her spiritual development and in the domestic arts. Her exemplary embroidery was a tribute to her Abenaki elders, who had passed on the skills at intricate needlework for which their nation was famous. But Esther showed equal promise in her academic subjects, in music and in mastering the intricacies of French etiquette.[30] That she received such glowing school reports suggests that she may have already begun to regard the convent as more than just a stopping point on her journey back to Wells.

Within a month of Esther's arrival, the priest who attended the girls at the boarding school considered her so spiritually advanced that he recommended her for First Communion. This was another compliment to her Jesuit teachers at Norridgewock and Odanak. She spent February and March preparing for this ceremony, where she would receive the sacrament of the Eucharist wearing a white linen dress held by a leather belt, a cap of white taffeta and a white veil.[31] Already Father Bigot's plan for Esther's future appeared to be unfolding smoothly.

Esther may have been helped in her transition from life in the Jesuit missions to the Ursulines' highly ordered boarding school by the other English captive girls who were among her fellow students.

These girls had followed the well-worn path from a Mohawk, Huron or Algonquin village into a French family, where a patron paid for their education. They usually stayed on a few months before being sent back to New England, or they married local men, converted and made their home in the French colony. Those who expressed a desire for the novitiate, however, were exceedingly rare.

As Esther prepared for her First Communion, her ties to the French Catholic community were growing stronger. If she needed inspiration, she could turn to Sarah, also known as Marie-Anne Davis, now Sister St. Benoît. Another English captive, she had briefly lived with Governor de Vaudreuil before Father Bigot brought her to the convent school, where she was "loved by the whole community." Her name first appears on the boarding-school register as "Agathe, *l'Angloise*" on February 6, 1696, and two years later, the bishop of Québec, Jean-Baptiste de Saint-Vallier, asked that she be admitted as a novice.[32]

The Ursulines were so eager to take their first English nun that they accepted her without a full *dot*. Sister St. Benoît had several benefactors who contributed towards her dowry as a choir nun, "but the larger part was given by the Community because of her vocation and because she sacrificed her country for her faith." On March 19, 1699, Marie-Anne finally entered the novitiate, and she took her vows on September 14 of that year. Although she was the Ursulines' first English nun, fifteen other English captive girls had been educated in the boarding school before Esther's arrival in 1709.[33]

On March 7, 1708, Margaret Bourchemin, who had lived among the "savages" for a year, moved from the Château St. Louis to the boarding school, just as Esther later would. In October of that year, Madame de Vaudreuil brought another English captive, Madeline du Fort, to the nuns for six months' schooling. The

Ursulines had years of experience teaching "*les Angloises*" and the Native *séminaristes,* so Esther's teachers were sympathetic to any problems she had in adjusting to their rules and customs.[34] Even Mother Migeon, who had entered the convent when she was ten, had a connection with an Englishwoman who was a relative of the Wheelwrights. Her mother, the wealthy Montréal widow Catherine Gauchet, had employed as a servant Esther's aunt Mary Plaisted, who was taken in the York raid of 1692 with her daughters, the Sayward sisters. Esther entered a community of women whose experience of captivity, redemption and exposure to Native cultures mirrored her own. She lived with girls who understood the strangeness of living with a French Catholic family or the confusion, loss and disorientation of moving from an Abenaki wigwam to the vastness of the Château St. Louis. These captive girls spoke Abenaki and may even have known Esther's clan members or been regarded as blood relations. Like Esther, they had witnessed the murder of parents, siblings and friends during the frontier raids but had adjusted to this grievous loss.

Esther, however, stands out among this exemplary handful of captive girls. She had a father who was actively campaigning to bring his daughter home and would be cruelly disappointed. So began what Father Bigot would describe as a period of "continual waverings between grief and joy" for his protegé, who loved her new school and may have already believed in the Jesuits' vision of her future as a *religieuse,* but mourned her lost family.[35] According to the Ursuline annals, Esther had alarmed the Marquis de Vaudreuil by speaking so soon of a religious vocation. The annals record that "Miss Wheelwright's only desire was to prolong her stay in the monastery, and even to share the life of her pious convent mothers."[36] But Esther had become a political problem because the marquis was under increasing pressure from Governor Dudley to finally bring the captive exchanges to a close.

At the same time, the stakes were high for Father Bigot. His three decades of work in the colony's most remote missions had left him "exhausted in strength and assailed by fevers." He complained that his rheumatism and asthma were growing worse, and by 1710, he was forced to give up his post as superior general. Denied a martyr's death, the Jesuit looked forward only to "consummating the holocaust of his life." Esther Wheelwright was the last of his long line of English captive protegés, and her vocation would be a lasting testament to the Bigot brothers' work. It would also play well at Louis XIV's court, where Louise-Élisabeth de Joybert could offer Esther's vocation as tangible proof of Canada's success in developing as a Catholic colony.

While living at Versailles with her youngest children in 1712, Louise-Élisabeth befriended Jerome de Pontchartrain, the powerful minister of the marine and the man responsible for the colony's affairs. (She became the under-governess to Louis XIV's grandson, the Duc de Berry, the same year her husband was recognized for his work in Canada by being made a commander of the Order of Saint Louis.) Pontchartrain listened to her opinions and was moved by her support for the Jesuits' campaign to educate the "savages" and Protestant captives of New France.[37] This may have helped Father Bigot's quest to find a French lady willing to pay the *dot* for a Protestant convert taking her vows as a *religieuse*. By the time Father Bigot had succeeded in attracting such a patron, he had already raised fifteen hundred *livres* (paper notes) to fund Esther's spiritual education, further evidence of God's "invisible hand" at work on behalf of her endangered soul.[38]

But if God moved in mysterious ways, the Marquis de Vaudreuil did not. He had much more mundane concerns, such as the financial burden of keeping Esther in Québec, since he had the considerable expense of housing her at the château when she was not at school. Vaudreuil had already attempted to recoup his expenses by presenting Pontchartrain with an itemized bill for Esther's clothing, food and housing. This was common practice in both colonies, where expenses were paid by the Crown, but it had become a sore point with the Vaudreuils. The marquise even raised the matter with the minister, pointing out that the couple had "fed and lodged . . . for nearly a year the daughter of the Governor of a small place . . . that had cost the said Sieur de Vaudreuil a great deal, without his having been repaid one *sol* [copper coin], although his predecessors were paid at the rate of four *livres* a day for the English officers whom they had as guests."[39]

On July 18, 1710, Father Bigot used his anonymous patron's fund to pay a second year of school fees for "*la petite* Esther '*Angloise*'." This suited Vaudreuil, since it relieved him of any expense and also meant that Esther was cared for until the negotiations with Boston for all the captives in New France could be completed. Then came news that presented an immediate complication to Vaudreuil's plans to redeem Esther to her parents: the English girl had asked to enter the Ursuline novitiate as a choir nun. The council of sisters met, decided in Esther's favour and set as the date for her entry the Feast of St. Ursula, on October 21. Vaudreuil realized that unless he acted swiftly, the matter might blow up into a diplomatic incident, since his failure to return Esther would upset her parents and, potentially, Governor Dudley. The marquis sent a message to Mother Migeon that Esther must finish out her school year and then return to the château before the feast of St. Ursula.[40] Meanwhile, arrangements would be made for her journey back to New England.[41]

If Esther had already shown signs of a true vocation, she must have realized how influential Father Bigot was in arguing her case. But Vaudreuil had his own agenda, and what followed for Esther was a period of terrible uncertainty. She became the centre of a power struggle between her Protestant parents and her Catholic patrons that echoed the larger religious conflict being played out across two continents. The outcome would determine the course of her life and shape a critical chapter in Canadian and British colonial history.

CHAPTER 11

Le Dossier Wheelwright

I SETTLE INTO MY ARCHIVAL ROUTINE—WHITE COTTON
gloves, laptop and notepaper assembled on the long wooden
table beneath the high window—and slowly plod my way through
large vellum volumes and letters that record Esther's place in the
convent's remarkable history. Every day the past becomes a more
elaborately detailed landscape and characters emerge with their
personal quirks. I begin to decipher handwriting styles and archaic
French spellings.

This afternoon, the archivist leaves me a thick file entitled
"Esther Wheelwright *et famille,* s.d. 1713–1986." It contains correspondence spanning the three centuries in which my relatives made
pilgrimages to the Ursuline convent and corresponded with the
nuns. My uncle Peter and his wife, Barbara Wheelwright, who originally told me the story of Esther, came here in the 1980s, although
I have no idea what they were hoping to find. I discover through
these letters that Esther was lodged firmly in the family mythology
among my relations in Australia, Britain, Canada and the United

States. I am, it seems, following a well-worn path to the convent to understand the mysteries of Esther's life as a captive and her decision never to return to her family in Wells.

Shuffling through the letters and cards, I discover that Ned Wheelwright had corresponded with the novelist William Kirby on December 23, 1897. Kirby's portrait of Esther in *The Golden Dog,* a novel based on his nineteenth-century research, demonstrates the American historian Jill Lepore's argument that "the best novels boast a kind of truth that even the best history books can never claim." In Kirby's case, he wanted to know what Ned knew about Vaudreuil's decision to return Esther to the Ursulines, despite his obligation to the Wheelwrights.

Ned replied, "My kin . . . have the tradition that the governor's son fell in love with Esther and that was the reason she was placed in the convent. You say the governor adopted Esther. The tradition runs, and the records show, that he brought her up as his own daughter but I should hardly think that he could have adopted her, that is, legally." Ned had taken pains to chronicle Esther's story, even gathering oral histories from family members, and this detail about a suitor is remarkably consistent throughout its telling.

I'm pondering this on my lunch break as I head across town to the library in the Frères des écoles chrétiennes to consult the *Dictionary of Canadian Biography.* The entries for the Marquis de Vaudreuil, however, prove disappointing; there are no candidates among his sons who fit with Esther's dates at the Château St. Louis. His eldest, Louis-Philippe, was already an ensign in the French colonial regulars, and the younger sons, Pierre, Philippe-Antoine and François-Pierre, were also serving in the military, while Joseph-Hyacinthe was then just four. Perhaps it was another aristocrat or a visitor to the château who had become infatuated with Esther?

Back in the archives, I trawl through the Wheelwright file for more clues. Then I turn to Father Bigot's testimony of those "years of anguish," when Esther had no idea whether her future lay in Québec or Wells. He describes how he comforts her when she is "all bathed in tears," her moods swinging like a pendulum, her mind seized with unnamed terrors. When she leaves Québec for Montréal with Vaudreuil in 1710, Bigot says that "old wounds" are reopened and Esther senses a "storm about to burst upon her." The language suggests that a violation has been committed against her—one even worse than the captivity that separated her from her parents. Or Father Bigot, who delivered these words in a sermon, may just have been a bit of a drama queen, playing to his audience and building up the tension of Esther's conversion.

Where the old château once stood—on the south side of Cap Diamant, more than three hundred feet above the St. Lawrence—is the Citadelle of Québec, the official residence of the governor general of French Canada. As I walk back to my hotel later that day, I look down from the walls into the steely water, wide as a sea, wondering about the clash between Father Bigot's anguished, almost suicidal teenager and the convent's *demoiselle*, who was "the delight of the Château St. Louis with her wit and grace."

The river brings me back to Esther travelling in that canoe up from St. François in 1708. Back at the hotel I look up an email sent to my sister Penny by John Demos, a historian and the author of Eunice Williams's biography, *An Unredeemed Captive*. Taken captive from Deerfield, Massachusetts, six months after Esther, Eunice married a Mohawk and also refused to be redeemed. Demos had found, at the Historical Society of Pennsylvania, a letter written by Eunice Williams's sister, also named Esther and taken captive herself in 1704.

After Esther Williams was redeemed to Deerfield, she corresponded frequently with the English captives in New France and wrote to her brother Samuel on February 28, 1710, repeating gossip circulating in Québec that John Wheelwright's daughter had given birth to an Indian child. Esther Williams may have been especially sensitive to such gossip because of Eunice's decision to stay in the French colony with her Mohawk husband. Demos believed there was "something behind" this rumour, however, and suggested that either the Ursuline convent or a convent in Montréal would be a possible place for Esther Wheelwright's lying-in.

I close my laptop. Inspired by the men and women battling it out for medals at the World Police and Fire Games, I change into my running gear and head down the rue des Remparts to the docks in the gathering dusk. To my right, Québec's famous rock face rises up, sheer and imposing; to my left, the river swells where boats are loading up with passengers for the evening cruises. I remember my own awkwardness at fourteen and wonder what it meant for Esther to encase her body in a full-length habit of heavy black serge; she would never run or swim again, never have another set of eyes upon her naked limbs, never give or receive an intimate caress.

That twitch of certainty returns, always from nowhere, and my hunch grows that something happened to Esther between the time she arrived in Québec in 1708 and her return to the Ursulines four years later. The rumour about her child "with an Indian" seems easier to disprove than to prove. But if it was true, then Father Bigot covered up a mortal sin by telling the noblesse of New France an exquisitely edited account of Esther's life. In his sermon at her investiture, he took pains to emphasize her purity despite the "perils to her innocence" among the Abenakis.

Would Father Bigot risk his reputation on his last great

English convert if she had borne an illegitimate child? Such unfortunate women were then considered spoiled goods, and rape was merely deemed the violation of another man's property under French law.

Perhaps the anguish that Father Bigot observed was ignited not by her fear of renouncing Catholicism but by some other catastrophic event—that it was some other fresh insult that opened her "old wounds." If a garrisoned soldier or drunken guest in the Château St. Louis had pressed his interests on Esther, she would have had no one to protect her.

I jog my way up the rue de la Montagne, making a promise to myself to cut through the romance to find the source of Esther's anguish.

CHAPTER 12

Years of Anguish

IN THE LATE AUTUMN OF 1710, ESTHER LEFT THE Ursulines' tranquil convent for the Château St. Louis, exchanging her peaceful schooldays for hours of idle conversation about *coiffures*, the latest fashions and the news of the colony's aristocratic families. As Vaudreuil's guest, she was expected to attend the military reviews, banquets and all-night balls, which left considerably less time for reading, lessons and prayers. But according to the Ursulines' history, Esther rose to the challenge, charming her blue-blooded hosts and their guests as she mingled among them dressed in borrowed gowns, stays, shawls and shoes.[1]

Before Esther's departure from the boarding school, the Ursulines carefully considered her spiritual training. Indeed, the Mother Superior discussed the matter with her senior nuns, many of whom had taught Esther, on October 1, 1710. Their dilemma was clear: the "Vullerith" parents had consistently demanded their daughter's return, but Esther, the sisters believed, had shown a clear vocation and demonstrated the qualities needed to become an Ursuline.

The nuns were weighing the spiritual progress made by Esther under the instruction of Fathers Rale and Bigot against their own observations of her eighteen months at the school. They unanimously agreed that she possessed the virtues "of a great gentleness, of wise and virtuous conduct, joined with a fervour which . . . appeared most natural." Loved and respected, she showed no sign of the "*ennui*" to which her schoolmates were susceptible.[2] Even though they believed Esther was younger than her fourteen years, the nuns supported her request to enter the novitiate. Whatever the outcome of the captive negotiations, if Esther chose to defy her parents, it would be with the Ursulines' blessing.[3]

Like Father Bigot, who saw Esther's vocation as a glorious testament to his mission's success in converting Protestants for New France, the Ursulines had an agenda. Eager for recruits with Esther's intelligence, artistic talent and spiritual qualities, the nuns were keen to accept the "*petite 'Angloise'*." During the war, few French novices were able to make the dangerous Atlantic crossing, so the Ursulines were forced to fill their ranks from a small pool of suitable colonial daughters. Their numbers had sunk dangerously low, with only one novice choir nun, Mother Geneviève de la Grange de St. Louis, joining the community in the previous four years.[4] The Ursulines even allowed Father Bigot to pay half the usual fee for Esther's dowry. They felt justified in their actions because they believed Esther was "in danger of returning to her native land and being lost."[5] Esther's request had become a mission of spiritual mercy.

Father Bigot described the brutal drama Esther endured over the next two years, after Vaudreuil moved her back into the Château St. Louis. She felt torn between the Wheelwrights and the convent, and even suggested that a martyr's death would be preferable to her emotional suffering. "I myself am witness, Lord, to what tender expressions she conjured you a hundred times, all bathed in tears, to be pleased to put an end to her fears and alarms in death," he wrote. Esther's longed-for reunion with her family was closer than ever to becoming a reality, and she was devastated. She cried bitterly, begging Father Bigot to send her back to St. François, where she had enjoyed a "blessed" and "kindly" captivity. But she could not, and would not, return to Wells.[6]

Although Father Bigot and the Mother Superior were influential figures in the colony, the decision ultimately lay with Vaudreuil. While Father Bigot assured his protegé that "no one was thinking of sending you back to your homeland," this was simply not true.[7] Vaudreuil had to seriously consider returning this important captive to New England as a way of fulfilling his political obligation to Dudley and recouping his expenses for her lengthy stay. Although she was no longer a minor, he had strong incentives too, since her conversion to Catholicism was insufficient grounds to keep her in Québec if the Wheelwrights refused to believe its legitimacy.[8]

Now began an agonizing limbo for Esther, and for Father Bigot, as ambassadors arrived from New England to press Vaudreuil to exchange the remaining captives. Among them was Major John Livingstone, who arrived from Boston in December 1710 charged with bringing the English prisoners home. After a perilous journey, the major made it in time to enjoy the New Year (celebrated on December 21) and Christmas festivities. His journal hints at a constant round of entertainments that might have irked an aspiring nun like Esther. On December 10, 1710, he wrote of a banquet where the "Governor, Gentlemen and Ladies of ye town [who] were guests . . . were diverted with music and dancing." The next evening the major was again "treated nobly," and a fortnight later, at the Intendant's residence, he listened to an ensemble of trumpets, small drums, flutes and violas while the guests danced. Rather breathlessly for a Puritan officer, Major Livingstone described a fine supper with "at least 50 persons of distinction and ye whole entertainment in great splendour."[9]

According to the Ursuline historian, the soulful adolescent Esther dismissed as "fickle joys" the adult pleasures of these "brilliant circles" of evening entertainments, preferring the contemplative routine of the convent.[10] The Ursulines actually approved of periods when a girl with a promising vocation was sent back into the world, "to test and strengthen her resolve."[11] But Esther was especially vulnerable, since she had no family to protect her from unwanted male attention or the temporal delights that surrounded her. As Marie de l'Incarnation once wrote about these corrupting influences, "[They] are deadly poison for the Religious, especially for the young and attractive . . . Without special protection from God, virtue suffers in the Parlour."[12] Esther could only wait for the colonial governments on both sides of the border to decide her fate.

As the holiday season dragged on, Major Livingstone presented Vaudreuil with a cache of letters, among them a special plea from the Wheelwrights for Esther's return that was sealed in a tin envelope.[13] By December 27, he was growing "very uneasy at so long a stay" in Québec, and despite the bad weather, he began preparing to leave for New England. On January 1, Major Livingstone met with the English captives in Québec, giving them small allowances of cash, taking letters for their families and passing on news from home. Vaudreuil urged patience, warning Major Livingstone that if the negotiations were not conducted properly, this might trigger a new rash of kidnappings.[14]

While the colonial powers used the captives as bargaining chips in the battle for political control, Esther grew increasingly anguished about her future. Over that winter and into the spring, Father Bigot watched her mood swing wildly, from a sparkling confidence in her vocation to terror at the thought of returning to Wells, where she would be forced to reconvert. To which family and religion did she belong, really? The question tormented her, and she knew that whatever decision she made, she was bound to disappoint her English parents or the Jesuit fathers, the Ursulines or her adoptive Abenaki parents.[15]

By February 1711, Vaudreuil had made arrangements for Esther's journey home, but it would be another five months before the roads and rivers were navigable. In July, his servants bundled up her clothes, Bible and other belongings for the trip south to Montréal. The city was meant to be a transit point back to Wells, and Father Bigot described how the thought of travelling there "reopened old wounds" for her. But if she pleaded directly to Vaudreuil, her putative guardian, he showed little sympathy. "Everyone is deeply touched by this," wrote Father Bigot, "but they do not think that they should give in to you."[16]

That summer, when Vaudreuil's party canoed down the St. Lawrence, Esther and Johnson Harmon, an English prisoner and a friend of John Wheelwright's, accompanied them as far as Trois-Rivières.[17] After a brief stop at the settlement, where Esther stayed at the Ursuline convent, they continued to Montréal, where she was deposited with the Hospital Sisters of St. Joseph at the Hôtel-Dieu. Here she was invited to join the nursing sisters in "the constant practices of the religious life," which suggested that despite the current maelstrom, her vocation was strong, and that her training as a novice could continue informally.[18]

Once rid of his young charge, Vaudreuil retired to his summer residence to deal with disturbing reports that Governor Dudley was planning a naval or military attack on Québec. If this were true, all prisoner exchanges would be suspended, including Esther's. But the rumours proved to be false, and several weeks of peace prevailed as Vaudreuil made the final arrangements with the authorities in Boston for Esther's return. The sooner Wheelwright's daughter was gone, it seemed, the better. As he wrote to Dudley,

> *Mr. Wheelwright's daughter being no longer considered a prisoner [since her redemption from the Abenakis] I await only a safe and fit opportunity to send her back although she does not wish to return. As her brother speaks French, he can, with a passport from you, come and seek her, and it will not be my fault if he does not take her back. I will give him every possible help and the change of her religion shall not be a strong enough reason to oblige me to keep her.*[19]

John Wheelwright, the brother delegated to meet Esther, was the eldest of the Wheelwrights' ten surviving children and a well-educated young man of twenty-three who had settled in Boston. Within a decade, he would be a rising star among the merchant class, selling English imports that ranged from indentured servants to Cheshire cheese and nails. By 1727, John had used his contacts among the Native peoples to expand his business into the thriving fur trade, and soon had made enough money to buy a warehouse on the Boston docks.[20] Although the Wheelwrights were clearly eager to get Esther back, John may have had his own agenda—a trip to Montréal would enable him to expand his contacts in New France, even though war had temporarily suspended trade between the colonies.

But finding that "safe and fit opportunity" for Esther's return proved difficult. In August, the governor had intelligence that an army of 2,300 English soldiers was preparing to attack Montréal, while another force of 6,700 was heading for Québec.[21] On September 7, 1711, Vaudreuil returned to Québec to await the English fleet. John's journey north would be put on hold for the duration.

In 1711, Montréal was still home to many English captives who had been sold by the Native peoples to the French colonists as domestic servants. If these captives were not exchanged first, they could work off their own ransom payments or convert to Catholicism. If they changed religion, they were granted permission to live as free citizens. Over that summer and early autumn, Esther discovered a network of Englishwomen, many of whom had defied their families to remain in the French colony, where they married well, owned property and ran businesses or, more rarely, entered a religious order. These Englishwomen had been persuaded to reject their Puritan beliefs for the Catholic message of redemption through Jesus Christ, a vision that cast their experience as captives within a meaningful narrative.

Meanwhile, Esther was living with the Hospital Sisters at the Hôtel-Dieu and meeting members of her own family, former captives who had been taken during Queen Anne's War and subsequently made their homes in New France. At the heart of this network was a French cleric with a mission to convert the English captives and forge their Catholic bonds through baptisms and marriages. Like the Bigot brothers, Father Henri-Antoine Meriel, a Sulpician who had arrived from Paris in 1685, looked for promising girls to be educated—in his case, at the Congrégation de Notre Dame, where he was confessor to the nuns and the pupils. He was adept at finding sponsors for these captive female converts, and he counted among his success stories Esther's cousins the Sayward girls, who were taken during the raid on York in 1702.

Just over the little hedge that separated the Hôtel-Dieu from the Congrégation de Notre Dame lived Esther Sayward, now baptized as Marie-Joseph. She was finishing out her school year before marrying Pierre de Lestage, a prosperous Montréal merchant. Marie-Joseph's sister Mary had also done well under Father Meriel's instruction. A Congrégation graduate who had taken her vows as Sister Marie des Anges, she taught religious instruction at the small mission of Sault-au-Récollet, on the north shore of the island of Montréal, for more than a decade.[22] Among Sister Marie des Anges's pupils was Mary Silver, a captive taken from Haverhill, Maine, in 1708. A sponsor was found to pay for Mary Silver's education and training at the Congrégation de Notre Dame, and she eventually joined the Montréal convent of the Hospital Sisters of St. Joseph.

The ties with Esther were close, since Vaudreuil had stood as Mary Silver's godfather at her baptism a few months earlier. Her story illustrated how it was possible to defy the emotional pleas of your family and enter a religious life.[23] Of course, the Puritan families back in New England were horrified by these conversions. When news of Mary Silver's conversion reached Mary Wainwright, her widowed mother, she submitted a petition to the General Court in Boston for her daughter's return, fearing that "her soul is in very great danger if not already captivated." Determined to follow her vocation, Mary, who was eighteen, refused to return home and instead suggested that her mother should "embrace the holy Catholic faith."[24]

Esther's cousin Hannah Parsons (now Catherine) had also made the journey from Maine to Sault-au-Récollet, where she was baptized in January 1704 by Father Meriel. If the girls needed any further reassurance of Father Meriel's understanding of their background, he might have mentioned his friendship with the Wells minister Reverend Samuel Emery, who had baptized into the First Church of Christ both Esther and Hannah's own sister, Abigail, who became the "adopt[ed] child of John Wheelwright" in 1706.[25] Mary Sayward may have taught Hannah at the mission school before Hannah moved to Montréal, where she became a French citizen in 1713 and later married a French officer, Claude-Antoine de Berman.[26]

While Esther waited for her brother, Father Meriel bonded her more closely to the Anglo-French community by inviting her to stand as godmother to a local child. Dorothée De Noyons was the sixth child of Abigail Stebbins, who had married a Frenchman named Jacques De Noyons in Deerfield before the couple were taken captive in 1704. The family was well known in the colony; Vaudreuil was Abigail Stebbins's godfather, and her godmother, Marguerite Bouat, was the wife of Antoine Pascaut, the royal treasury clerk. When Esther stood for Dorothée, her social credentials were listed in the baptismal record, where she is described as "daughter of Mr. John Wheelwright, Justice of the Peace at York and member of the sovereign council of Boston." Either Father Meriel or the other English citizens were certainly aware of John Wheelwright's formidable reputation. The godfather was eleven-year-old Augustin-Nicholas le Moyne, son of an important colonial aristocrat.[27] Esther and Nicholas promised to help raise and educate little Dorothée as a Catholic if her parents died, a serious responsibility in a period of high mortality and periodic epidemics.

Completing this circle of captives were the Storer girls. All three were taken from Wells with Esther in 1703, and all were converts who had married into the elite of French colonial society. Priscilla Storer worked as a domestic for a Montréal merchant, Pierre Lanequet, before she was baptized at nineteen and married Jean-Baptiste Dagueil, a wealthy officer. When Esther arrived in

Montréal, Priscilla was pregnant with her first child.[28] Her younger sister, Rachel, was baptized on April 16, 1706, and within twenty-four hours had married Jean Berger, a former soldier and painter, much to the dismay of the Protestant captives.[29] Their cousin, eighteen-year old Mary Storer, who was said to be "beautiful . . . with attractive manners," refused her father's impassioned pleas to return home and instead married a merchant, Jean Gaulthier, in Boucherville on November 20, 1708.[30]

What was the incentive for these Englishwomen to remain, at the risk of severing ties with their extended families across the border? One possible explanation is that life in New France offered them a wider range of choices than they could enjoy in the English colony. An ideal Protestant wife was expected to obey her husband and follow his wishes in all earthly matters. In the meetinghouse, she was a member of the congregation but never a religious leader. Honoured for their submission, wives were openly, publicly and demonstrably lesser citizens than their husbands, sons and other male relations.[31] But women, especially those with skills, were welcomed in New France, where single men outnumbered them by roughly ten to one.[32] With so much choice, English captive women often made much better marriages in New France, and they could become both landowners and businesswomen, as several English-women did during Esther's lifetime.

While living at the Hôtel-Dieu, Esther was also surrounded by young Frenchwomen who were weighing their choices between marriage and the convent. Although these daughters of colonial merchants and officers had been spared Esther's captive experience, they, like her, often had to thwart their parents' plans in order to seek a spiritual life. Among them were Marie-Charlotte and Catherine de Ramezay, the daughters of the Montréal governor (and future acting governor of New France), Claude de Ramezay. Marie-Charlotte and Catherine shared Esther's distaste for the "fickle joys" of aristocratic social events. They resented being forced to attend a late-night soirée following a regimental review at the city's military fortifications. Up early the next morning, the girls protested to their mother:

> You are as pale this morning, dear mother, as if you'd been in bed a whole month. It's this wretched ball that's wrecked you. As for us, we've slept from eleven until eight in the morning, we're going to sleep some more in the carriage, and it was with greatest difficulty that we attended Mass . . . Tell us, dear mother, doesn't this noisy and dissipated life vex you?

Madame de Ramezay confessed that she would prefer a quiet country life on the family's estate, but she insisted that duty to the Crown came first. "What would people think of us if we refused to associate with his Majesty's officers, with high-ranking people?" she asked. After coolly assessing their future, the sisters asked to attend the Ursuline boarding school in Québec; Marie-Charlotte entered the novitiate at the Hôpital Général de Québec, while Catherine became a novice in the Ursuline convent. The sisters wished, they said, to "embrace a state which never offers such vexations."[33]

❧

As the weeks passed and John Wheelwright failed to appear, the emotional ties that bound Esther to the French colony grew deeper. John's journey was likely postponed because heavy rains that summer had washed out the roads between Boston and Montréal, making them impassable.[34] Then, in September 1711, journeys north from Massachusetts were cancelled when Admiral Hovenden Walker led a naval fleet down the St. Lawrence in an attempt to attack Québec. The attack was foiled, however, when a tempest blew up along the river and dashed the English ships against the rocks at Île-aux-Oeufs, forcing a humiliating retreat.[35] Dorothée De Noyon's baptism on October 3, 1711, coincided with victory celebrations when news of Walker's defeat reached the city.

Even if John had been able to navigate the rough route north, the weather soon made it impossible, and thus Esther's sojourn in Montréal was over. Before winter set in, she returned along the plains of the St. Lawrence River, past the large land estates, to Trois-Rivières to stay again for a few days with the Ursulines there. Once back in Québec, Esther lived at the Château St. Louis while Vaudreuil wrote again to Dudley, proposing another exchange of prisoners. Father Bigot, in the lull between giving up his post as superior general and his return to France, where he would act as procurator of the Canadian missions, made time for his protegé.

Vaudreuil's letter eventually produced results, and in the summer of 1712, a delegation arrived from Boston to continue the exchange of prisoners. Lieutenant Samuel Williams (the son of Reverend John Williams and himself a former captive) had travelled north with John Nims, Ebenezer Warner and Jonathan Wells, all of whom had female relatives in the French colony.[36] When, on June 15, 1712, Governor Dudley had announced the details of Lieutenant Williams's expedition to Québec before the Massachusetts Assembly, John Wheelwright was among the delegates listening in the chamber. He was no doubt well aware that this delegation represented his last remaining hope for Esther's return.

Although the Wheelwrights feared losing their daughter to the French Catholics, she was actually safer in Québec than in Wells, which still experienced periodic attacks. In July 1712, one of Wheelwright's African slaves had been taken captive while working in fields near the garrison.[37] Indian warriors then attacked the garrison itself, and there was an exchange of gunfire. Captain Wheelwright also discovered young Jonah Titus, killed in an ambush near his home. He wrote to the boy's father, Joseph Titus, after finding the boy's corpse riddled with bullets. "I provided for him a coffin and lining to bury him in for which I was satisfied . . . It was the will of God to dispose of your son and it is a matter of consolation that you have no reason to mourn as one without forgiving, for your son conducted himself nobly."[38]

That autumn, disaster struck the nuptials of Esther's eighteen-year-old sister, Hannah, to Elisha Plaisted.[39] Several men from the wedding party were returning to Wells after the celebrations when they noticed two horses were missing. When it was clear that the riders had disappeared, Joshua Downing, Isaac Cole and a militia officer, a Sergeant Tucker, headed out to find them. Warriors killed Downing and Cole on the road to Wells but took the officer captive. When the rest of the wedding guests heard gunshots, the men rode towards the fields, where they were ambushed by 150 to 200 warriors who stopped the men "by killing their horses under them." Hannah's bridegroom was taken captive, although he was later ransomed and reunited with his bride. Among the guests was Captain Johnson Harmon, lately returned from Québec, where he had travelled with Esther and Governor Vaudreuil to Trois-Rivières.

The English officer most likely brought the news, or confirmed the rumours, that Esther had converted to Catholicism and now intended to take her vows with the Ursulines. Her soul indeed was in mortal peril. When the Massachusetts delegates met with Esther in 1712, they brought letters and pleas from her parents to return home. But under the guidance of Father Bigot, her teachers at the Ursuline school and her English captive friends and relations in Montréal, Esther turned aside these invitations. The Ursuline historian records that she "was closing her eyes to every seductive appeal of her heart, inviting her to return to her country, and to see her family again."[40] The four Englishmen, strangers who spoke neither French nor Abenaki and were actively hostile to her religion, were simply "not forceful enough to persuade her."[41] Lieutenant Williams reported back to the Massachusetts Assembly on September 24 that he had persuaded only nine English prisoners to accompany his party south.

What Esther could not have realized when she faced Lieutenant Williams was that a vicious rumour about her had been circulating among the English colonists. Samuel's sister Esther Williams, taken to Odanak from Deerfield in 1704 and redeemed the following year, wrote frequently to the English captives in Canada. On February 28, 1710, she penned a letter to Samuel, repeating gossip from the captive network in Québec that "Wheelrite's daughter is with child by an Indian."[42] Whatever the truth of the rumour it may have galvanized the Wheelwrights into making one last effort at Esther's redemption.

Father Bigot observed Esther closely during those two years when her future, over which she had no control, remained so uncertain. While she anguished over her decision to remain, Vaudreuil relented to her desire for a spiritual life and the entreaties of Father Bigot and his wife. On October 2, 1712, the Ursulines recorded that the English girl named Esther "aged about 15 and one-half years" (she was actually a year older) began her postulancy. Father Bigot provided the dowry, which was usually paid by the novice's father, and another sum for the trousseau, which included chemises (a long, loose shirt worn instead of underwear), stockings, wimples, hand-kerchiefs, nightcaps, bed linens, table napkins, a place setting, some furniture and a gift for the altar.[43]

While the long-fought war between France and England stag-gered towards its close, deep within the cloister Esther was at least physically protected from any further attempts to force her home. The Ursuline convent offered her a security she had not experi-enced in any of her many homes. Even though she was giving up the temporal world, and the prospect of seeing her family or home-land ever again, she had at last found what she hoped would be an inviolable sanctuary.

PART 2
Esther's Vocation

CHAPTER 13

Le Musée des Ursulines

*I*N MY LITTLE CELL OF A HOTEL ROOM, I AM TORN
between the lonely intensity of an archive junkie and my itch
for contact with real people. So I call London, where sports day at my
daughters' primary school is already over. My elder daughter has won
a medal for sprinting through a waterlogged park in a summer down-
pour, her crown as the fastest girl in the London borough of Lambeth
untouched. Her younger sister lets me speak only to her furry mon-
ster, and he demands to know when I'll be home. Guilt-ridden, I give
my standard answer: "Before you know it."

I ring off and distract myself with my battered copy of *I Leap
over the Wall*, Monica Baldwin's engaging memoir of her life after
leaving the contemplative order where she lived for twenty-eight
years. Baldwin metaphorically vaulted her way back into Britain in
the midst of another war after entering the convent in 1914, on the
eve of the Great War. She had been so cut off from the world that
only when the church bells announced the Armistice did she know
that the First World War had ended.

Most novices, Baldwin observed, entered a religious order to escape an unhappy love affair or because they wanted the peace and stability of a spiritual life. Those with a true vocation were rare and "possessed by a kind of burning hunger and thirst for God, which only he himself can satisfy . . . And those who experienced that contact declared unanimously that it can only be described as a foretaste of the bliss of heaven." In the absence of Esther's own words, I wonder if her entry into the convent wasn't provoked by a combination of all three. Her early Puritan life was certainly shaped by a "hunger and thirst for God." She may have been exposed to unhappiness, or worse, with a man. And the convent did offer her peace and stability.

Piecing together Esther's experience, I uncover an interview I did for a British newspaper with Karen Armstrong, a theologian, former nun and author of *Through the Narrow Gate: A Nun's Story*. As an urbane, fiercely intelligent and highly intellectual woman, Armstrong seemed an unlikely candidate for the convent, a fact she seemed to acknowledge when she told me, "Very few people can be nuns, very few people can live a life that's wholly celibate, wholly without material possessions and submit [themselves] wholly to a religious authority and become a mature person." When I asked her why she had left after seven years, she said simply, "I knew that I didn't have it." There was a lingering hint of chagrin in Armstrong's statement, even though her post-convent life has been extremely successful by anyone's standards—she has written more than twenty books and travels the globe advising religious leaders.

I fling Baldwin into my bag and decide that this morning I will raid the Ursuline bookshop for sources that might help me tackle my struggle to understand the meaning of a vocation. I was raised a lukewarm low Anglican, and my intellect can't quite grasp what it means to love God so deeply that you are willing to give up your family, love, sexual passion and children to spend a lifetime in prayer.

When I arrive at rue du Parloir, I realize I haven't yet visited the Musée des Ursulines de Québec and head there first. When the original museum opened in June 1936 (in the current archive room), the American paper magnate William Bond Wheelwright was invited to attend. Business kept him away, but as a Protestant, he wrote to the Ursulines expressing his kinship with "our Holy Sisters whose predecessors instructed and cared for our kinswoman Esther Wheelwright, whom God protected among the Abenakis in the wilderness."

The new museum, opened in 1964, is a tribute to modern architectural design; display cases flooded with soft light fit comfortably with the embroidered, woven, carved and gilded works of centuries of Ursuline artists. I climb the wide polished stairs to a display of an eighteenth-century nun's cell. On a wall hangs a brass bed warmer and beside it a small writing desk with a quill poking from the inkwell. There is a narrow wooden bed made up with linen sheets, covered in a grey woollen blanket and topped by a high canopy. I resist the temptation to lift the pristine covers and climb into the perfectly made bed, cross my arms across my chest and soak up the experience.

I wander into the next room, where I am mesmerized by a nun doll that lies in a gilt-edged glass box. Her pale face is visible beneath the wimple that sits low on her forehead, her hands hidden inside her black serge robe. Her clothes—sixteen separate hand-stitched items—replicate an Ursuline choir nun's habit in every detail. Known as "the Form," the doll was traditionally kept in a triple-locked cabinet as a teaching aid for the Ursuline students and a template for the convent. Any disagreements over or questions about the habit could be checked against the Form, thus ensuring its consistency from year to year.

The appeal of this peaceful, prepossessing space is obvious: it gave Esther a needed sanctuary from her childhood trauma. Everything from the chapel and the convent rooms to the surrounding grounds suggests a severe and simple dignity. But to achieve that spiritual state as a choir nun, Esther had to give up her individuality and, as Baldwin describes it, "allow the Rule to mould [her] according to the pattern of the Order to which [she] belong[ed]."

Perhaps because the search for individual identity is what drove my generation of women away from marriage and into university and careers, I stumble over this idea of such extreme sacrifice. I cannot turn off the sceptic within, who doubts that Esther could have made this decision on her own. There was always in the background the persuasive and invisible hand of Fathers Bigot, Rale and Meriel.

Once I'm back downstairs in the bookshop, an Ursuline sister disarms me with the story of her own calling. Dressed in a plain-coloured smock, her grey hair parted into wings that sweep out from her face, she patiently combs through her stock for books relevant to Esther's story. After carefully piling a stack next to the cash register and punching in my purchases, she explains how she fell in love with Jesus as young girl. She tells me that she knew "no man would ever give me what Jesus could or love me as much." It is a moment of reverie, as still happy remembering her childhood epiphany, she smiles while writing out my invoice. I smile back, lost for words.

Back at my desk in the archives, I take out my laptop as the morning chorus is in full cry. As I'm setting out my books, I ask the archivist about Esther's vocation. The nuns believe, just as Father Bigot did, that Esther was destined to become a member of the Ursuline community. It was a calling from God that Esther responded to with generosity.

All the nuns I've met here have a sense of humour. They're smart, consummate diplomats and seem to lead busy lives, even though most must be well past sixty. These are not relics of a medieval system—they have a relationship with the world, too. But in the early eighteenth century, Esther had the added burden of heresy to contemplate. When she took her vows, she was turning her back on Reverend John Wheelwright's impassioned mission to complete the unfinished Reformation. She was her parents' worst nightmare.

Like all those generations of Wheelwrights who've trekked up to the convent, I am trying to make sense of pieces that don't quite fit. Father Bigot's story—that Esther was destined for "great things"—is persuasive and laudatory, so it's easy to imagine the power he exerted over his protegé. But I'm alarmed that he portrayed John and Mary Wheelwright's efforts to redeem their daughter as an act of "snatching her away from [God]." I'm troubled by his story that Esther begged the nuns to let her enter the novitiate, and that she felt only anguish at the thought of going home to her family.

Esther left no record of her story, so I am feeling my way through it, relying on my emotional connection to her to fill in the blanks where the black hole of documentation gapes wide. But this story refuses to shape itself into one of a simple religious conversion.

Later in the day, I turn away from the vellum books on the desk and look up at the exquisite blue angels with their polished cheeks and bright dresses to ponder the depths of *la vie spirituelle* as the afternoon turns into dusk behind the high stone walls.

CHAPTER 14

An Ursuline Novice

*I*N ESTHER'S EARLY PURITAN CHILDHOOD, ENTRY INTO heaven was far from assured. Only the purity of a believer's thoughts and actions across a lifetime could guarantee admittance, while hell, with its everlasting pain, beckoned to everyone. Although the other English captives—Marie-Anne Davis, the Sayward sisters and Mary Silver—defied their mothers' religious beliefs, Esther was alone in rebelling against a living father. As the symbolic head of the household, a state representative and the inheritor of Reverend John Wheelwright's beliefs, Esther's father was an indomitable figure. Ironically, it may have been the narrative of her great-grandfather, the religious dissenter, that inspired her to keep faith with her adopted religion and enter the novitiate in 1712. After all, she had inherited the legacy of his spiritual passion, the sacrifices he made for his cause and the stubborn courage of his convictions.

Esther most likely had other options if she wanted to stay in the colony. She would have been regarded as a suitable bride for an aristocratic husband, since women were in short supply. But instead, she chose a highly regimented and disciplined life organized under rules, laid down by the Ursuline congregation in Paris, that made no concession to Québec's culture or climate. Her daily existence was the antithesis of the quotidian life at the Château St. Louis, where the focus for young ladies was on elaborate meals, embroidery, sleigh rides, all-night balls, fashion and finding an appropriate suitor.

Once Esther's contract to enter the convent had been settled in the autumn of 1712, the Mother Superior, Le Marie des Anges, and two of her *discrètes* led the postulant to the choir, the space between the altar and the nave, to receive a blessing. From that point on, the mistress of the novices would guide her in a life that would revolve around prayers, meditation, spiritual readings, confession and communion. For the first three months, Esther lived as a postulant, wearing secular dress but participating in the conventual daily routine. After this first taste of monastic life, she embarked on an eight-day retreat within the convent, fasting and maintaining a strict silence to prepare for her clothing ceremony, or *vêture,* on January 3, 1713, when she would be handed her white veil and her habit. When she emerged on the final day, she would also take her religious name, Sister Marie-Joseph de l'Enfant Jésus, and join the Ursulines' elite choir nuns. She would learn the Latin chants and prayers of the Divine Office, as well as preparing to teach in the Ursuline school and serve in the order's administration.

Without the endorsement of Father Bigot and the Marquise de Vaudreuil, Esther might have entered the order as a lay nun, or *soeur converse.* These women were usually the daughters of local farmers, and they were responsible for the most physically demanding work in the convent's stables, gardens, kitchens and laundries. They offered their labour instead of a dowry and performed domestic work rather than the prestigious rites of the Divine Office. Traditionally, they formed the end of every procession and wore a modified habit. They did not sing in church and read only with the Mother Superior's approval (and, if illiterate, were not always taught to read). The principle was that "those who had nothing in the world may not seek in the convent what they never had outside of it." The lay nuns were not consulted about the community's day-to-day operations.[1]

So it was a measure of Esther's value to the convent that even with a half-price dowry, she was admitted as a choir nun rather than relegated to this relative drudgery.[2] A Paris-educated veteran of forty years, the Mother Superior had welcomed Esther as a boarding student in 1709 and had carefully assessed her qualities.[3] Since the Rules forbade the order to receive any woman by force (a temptation for parents of a daughter with poor marriage prospects), Le Marie des Anges had to weigh Esther's true spiritual devotion. She believed the English captive had come of her own free will and pronounced Esther an excellent candidate for the novitiate.[4] For Father Bigot, the Mother Superior's agreement was the realization of his dream of rescuing Reverend John Wheelwright's great-granddaughter from the hell to which her ancestor's misguided faith had condemned her. With only weeks left before he returned to France, her *vêture* would be his final public triumph.

❧

Before Mass was heard that January morning, elaborate preparations had already begun. Monsignor Charles de Glandelet, the Ursulines' ecclesiastical superior, blessed with holy water the sixteen separate pieces of Esther's new habit, including her linens and a choir mantle. The younger nuns scattered dried flowers and sweet-smelling herbs across the choir's floor before the sexton covered it in a large grey serge carpet. A chandelier was set upon the altar, where the postulant's candle would be placed during the sermon. In a small room that led to the choir, the sexton neatly arranged the blessed clothes, which included a grey serge petticoat, plain leather shoes, a bonnet, a headband, a wimple and a veil.[5]

That morning, Esther dressed in a bridal gown paid for by Father Bigot in lieu of her parents. A Mass was held in her honour in the small, whitewashed sanctuary at the eastern end of the monastery. Later that afternoon, there would be a good crowd to witness her *vêture*, since a captive English girl taking vows in the Ursuline chapel was a rare and curious event.[6] Dressed in fur coats, their hands buried in muffs and their bodies covered by rugs to keep out the bitter cold in the unheated chapel, the family of the Marquis de Vaudreuil joined in the plain wooden pews many of Québec's nobles, who had known Esther at the château.[7] If any evidence was required of the order's urgent need for fresh blood, the worshippers had only to observe that Sister de la Grange de St. Louis was the sole black-veiled novice among the congregation.[8] Behind the sanctuary's grille (a latticed wooden screen that protected the nuns from public scrutiny) sat the boarding-school students.

The cross bearer then passed through the gate and entered the choir, followed by Esther and the rest of the monastery's aspiring nuns in pairs. They genuflected in the middle of the room and arranged themselves along the pews, with the eldest nearest the grille.

Esther paused and told the congregation, Monsignor Glandelet and the Mother Superior that she was ready to enter the order.

I have separated myself from all that the world holds dear and delightful, but I have done so willingly, and I consider such a loss my greatest gain . . . Here when one is weary of attendance to duty, another supplies her place; while one reads, many are edified . . . All will love me truly without guile, without flattery.[9]

All that mattered to Esther now was the small community of Ursulines who would live with her throughout her adult life and her duty to God. She would cease to be "Wheelwright's child," a sister to her far-away siblings and a daughter to her grieving parents. Although she was exercising her will in rejecting their Protestant faith, this would be her last individual act. From that moment, her own desires would be extinguished and her actions would be made for the benefit of her community. Her cloistered life would be hard, silent and austere, but also full of opportunities for a quiet heroism.[10]

Mother Le Marie des Anges held Esther's right hand while her assistant, Mother Poisson de St. Jean l'Evangeliste, held the left. As the three moved towards the altar, the Ursuline pupils chanted in harmony until Esther knelt to receive the Mother Superior's blessing and her new name. For the first time, Le Marie des Anges addressed her publicly as Sister Marie-Joseph de l'Enfant Jésus. As the monastery bell rang, the choir began to sing the Latin hymn "*O Gloriosa Virginum*":

> *Mary! Whilst thy maker blest,*
> *Is nourished at thy virgin breast,*
> *Such glory shines, that stars less bright*
> *Behold thy face, and lose their light.*

Before Esther stepped inside the cloister, she made a low curtsey in front of the Blessed Sacrament and knelt with folded hands.[11]

Monsignor Glandelet blessed a lighted candle and handed it to her. After the prescribed prayers, Esther rose, placed the candle in a holder and sat beside Mother des Anges.

Now it was time for Father Bigot to deliver his sermon on his protegé's life. Before the assembled parishioners shivering in the pews, the priest presented a story of Catholic triumph over the dark forces of Protestantism. The congregation had front-row seats to "a day of inexpressible happiness" as Father Bigot witnessed his "dear protegé" enter the religious life. He recited Psalm 138: "Though I walk in the midst of trouble, thou dost preserve my life; thou dost stretch out thine hand against the wrath of mine enemies, and thy right hand shall save me." Through God's power, the Jesuit father explained, Esther had been "happily transplanted from a sterile and barren land, where [she was] to be a slave to the devil of heresy, to a land of blessing and promise, where [she is] enjoying the sweet freedom of God's children."[12] This was a pleasing contrast for the seasoned officers seated in the pews; Esther was cast as a flesh-and-blood rendering of Louis XIV's desire for French Catholicism to defeat his English Protestant enemies.

After a few more celebratory remarks, Father Bigot traced the arc of Esther's childhood. He described her suffering during the raid on Wells, when many English children had perished. Esther, he said, survived only to be "plunged into the bitter loss of everything [she] cherished most in the world." The "savages" forced her through the vast, tangled forest, where she struggled alongside foreign men "who cared little that [her] steps could not keep pace with theirs." This was the nearest a young woman could come to a martyr's experience in the French colony, and only God's desire, Father Bigot believed, kept her alive on that brutal journey to Norridgewock. "God became manifest" to Esther there, just as he did to Joseph in his biblical captivity, and he prepared her for great things through her gift for languages. In her catechism lessons, Father Bigot watched with delight as Esther's spark of religious conviction was ignited, displacing her "despairing thoughts of captivity."[13]

The possibility of Esther's becoming a *religieuse* was soon apparent to Father Bigot, who drew a parallel with her namesake, the Jewish orphan who became Queen Esther to Persia's King Ahasuerus and saved her people from genocide. Both women had learned that "harsh captivity" prepared them for leadership. No doubt the fashionable ladies seated before Father Bigot knew of Jean Racine's play *Esther*, first performed by the Ursuline-educated schoolgirls of St. Cyr, at Versailles, a few years earlier. The congregation was encouraged to believe they were witnessing a real-life biblical drama in the theatre of Esther's profession.

Father Bigot circled round the sticky ethical problem of the Wheelwrights, who were even then fighting to bring their daughter home. His sermon acknowledged the "loss of their cherished daughter" during the raid, and the priest said that when they learned of "the dreadful harshness of her savage life there was nothing they would not have done to free [her] from such slavery." In Father Bigot's narrative, however, it was not the Wheelwrights but the Vaudreuils who "compassionately felt the sorrows of a mother and father afflicted with the loss of a daughter they dearly loved, taken from them by a tragedy of a cruel war." Even though the Marquis de Vaudreuil was indirectly responsible for Esther's captivity and had complained about the cost of keeping her, Father Bigot presented their relationship as affectionate. The marquis, he said, was "a kind Governor who was prepared to act as father to [Esther], and from whom [she] soon earned esteem and tenderness."[14]

Father Bigot reminded the ladies of the congregation that

their travails paled in comparison to those of Sister Marie-Joseph de l'Enfant Jésus, who was "less a subject for imitation than for admiration." These bewigged and perfumed wives had not the piety or the modesty to copy Esther. "No, no, *mesdames*," he scolded. "She would never compromise holy religion for this love of the world, this love of pleasure that dominates you, for the boundless extravagances of these immodest fashions to which a strict modesty would never be susceptible."[15] He then went on to assure the congregation that Esther had remained pure among the family of nameless "savages" with whom she lived, even though captive women lived without fear of being raped or forced into marriage. But given the rumours circulating through the English captive community about Esther's "child by an Indian," perhaps Father Bigot was simply dispelling any suggestion that his protegé was damaged goods.

After more than an hour in the freezing pulpit, with the light failing fast on a winter's afternoon, Father Bigot rolled up his parchment, which would be given to the community as a souvenir of the event, and concluded his sermon. Mothers des Anges and Poisson de St. Jean l'Evangeliste then led Esther back to the grille for the final part of the ceremony, "the momentous question of vocation."[16] This part had the solemnity and joy of a wedding ceremony—and would generate as much gossip among the congregation.

Monsignor Glandelet asked, "My daughter, what do you seek? The mercy of God, the holy habit of religion, the charity of the order, and the society of the Mothers and Sisters?" She replied, "Yes."

Glandelet then turned to the Mother Superior. "Have you inquired into the other points necessary to be known, for those who inquire into religion, and are you fully satisfied?" he asked.

Mother Le Marie des Anges replied, "Yes, Father."

The monsignor returned his attention to Esther. "Daughter, do you firmly intend to persevere in religion to the end of your life, and do you think you have the strength to bear with constancy this sweet yoke of Our Lord, Jesus Christ, for the love and fear of God alone?"

Esther replied, "Relying on the mercy of God and the prayers of the Mothers and Sisters, I hope to be able to do so." She then curtsied and knelt before Glandelet.

He clasped his hands in prayer. "What God has commenced in you, may he make more perfect. May he banish from your heart the devil and his works."[17] Esther replied, "Amen."

The novice rose, curtsied once more and then slowly withdrew from the chapel as the choir sang "*In Exitu Israel de Aegypto*" (Israel's exit from Egypt), the nuns' expression of joy at being delivered from earthly bondage.

Behind closed doors, Esther was helped to undress before her pale locks were closely cropped from her scalp. There were seven separate items for the *coiffure* alone. Around Esther's freshly shorn head was wound a band of linen, which was then covered by a close-fitting cap. Next, a second piece of linen was pulled tightly across her forehead and tied at the back with strings. Another sister passed her a cotton chemise, then a gown made of grey cotton, and finally a black serge gown. Then came that symbol of poverty: her long black habit of heavy serge. A "day veil" made of fine carded wool covered her head and ears, and fanned out to the shoulders beneath a starched *barbette* that covered her breasts. Over this was pinned a long white veil, which fell on either side of Esther's head to just above her elbows. Between this and its lining of starched white linen was a piece of cardboard stiffened with strips of cotton. Her veil was mounted on an under-veil and held down with metal hairpins imported from the Mother House in Paris. She stepped into pair of black shoes made from French leather and stitched together by the convent shoemaker. Except at her death, no one would again see her unclothed body, and every tender, sensual feeling would be focused through prayer and meditation.[18]

Esther emerged into the sanctuary as the choir chanted in Latin, "*Quae est ista quae ascendit de deserto?*" (Who has ascended from the desert?). With her eyes modestly downcast, she glided towards the grille, where Mother Le Marie des Anges bound her waist with the symbol of obedience, a heavy leather cincture. The habit and veil were symbols of her departure from the world and her inclusion in the Ursulines' spiritual family.

Finally, the choir mantle, the symbolic robe of immortality, was placed about her shoulders as the celebrant implored, "O Lord, hear our supplications and deign to bless thy servant, whom we have just clothed in the habit of this holy order."[19] The Ursulines each renewed their vows of spiritual love and devotion in a "contest of sorts, in which the elders seem to vie with the newly elect in fervor, in happiness, and in gratitude." It was a celebration of the joy of leaving the temporal world "for the love of Our Lord, Jesus Christ."[20]

Then Esther sank to the floor, her arms outstretched in imitation of Jesus on the cross, while the hymn "*Veni, Creator Spiritus*" (Come, creator spirit) was sung and the celebrant called down further blessings upon her.

She rose and slowly passed down the waiting lines of her sisters, who gave her the kiss of peace while singing Psalm 133. The ritual ended as Sister Marie-Joseph de l'Enfant Jésus followed her community out of the choir and into the intimacy of the cloister. As the last nun slipped through the heavy wooden door, a key turned three times, signalling their symbolic departure from the world.

Watching throughout was Father Bigot, who would sail back to France that spring to take up his post as procurator of the missions in New France, satisfied that Esther was finally safe from harm. No one, he believed, could now send her back to that "heretical land" and force her to re-convert.

❧

So began Esther's life as novice. She would live in a separate wing of the dormitory with the other novices (two girls took their white veils soon after Esther) during a period of training not unlike a modern military boot camp. Once in this "little world," Esther no longer had permission to communicate freely with her friends, her family or even the other novices. She lived with these other novices, slept in a dormitory with them, shared meals with them at a separate table in the refectory and took her recreation with them, but she could not speak to them without permission.

For the first year, she would learn the basics of religious life— how to pray and approach the sacraments, how to recite and chant the Divine Office, and how to examine her conscience. Esther and the other novices learned to think of themselves as small, undeveloped and totally dependent upon God. Marie de l'Incarnation compared them to a little sister whose "breasts are not yet formed."[21] They would blossom through the prayers, devotions, meditation, classes, meals and recreation—all of which were scheduled with clockwork precision; the Rules even prescribed how a novice should sit, move her body or hold her hands. The novitiate was designed to be hard because it tested each young woman, breaking her in the monastery's cycle of discipline and prayer.

Esther was taught that every concession to the self had to be regarded as impure, and therefore that she had to extinguish any thought or desire not focused exclusively on God. As one contemporary nun wrote, describing this process, "She is locked into the Noviceship to wrestle with God, her jealous and demanding lover."[22] She followed a routine that was designed to break her spirit and ego so a new self could be formed in place of the old one. The young women began each day long before the sun rose over the Île d'Orléans. At 3 a.m., a lay sister lit a fire to warm the spartan dormitory. Esther's cell—a narrow bed covered in a thick woollen blanket surrounded by thin curtains—was small, with bare walls decorated only with holy images and a crucifix. In a corner, a little desk and chair were her only other furniture. There were no luxuries, not even warmth. Heat from the stove in the corridor was so ineffective in deepest winter that even with doubled woollen blankets and serge coverlets, the novices sometimes slept in their shoes.[23]

At 4 a.m. the rising bell rang, summoning the sisters to wash, dress and join in the procession for 5:30 Mass, when they would recite the Divine Office. Each side of the choir would take turns singing or saying versicles, in a form of call and response. This was followed by fifteen minutes of reading, after which each nun went to her respective duties.[24] Mass was observed several times daily—at the Night Office, Lauds and the Little Hours (Prime, Terce, Sext, None, Vespers and Compline)—so that five or six hours of Esther's days were spent in the official praise of God.[25]

At the end of the grand silence at 9 a.m., the buildings would erupt with noise—the nuns' shoes ringing down the corridors, the children filing into their classes in the Ursuline school, the lay nuns clattering in the kitchen on the lower floor.[26] At 10:15 a.m. the nuns made an examination of conscience (a review of their sins), and then at 10:30 a midday meal was eaten, silently, in the refectory while

1. A portrait of Reverend John Wheelwright, Esther's great-grandfather

2. The headstone of Samuel Wheelwright, Esther's grandfather, in Wells, Maine

3. The only surviving image of the headstone of Esther's father, John Wheelwright, in Wells, Maine

4. *The Capture of Esther Wheelwright*, painted for
St. Mary's Church in Wells, Maine

5. *Abenaki Man and Woman at the Mission Village of Bécancour*, early eighteenth century

6. *Mi'kmaq encampment near Halifax, Nova Scotia*

7. *Plan du village des Abenakis Lévy en l'année 1704*

8. *A Plan of the Inhabited Part of the Province of Québec*

DEATH OF FATHER SEBASTIAN RALE OF THE SOCIETY OF JESUS.
Killed by the English and Mohawks at Norridgewock, Aug 23, 1724.

9. *Death of Father Sebastian Rale of the Society of Jesus*

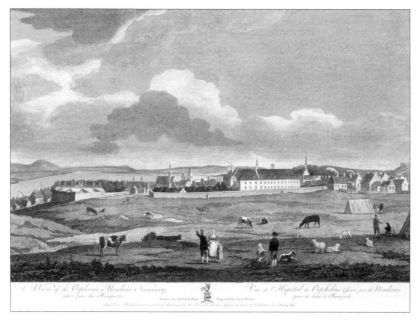

10. *A View of the Orphans' or Ursulines' Nunnery (Québec)*

11. *A View of the Jesuits' College and Church*

12. Miniature portrait of Mary Snell Wheelwright as the Madonna

13. Portrait of Mother Esther Marie-Joseph Wheelwright de l'Enfant Jésus

MENS SIBI CONSCIA RECTI

14. Nathaniel Wheelwright, Esther's nephew

15. The silver *couvert d'argent* set with the Wheelwright family coat of arms, given to Esther by her nephew Nathaniel Wheelwright in 1754

16. Examples of the porcupine-quill boxes made by the Ursulines
under Mother Esther's direction, c. 1760

17. Esther Wheelwright, daughter of Thomas Wheelwright of Norfolk,
Virginia (left), and her cousin Margaret Davis, c. 1897

one sister read from a saint's biography or a theological text. The convent followed the Rule of St. Augustine: "Listen without noise and contention to what is read to you at table, in order that not only may the mouth receive food, but that your ears may be filled with the word of God."[27]

Since the ecclesiastics ruled that only two meals were needed for a healthy life, this midday meal served as breakfast and lunch.[28] Serving and eating were highly regulated and offered the nuns opportunities for "mortification of the palette," where they tasted morsels they disliked or refused food they enjoyed. Food was only fuel for God's work, in their minds, and eating for pleasure was gluttony.[29] After the meal, Esther would walk with another novice to the recreation room, chanting in Latin, *"Deus det nobis suam pacem"* (God give us his peace).

Entering the large recreation room, Esther was taught to kneel and repeat the *Ave Maria* before kissing the floor and taking her seat round the cast-iron stove. She would unfold a parcel of knitting, sewing or mending with the other novices, whose seating was chosen in strict rotation. On a plain centre table, two lighted candles measured out the forty-five minutes when the nuns could speak and laugh freely, like a "family circle without its anxieties and cares . . . [a] society, without its tedious forms and shallow compliments." On Sundays and feast days, such recreation might be extended to an hour. At noon, the church bells announced the Angelus (prayers including the Hail Mary), which was followed by another fifteen minutes of communal reading. Esther sat with the lay sisters, who, aside from those in the kitchen, would join the choir nuns in mending or knitting.[30]

At 2:15 p.m. the nuns recited their prayers of Vespers and Compline, and then supper was served at 5:15 p.m., followed by another recreation period, when the nuns, although afforded little privacy, could write letters. Every day, Esther walked with the other novices through the spacious and immaculately tended convent grounds, which included beds of flowers grown from imported seeds and bulbs, vegetable gardens, fields, stables and orchards with plum and cherry trees. Marie de l'Incarnation had planted an ash tree, where the nuns still instructed their students on warm summer days.[31]

When the nuns' duties were finished, at 7 p.m., the Angelus was rung again. After reciting Matins and Lauds, the nuns made another examination of conscience, listened to the Mother Superior's points on the following morning's meditation and retired to the dormitory to receive her blessing. A bell rang at 8:30 p.m. so the nuns could be in their cells before 9 p.m. to sprinkle their narrow beds with holy water before climbing under the blankets to sleep.[32] Esther was expected to change her linen (underwear) weekly and her bed sheets monthly, while her robes were renewed annually. The Rules dictated that she be well groomed, periodically cutting her hair and remembering to wash her hands, mouth and teeth, and once or twice in the summer, her legs.[33]

As a novice Esther would learn habits designed to limit earthly distractions and to develop detachment. Père Jérôme Lalemant, who devised the Rules that the Québec Ursulines observed, believed the vow of chastity involved "the sacrifice of all other bodily pleasures and goods, even those that are lawful and indifferent, and a placing of all . . . at the disposal of Jesus Christ, her beloved spouse." To obey this command, Esther was taught never to touch another person unnecessarily, to control her tongue, to eat moderately and to avoid profane goods and "the use of all other things that give pleasure to the senses."[34] She was forbidden from swinging her arms and learned to keep her hands clasped together above her waist. To hurry was a breach of decorum, so her steps were short and measured, with her head bent slightly forward. To raise her eyes, even for a moment, without strict necessity was also a serious breach of the Rules.[35]

Mistakes were punished with a public penance in the middle of choir or during dinner. Every novice knew that whenever she broke the Rules, this would count against her when the Ursuline assembly decided whether she should take her final vows. During this testing period, Esther, like all other novices, observed only selected parts of the convent's Rules. Once she had mastered walking, sitting, bowing and standing "religiously," she might be instructed in ringing the heavy church bells. She learned certain versicles (short sentences said or sung by the priest to which the congregation answers), memorized antiphons (sung or said after a psalm) and read the martyrology (lives of the martyrs).[36]

The hardest test for many novices was the restriction against forming close friendships in the novitiate, since this was regarded as "cheating the Divine Bridegroom." To ensure internal harmony, nuns were prohibited from seeking solace from the extreme loneliness of religious life through any intimate relationship.[37] According to Marie de l'Incarnation, there were sound reasons for this seemingly harsh rule, including the "particular friendships and intrigues [to which] such cloistered persons, especially women, are subject."[38] As they would in any monastic order, the women struggled to balance factionalism and common love, individual rights and communal demands, temporal needs and extravagance.[39]

Whenever difficulties arose, it was the responsibility of the Mother Superior, revered as the representative of Christ, to settle disputes. As a novice, Esther was trained to admit lapses such as forgetting to take holy water when entering the community or choir, failing to respect the Mother Superior and failing to respect her vows. Obedience was expressed through ritualized punishments that involved "instruments of penance" to mortify the flesh; usually nuns performed these punishments privately in their cells each week.[40] They used a scourge, a thin, waxed cord knotted into five or six little tails, to whip their backs until they bled. The metal "discipline" had thicker tails that cut and stung the skin even more effectively. Esther might have also used silver barbs or brass-pointed belts against her flesh, or she could have worn a wide horsehair belt strapped between her legs with the ends left loose to prick her skin.[41] Other punishments included standing in bare feet upon the convent's stone floors throughout the night or traversing the Stations of the Cross every hour from midnight until 9 a.m.[42] Penances for misdemeanours usually included taking on hard and unpleasant jobs, such as trudging up and down the stairs from the washroom on the lower floor with aching armfuls of wet washing.[43]

Esther's education included the principles of mortification: to welcome suffering (heat, cold or unpleasant people), to always choose the harder option, to seize every opportunity for self-denial but to omit ordinary penances when unwell.[44] During Lent, "when the spirit of penance is in the air," these practices were very popular among the *religieuses* and were believed to help a nun subjugate her body to the spiritual, "without which the highest adventures in the spiritual life can never be achieved."[45] There was always the danger, however, that such practices could become an obsession, as they had with one of Esther's contemporaries, Louise Pinguet-Vaucours, Sister St. Francis Xavier, who gained a reputation for being "over scrupulous and much given to mortification."[46]

Unlike the other Ursuline novices, however, Esther faced a unique threat to her new religious life. Throughout her first year in the novitiate, she received many letters from the Wheelwrights, pleading with her to return home. Since it was usual for letters addressed to a novice or professed nun to be read first by the Mother Superior, all of Esther's correspondence was a community matter. Even if she had wanted to return to New England, she would have had to convince her superiors and teachers that she was ready to renounce her faith. The Mother Superior could also censor letters before they left the convent, so it would have been impossible for Esther to contact her parents without the community's knowledge and consent.

⧆

The Ursulines realized the consequences for their English novice when the Treaty of Utrecht was signed on April 11, 1713, ending the Seven Years' War between France and England. Her status as a captive no longer protected her, and although she was not a minor, she could be persuaded to come home along with other English citizens. Several English commissioners were already making arrangements to collect their remaining compatriots, and Esther could still be among them. The peace also speeded up Father Bigot's recall to France, leaving her to face the Massachusetts ambassadors alone. The men arrived at Québec on February 16, 1714, to meet with Vaudreuil, and although he agreed that "all prisoners should have liberty to return," they wanted proof that the English captives were not being held against their will. Their suspicions had been aroused by disturbing reports of priests bribing captives to remain in the colony. Vaudreuil was unfazed by these rumours, claiming he could no more stop the clerics than he could "alter the course of the waters."[47]

Just as the Ursulines had feared, the "Bostonnais" arrived at the convent with "urgent letters" for Sister Esther Marie-Joseph Wheelwright de l'Enfant Jésus. Captain John Stoddard and his delegates were received in the parlour, where they spoke to Esther across a grille and passed her letters from her parents written in thick, dark ink and sealed with wax. Her brother John may have translated into French their longing to have "dear young Esther to return to them."[48] Despite her vows, Esther was deeply moved by the letters, and years later she would refer to the "infinite trouble" they caused her.[49]

But the peace treaty also enabled the return of Québec's bishop, Jean-Baptiste de La Croix de Chevrières de Saint-Vallier, who would prove a powerful ally for the Ursulines in their struggle to ensure that Esther remained to take her final vows. Among his first duties when he sailed back into the city after an absence of thirteen years was a canonical visit to the Ursuline convent.[50] The bishop, who had spent several years as an English prisoner, shuffled into the Ursuline chapel as the choir sang the *Te Deum* before a visit to their recreation room. Among the novices was the Ursulines' famous "daughter of Albion," who curtsied before kneeling to kiss the bishop's ring and dutifully answer his questions.[51]

After speaking with Sister Esther Marie-Joseph, Bishop Saint-Vallier discussed her complicated situation with the Mother Superior and her council. Esther had new fears "that her relatives would make more vigorous efforts to get her back again that spring," since there was no longer any legal reason for her to remain in Québec.[52] She had convinced Captain Stoddard that her desire to stay with the Ursulines was genuine—that she was not being held against her will but had taken her vows as a *religieuse* to remain within the cloister throughout her life. Satisfied, Captain Stoddard wrote in his report to the Boston authorities that he had spoken with "some English nuns, whom we found well pleased with their present circumstances."[53]

But whether this was enough to satisfy John Wheelwright and Mary Snell was another matter. The Ursulines realized that the best hope Esther had of ensuring her future in the convent was to take her final vows before a second English delegation, or indeed the Wheelwrights themselves, arrived in Québec. This gave the Ursulines a powerful incentive to shorten the date of Esther's training by more than a year, an unprecedented decision.[54] The Mother Superior met with her assembly to consider the evidence: Esther had for so many years lived away from her family; she no longer spoke English; and she was now an adult under French law. The nuns also contemplated "the changes that might have taken place in her family," as well as Father Bigot's conviction that God had ordained Esther to join them.

The case went up to the highest ecclesiastical authorities in the colony, with the prelate and Bishop Saint-Vallier meeting to review the merits of Esther's case. During the bishop's canonical visit, she begged him to allow the date of her vows to be moved forward.[55] Saint-Vallier, still smarting from his own five-year exile in England, may have easily sympathized with the young novice's fears of being forced back into the Protestant religion. He agreed, and the matter went back to the Ursuline council, which set the date for her final vows as April 12, 1714.[56]

On April 12, the nuns prepared the little sanctuary where Esther had received her novice's white veil just a year earlier. While the nuns silently arranged the flowers and the linen, polished the pews and the chandelier, Esther lay prostrate at the foot of the altar. The nuns smiled to one another, each remembering the day when she "savored a similar joy." Esther had spent the previous week in solitary retreat, contemplating the sanctity of her religious vows and her final entry into a spiritual life.

Later that day, a bearer carrying a crucifix led the Ursuline sisters into the chapel as they sang the *Magnificat*. This would be a private ceremony for the order only. The stooped and shaking Bishop Saint-Vallier officiated in mitre and robes, bearing his crozier.[57] He blessed the precious black veil folded on its silver salver amid the flowers and candles of the altar, praying,

> *O God, may this garment be blessed with most abundant blessings, may it be consecrated, holy and immaculate. Thou art the leader of the faithful and the saviour of the whole body; here is the veil which will cover thy servant for the love of thee and thy blessed Mother; cover her thyself with thy protection so that, pure in soul and body, she, in company with the wise virgins, may also be introduced by thee to the nuptials of eternal happiness.*[58]

Esther advanced to the grille and knelt down before the bishop, a glowing taper in her hand, then asked to be admitted, "although all-unworthy," to the profession. At Holy Communion, Mother Le Marie des Anges asked her to "offer to God the sacrifice of praise."

The nuns replied as a chorus, "And render your duties to the Most High."

Esther responded, "Yes, I shall offer my vows to the Lord; I shall offer them in the presence of his people and in the house of my God."

Esther then made her solemn betrothal to her only spouse before the bishop:

> *In the name of Our Lord, Jesus Christ, and in honour of his most holy Mother, of our Blessed Father St. Augustine, and of*

the blessed St. Ursula, I, Esther Marie-Joseph Wheelwright,
called de l'Enfant Jésus, vow and promise to God poverty,
chastity and obedience and to employ myself in the instruction
of the little French and Indian girls.

She agreed to follow the Ursuline constitution and the authority of the Holy Fathers under the bishop of Québec. Then she genuflected and received the host as Bishop Saint-Vallier prayed. She was renouncing earthly secular love, all ordinary satisfaction and personal fulfilment to take her place within the institution of the Catholic Church.

The Mass moved to its close as Esther sang three times, "Receive me, Lord my God, that I may live!" Her tone was plaintive and supplicating at first but rose in strength as she spoke. As her long black veil was draped across her wimple, she heard the Mother Superior make her perpetual commission: "Receive this sacred veil, symbol of modesty and continence, and bear it without stain to the judgment seat of Jesus Christ, that you merit it to dwell in life eternal and to live forever and ever."[59]

Esther lay face down on the stone floor, her arms flung out in imitation of Christ on the crucifix. Then a heavy funeral pall was laid over her body, covering her completely in a symbolic death while over her surged the chanting of the *Te Deum*. Then she rose to face her sisters, offering them the kiss of peace, strong and serene. She was leaving "the sea of the world, never to return."[60] These women assumed that they would remain within the cold, clean spaciousness of the cloister even after their death.

But God and human forces well beyond her control had other plans.

CHAPTER 15

La Fête nationale du Québec

*I*T'S JUNE 24 AND I AM MUTTERING INTO MY TAPE recorder as I pass the brutalist concrete architecture on Québec's rue René Lévesque, trying to organize my thoughts before I meet Professor Denys Délage, an expert in North American Native history who teaches at the Université Laval.

"Hey! You CBC?" a guy wearing a cap with a Montréal Canadiens logo shouts at me from across the street.

We're a stone's throw from the CBC studio on rue St. Jean, so I could be a radio journalist working on a story. Or perhaps a patient on day release experiencing auditory hallucinations. Take your pick.

"A writer," I shout back, feeling caught out in my reverie. "But not with the CBC." The man and I exchange an awkward half salute as he says, "Have a good one."

The whole city is heaving, tourists and locals alike humming and swaying along with the music of Québec artists like Beau Dommage, Harmonium and Offenbach—an infectious, shared joy on a humid summer afternoon. With a stab, I realize how much I love Canada, even when my life is elsewhere.

The tall, bespectacled, soft-spoken Denys is waiting for me outside a café where a jazz band is playing. I'm late, but he doesn't mind. He's been listening to the music.

We walk west to Denys's home. In the hallway, Pitou, his Portuguese waterdog, marches smartly towards us, assessing the stranger with his soulful eyes. I am enchanted when he accompanies us outdoors to the backyard, which Denys and his wife have spent five years reclaiming from decades of junk.

"Everything was thrown into nature because 'nature' and 'dump' were equivalent," Denys says, guiding me through low shrubs and birches that sit on the edge of a steep rise. "I've introduced plants I found in the woods. I didn't buy any." We brush past an array of serviceberry, juneberry, shadbush, pembina, sweet viburnum, striped maple and Canadian elder. Denys points out the rare species of sugar maple, as well as the willow, box ash and common locust that were introduced to Canada by the first colonists in the seventeenth century and later by United Empire Loyalists like my relatives, who fled here after 1776.

As we walk along, the roar of the traffic is softened by the carpet of green that flourishes beneath a canopy of maples. "I'm trying to have as much diversity as possible," explains Denys, "and I'm looking for the rarest plants, to preserve them." Among the native species are several that were growing when Esther lived here: chokecherry, marsh marigold, hawthorn, phlox, wild onion and wild grape, whose fruit dry into raisins.

I also see maidenhair fern, which the Natives collected and sold to the religious orders. Denys speculates that the Ursulines cooked the leaves into a syrup that helped to prevent pulmonary disease.

Wild sarsaparilla, another popular medicine and a likely staple in the Ursuline dispensary, also grows here.

The dog has disappeared down the hill, and Denys calls him back: "*Viens, mon beau* Pitou."

We settle on folding chairs overlooking the fragrant garden, seagulls cresting the wind coming up from the river. I confess my failure to understand Esther's vocation, admitting to Denys that I'm feeling out of my depth and relying on intuition.

He reminds me of what the Ursuline convent must have looked and felt like to Esther when she arrived from Odanak. "The convent is beautiful. It is quiet; the architecture is exceptional. There is no war. There is a garden. The Ursulines sing in an extraordinary way, and singing was highly valued among the Indians," he says. "Being hosted with love in such a beautiful, serene space, it's understandable why she would have decided to stay."

But what about the Jesuits and the Ursulines? Was their influence so overwhelming that she had no choice but to take her vows?

"Sure there was strong pressure for Esther to become a nun," he says. "She was a spoil of war, and for the Catholics in the early eighteenth century, having any Protestant convert was a victory—but to have a little Protestant girl transformed into a nun was a huge triumph. It was the opposite of what was acceptable to Esther's family."

Denys agrees with my hunch that Father Bigot, Father Meriel and Mother Marie des Anges did everything in their power to convince Esther that the Ursulines were her salvation, and that the Catholic Church offered her the only sure route to heaven. If she returned to Wells, she would be condemned to eternal damnation. "The nuns and priests were convinced of their own beliefs," he says, "and were sure that it was not the best for Esther to return to her parents."

Pitou bounds up the hill and sniffs at a cold cup of tea near my feet. The sky is darkening; a storm threatens.

"We have no documents for this at all," says Denys, the wind now snatching at his words. "But we do know that these decisions were never taken by the person herself. Esther may not have known she was a spoil of war, or how important her conversion was."

So weren't the Ursulines and Father Bigot effectively stealing Esther from the Wheelwrights? Wouldn't we call this brainwashing or grooming if it happened to a kidnapped child today?

"Well, it's a scandal for us to see a religious order keeping a young woman and objecting to her returning to her family. But for the nuns, it was Esther's soul that was important, and the future of her soul in heaven. This was more important than her family, who were [perceived as] heretics."

Before I can begin to feel any righteous indignation on my ancestors' behalf, Denys reminds me about the Abenaki boy whom John Wheelwright captured or purchased for Esther's ransom. There were wrongs committed on both sides during this war.

Just then, the heavens open, and we head up through the garden to the house as the first raindrops fall.

"This boy also had a family," Denys points out. "But the Wheelwrights weren't concerned about them because they considered him a slave." In the Wheelwright garrison at Wells, he would have stayed among my family's African slaves and indentured English servants—people who, Denys says, had no rights at all.

Whatever coercion Esther experienced from her spiritual guides here in Québec, Denys explains, it must be understood within its historical context. I accept that.

After the rainstorm and a delicious dinner, I pat the dog, thank my hosts and head back along the city streets, frustrated that I can't wrench the past open, plunge my hands into its messy form and extract what I long to know.

The city is lit up for its own soirée, with jazz, rock and big-band music mingling up into the sky, past the Château Frontenac's gothic front towers and out over the St. Lawrence. I weave through the crowds and duck down a side street back to my hotel room and my doubts.

CHAPTER 16

Sister Esther Marie-Joseph Wheelwright de l'Enfant Jésus

*W*HEN ESTHER ENTERED THE URSULINE CLOISTER as Sister Esther Marie-Joseph Wheelwright de l'Enfant Jésus, she severed all ties with her family. The ensuing silence would last more than three decades. Although every professed nun in the French colony embraced the community's monastic life by limiting contact with her family to correspondence and occasional visits, Esther's case was extreme. There had been no approving father to pay for her trousseau of linens and silverware, no visits from her mother and siblings across the latticed grille in the convent parlour and little, if any, news about them from Maine. Her parents, who had fought so ardently for their daughter's return, learned to endure her absence, but they would never accept it.

As Esther adjusted to the convent's routine, the teachers and mentors who had guided her to the Ursuline school in 1709 were fading from her life. In 1713, Father Bigot sailed for Paris, where he died seven years later—news that reached the colony just as the

Marquise de Vaudreuil returned from Versailles. But if the governor's wife, now considered "a person of importance and power," took a renewed interest in the English novice, it was short lived. Esther's putative guardian, the Marquis de Vaudreuil, died in 1725, convinced that peace with New England would never last. "This colony will always be the cause of jealousy on the part of the English," he wrote prophetically in one of his last dispatches to France. "We have no more dangerous enemy to fear."[1]

The governor may have been alluding to the recent English massacre of Abenakis and Father Rale at Esther's former home of Norridgewock. After the Treaty of Utrecht, English settlers had increasingly encroached on Abenaki territory, claiming land and fishing grounds as spoils of war. With an explosion of new mills and dams along the rivers, the fish supplies had dried up, and the settlers' large, land-hungry families also pushed back Abenaki hunting territories and scared away their game. When this sparked a fresh round of border skirmishes from the French–Indian forces, the English blamed Esther's former teacher, Father Rale, placing a hefty bounty on his head.[2]

In August 1724, Captain Johnson Harmon, a friend of the Wheelwrights' and the man who had accompanied Esther to Trois-Rivières, led a force of 280 English volunteers to attack the Abenakis and seize the village priest. Even in the lexicon of eighteenth-century attacks, it was especially brutal, as the English soldiers fired on unarmed villagers fleeing across the Kennebec River, drowning many warriors, women and children. Back at the village, Lieutenant Benjamin Jaques broke down Father Rale's door as the priest was defiantly loading his rifle. The Jesuit was shot through the head, and the wife and two children of the sagamore Bombazeen were also murdered. The sagamore was later killed, and his scalp, along with those of Father Rale and twenty-six others, was brought back to Richmond, Maine, as a trophy. Four Abenaki men were taken prisoner, and wigwams were plundered of guns, blankets and kettles. The soldiers ransacked the church and smashed its "idols" before setting it alight.[3]

The shock of the massacre at Norridgewock reverberated throughout the colony, but it must have been especially painful for Esther and Dorothy Jordan, another pupil of Father Rale's, who had entered the novitiate as a lay sister in 1722. Although Esther had probably left Odanak before Dorothy's arrival in 1708, they shared the experience of living among the Abenakis and likely knew each other's family members. Dorothy, who had lived at Norridgewock until the age of eighteen, was initially sent to a French family by another Jesuit, Father Joseph Aubrey, to learn "the rudiments of education and refinement." When this experiment failed, however, she was brought to the Ursuline convent, professed as Sister Saint-Joseph and worked in the convent's laundry throughout her long career with them.[4]

The following year, another link with Esther's past withered away when the Ursulines closed their separate seminary for "the little forest girls," giving up their project of persuading Algonquin, Huron, Iroquois and Mohawk children to "adopt the civilization of European nations." The Ursulines believed there were enough Indian converts in the mission villages along the lower St. Lawrence to spread Catholicism. And so ended the Ursulines' goal of educating Amerindian girls, which had formed Esther's fourth vow at her investiture.[5] The map of her childhood and the people who had inhabited it was fast disappearing.

From the moment Esther became Sister Esther Marie-Joseph Wheelwright de l'Enfant Jésus, her individuality was subsumed by her community as fully as the habit covered her body. Records in the Ursuline archives mark her steady progress through the convent hierarchy as a teacher with increasing responsibility. But from 1714 to 1754, there is very little to find of Esther's internal world, no evidence of whether her life as a *religieuse* brought her the happiness and spiritual fulfilment she had imagined or how the legacy of her childhood shaped her adult life. There are no letters or diaries to reveal her feelings about her English family, her adopted Abenaki clan or the religious teachers who had determined her future.

What seems clear from the Ursulines' record of Esther's achievements over these decades, however, is that the strength of character and intelligence that had enabled her to survive the devastating separation from her family in 1703 now served her well within the convent too. Over the years she rose to become principal of the boarding school and to serve as mistress of the novices, before eventually enjoying great success as the order's Mother Superior.

Esther's extraordinary career began soon after she graduated from the novitiate in 1718, when she was appointed *maîtresse particulière*, or class mistress, in the boarding school where she had once been a student. Her duties were spelled out in twenty-seven articles written by the order's Italian founder, Angela Merici. The first principle was that all children were to be equally supported and encouraged. The nuns were also instructed to be friendly, to set a good example, to listen attentively, to show kindness in their conduct, to be patient and respectful.[6] Above all, the nuns were to work to provide their pupils with a sound religious education, preparing them for "a higher and more blessed life to come" in heaven. The girls were taught basic numeracy, literacy, and the artistic and domestic skills needed to become valuable colonial wives.[7]

Still, a distinctly political agenda underlay the Ursulines' pedagogy. The nuns shared Father Bigot's distaste for the colony's ladies, who demonstrated a "love of pleasure" and "boundless extravagances of these immodest fashions to which a strict modesty would never be susceptible." The Ursulines wished to disabuse their students of "the false values prevailing at the French court," where brocaded and perfumed ladies would turn away from the altar at Versailles to kneel before Louis XIV's throne.[8] Joseph de la Colombière, vicar general of Québec, said the Ursulines' mission was to inspire their charges with "contempt for the pomp and vanities of the world . . . All the young girls under your care should strive to become, by their piety, the living image of the most Holy Virgin Mary."[9] Through their quiet and consistent example, young teaching nuns like Esther hoped to clear up the confusion between the king and the true Father. The Ursulines' Rules, which set out an orderly regime of lessons and activities in their schools, paid close attention to preparing young girls for their First Communion.

Like the nuns, the students followed a life of strict routines and rituals. During Esther's three years as class mistress, her boarding students would have attended Mass with her before their morning lesson, which took place in a classroom plainly decorated with only a religious picture or statue. When Sister Esther Marie-Joseph entered the room, the girls were taught to rise and curtsy before sitting at their appointed chairs. The Rules stipulated that there should be a classroom assistant, known as a specialist, who gave instruction in reading, arithmetic or needlework. At a long wooden table, girls were given quill pens, inkstands, paper and writing models to copy. All instruction was individual or in small groups so that during the short school day (just four and half hours long), each pupil was focused and every classroom occupied. Classes were divided into groups of ten and supervised by a *dixainière*, an assistant who helped with the late-afternoon catechism lesson, distributed the school-books and reported misdemeanours.[10]

Pupils read from books kept in a locked cupboard. Each girl took her turn at reading (Latin in the morning, French in the after-noon) before studying arithmetic or sewing quietly in her place. Then each group would be called out by the writing teacher and taught for an hour before lunch. After the morning session, Esther's pupils returned for the afternoon (another two and a half hours), which began with a recitation of a devotional prayer, the Litany of the Blessed Virgin Mary. A second reading lesson followed, before more arithmetic and writing. At the end of the school day, the girls performed an examination of conscience, a spiritual recap of the day's events, before they were dismissed. One or two pupils were appointed to sweep the empty classroom.

There were clear rules concerning behaviour and activities in the classroom. Part of Esther's job was to ensure a harmonious social balance among her pupils, keeping a physical distance between the wealthier and the poorer children so that "those who are neglected, or who are not well kept and clean" would not "arouse disgust." This had to be accomplished without shaming the poor pupils, of course, and while showing "equal care and an equal affection" to every child.[11] The girls were also taught to respect their teacher and one another, but those who were sullen, lazy or noisy could be punished with "some little embarrassment," such as being made to stand while everyone else sat. The *dixainière* noted disputes, including "any tear-ing of clothes or playing naughty games." In the day school, prohib-ited activities extended to playing "with boys, striking one another or running in the streets as they came to school, or being noisy in the school hall or disorderly in the rank."[12] The school's principal, the *maîtresse générale,* punished more serious infractions, using a whip if necessary. The school encouraged the girls to learn self-control and consideration for others, principles designed to produce intelligent and confident adults.[13]

But there was time and space within this strict routine for Esther to indulge her love of crafts, music and dance. Religious ceremonies were always accompanied by music, often taken from the 120 manuscripts and liturgical chants that the Ursulines owned. In the chapel, there were concerts for the parents and for the congregation, and the nuns occasionally held joint recitals with the Jesuit fathers.[14] Esther was permitted to teach minuets and gavottes, dancing along with her students during the lesson. Artistic talent was also encouraged, especially through the needlework that kept the girls constantly busy. Whenever their schoolwork was finished, they were encouraged to sew slippers and gloves, which were then decorated with ribbons, coloured silks, threads, sequins and lace. The girls mended their own clothes and took turns folding them when their clean things returned from the laundry, ironing the cuffs and collars of their chemises. They kept the dormitory clean and tidy, set and cleared away their dishes in the refectory, made their beds and put away their books and games.[15]

The role of *maîtresse particulière* within the boarding school demanded a degree of maternal intimacy with each student, some of whom were as young as four or five. Most came at the age of ten or eleven to prepare for their First Communion, though, and stayed from two to five years.[16] Esther lived with the girls in the school dormitory, supervising as they washed, dressed, ate and prayed before their morning classes. A second mistress replaced her for the afternoon lessons, while Esther ate supper with the girls, then watched over them as they performed their examination of conscience and said their prayers before tucking them into bed. Students were taught to master "their passions and their bad inclinations" and to discover "their strongest impulses" (perhaps a coded reference to channelling adolescent sexual feelings into the spiritual realm).[17]

Esther's pastoral role stretched even to advising girls on their future husbands, since many convent pupils went straight from the boarding school to their wedding day. There were pressures on girls to marry young because unmarried European men vastly outnumbered women in the colony. Girls were instructed on the "danger to their salvation" from adult men who might take advantage of them. As Marie de l'Incarnation complained, "Girls in this country are on the whole better acquainted with dangerous matters than the girls in France. Thirty girls in the boarding school give us more work than sixty would in France."[18]

Whatever the challenges of imparting virtue and knowledge, Esther proved her competence and, by the late 1720s, had been elected the boarding school's *maîtresse générale*, an office she held for six years. This was a tough position, and Esther was responsible for managing the teachers and the parents, while also ensuring the quality of her students' spiritual education, monitoring their behaviour and doling out punishments when necessary. She supervised the teachers' pedagogy and their methods of discipline, ensuring in particular that no girl was deprived of food or exposed to the cold. Then there were school supplies to purchase, as well as daily attendance and academic progress records to maintain. And girls had to be tested periodically on their suitability for moving into a higher group (there were no grades or years). To guarantee the quality of the girls' meals, Esther ate with them.[19] Disputes between staff and parental complaints fell upon her shoulders. As *maîtresse générale*, Esther slept in the boarders' dormitory, where her duties could include nursing a sick pupil (a dangerous job in a colony that still suffered periodic epidemics of smallpox and other deadly diseases). If a child died, it was also Esther's responsibility to console the parents.

The nuns were aware that their pupils, who came from families wealthy enough to afford the school fees, had to be educated according to their social "rank and position."[20] Although the boarders' trips home were limited to weddings or christenings, the nuns indulged influential parents and friends if they dropped by for visits. Privileged girls, however, were reminded of their social obligations when the *maîtresse générale* invited them to donate cash or even worn clothing to those who sought help at the convent gates.[21]

The relationship between student and teacher outlasted the girls' sometimes short and sporadic school careers. Teaching sisters like Esther were regarded as spiritual advisers and mentors, often providing support long after the girls graduated. The convent was a place of sanctuary in times of personal crisis; an Ursuline might offer her prayers or, with the community's consent, food, shelter or even money. The nuns were proud of their graduates, occasionally making a neat pencilled note in the *Registre des entrées et sorties des petite filles* of prominent marriages. According to oral history, former students would sometimes return to the convent to pass their infants through the wooden turnstile that separated the parlour from the cloister for the nuns' inspection.

Esther's smooth running of the boarding school was crucial to the community's success, since it provided a steady income and kept a high profile among the colony's statesmen and church authorities. The nuns' education standards reassured prospective French colonists that Québec had teachers qualified "to instruct their offspring in virtue and learning."[22] They worked hard to ensure that all students had a solid Catholic education, using donations from the French Crown to offset fees for poor pupils and encouraging wealthy patrons to pay for English girls to board.[23] In the day school, even girls whose parents were unable to afford the fee of one *sol* (a copper coin) per month were given a place. (Each girl paid for her own ink and pens, and was expected to bring firewood during the winter.)[24]

The Ursulines needed to be conscious of their reputation beyond the cloister. During the 1720s, as Esther began her teaching career, her order was embattled. Religious women who ran reformatory institutions still played a vital role in France, but enthusiasm was waning there for the Ursulines' plan to save souls through female education rather than charitable work such as nursing or caring for the poor.[25] More than ever, the convent needed to maintain its good reputation and its excellent relations with the colony's best families—something it did through its students and through the choir nuns who served alongside Esther. Among these influential nuns were Catherine de Ramezay, the daughter of the Montréal governor; Charlotte de Muy, the daughter of Louisiana's appointed governor, Nicolas Daneau de Muy (he died at sea en route to Mobile, Alabama); and sisters Louise and Clare Gaillard, whose father was a naval commander.[26] The convent depended on the generosity of these "people of rank," who often visited to dine at the nuns' table, where names were dropped and favours rendered.[27]

Although Esther's immediate family was outside this system of patronage, her network of English Catholic cousins and friends certainly included "people of rank." They sent their daughters to the Ursuline school and even made donations to the convent. The year that Esther began her teaching career, her cousin Hannah Parsons was registered as a boarder, and she later sent her four daughters to the school.[28] Esther's former neighbour Priscilla Storer, who remained in contact with Esther Sayward (now Madame Lestage), also sent a daughter to the convent, in 1725.[29] And Madame Lestage herself proved an important patron. After the death of her first husband in 1717, she had risen to become the colony's most successful businesswoman and subsequently made many financial contributions to the convent. She may also have been Esther's only source of family news for many decades.[30] The cousins were close friends, and the wealthy Montréal merchant "never tir[ed] in generosity or in showing her affection for her cousin La Mère de l'Enfant Jésus."[31]

Madame Lestage journeyed back to Wells in 1726, bringing the Wheelwrights news of their daughter. John Wheelwright, who had paid for his children's education and ensured that his eldest son was taught French, must surely have appreciated his daughter's accomplishments as a schoolmistress. Unlike her sisters, who were destined to become colonial wives and to raise large families, Esther enjoyed the rewards of a professional life. In 1726, she rose to become a *religieuse vocale*, which gave her both the privilege of voting in the convent's assembly and the new title "Mother." As Esther moved through the community's ranks, she was given positions with increasing degrees of responsibility. After proving her "virtues and her talents" for handling raw recruits in the boarding school, she served three terms in the extremely important role of mistress of the novices.[32]

In Maine, there was also no prospect for a woman with artistic yearnings to see her work on public display, as Esther did. Crammed into her busy timetable was the hour each day where she developed her skills at delicate embroidery, making exquisite altar cloths and turning these religious crafts into "genuine works of art."[33] The elderly Mother Amyot de la Conception taught Esther to fashion silk flowers from wrought tapestry and birch bark, as well as to embroider and produce other fine needlework.³⁴ Mother du Bos de Sainte Marie Madeline, the only mixed-race Ursuline nun (her mother was a Huron), taught Esther to use these same materials in embroidery.³⁵

The Ursulines were proud of their community's artistic skills, especially the gilding of statues, carvings and altarpieces, which required hours of preparation and precise, careful work. Soon after Esther took her final vows, the convent began offering gilding services to Québec's churches to help defray the cost of furnishing a new chapel.³⁶ Ever since Marie de l'Incarnation brought the skills of "painting on thread" and gold embroidery from Tours in the seventeenth century, the Ursulines had become the city's most respected artists, so admired that Bishop Saint-Vallier sent nuns from the Hôpital Général to study their techniques.³⁷ The nuns had earned enough from these enterprises by 1734 to buy two large shipments of French gold and silver leaf for their new altarpiece and to gild their entire chapel, whose architectural design was based on that of Louis XIV's private study at Versailles.³⁸

As Esther approached middle age, she was appointed first portress, the literal keeper of the convent gate, that divide between the temporal and spiritual worlds. Mother Esther Marie-Joseph Wheelwright de l'Enfant Jésus greeted visitors and assessed their suitability for entry into a small antechamber paved with smooth flagstones and furnished with a table, stools and seats. On either side of the interior door was a wooden turnstile, through which the nuns could receive or deliver goods without being seen. Through it passed all the nuns' works of art, personal letters, messages, food and other parcels. This was the critical point of contact with the secular world and the place where family members, friends and former pupils brought news.³⁹

The novelist William Kirby imagined Esther in this role, describing her as a "tall nun, of commanding figure but benign aspect . . . gentle and sedate as became a woman of pure, cold and holy thoughts."[40] But if Esther was that imposing, middle-aged *religieuse*, she was not devoid of passion. During the 1740s, when France and England were once again at war, triggering renewed raids along the colonial borderlands, Esther's traumatic past began to intrude upon her cloistered life. The first interruption of her work and religious meditation was a letter from her mother that arrived in early August 1747. By then, Esther's English had grown so rusty that "a Person of virtue" was dispatched to translate it. The same day, Esther, with the Mother Superior's consent, composed a reply as a messenger waited to race down the rue de la Montagne from the Upper Town before his ship weighed anchor for Boston. Nowhere else in Esther's surviving letters does she express the mixture of affection, sorrow, anger and longing for her lost family. She acknowledged to Mary Snell her sadness at the news of her father's death.[41]

Two years earlier, suffering from gallstones and "other Distempers," John Wheelwright had drawn up his will. Illness had already forced him to resign as a York County probate judge, so he was organizing his affairs before meeting the "King of Terrors."[42] He listed his considerable assets, which would be divided among his wife, four sons and his surviving daughters. A share of his estate would also go to "my Daughter Esther Wheelwright if living in Canada whom I have not heard of for this many years and hath been absent for more than Thirty Years." Even after all that time, John still hoped that Esther might come home. He added a proviso that "if it should please God that she return to this Country and Settle here then my Will is that my Four Sons viz. John, Samuel, Jeremiah and Nathaniel each of them pay her £25 it being in the whole £100 within six months after her Return and Settlement."[43] If Esther left the cloister, she could live again quite comfortably in New England on her father's legacy.

The idea that Esther might suddenly leave the Ursuline monastery after almost three decades as a nun was another vain hope and suggests the poverty of communication between Wells and Québec. The Wells historian Edward Bourne claims Esther wrote to her father "from her captivity [with the Abenakis] and perhaps several times," which kept alive John's hope for her return "to gladden his fireside, even to his last days."[44] Either the Wheelwright parents had no concept of the deep spiritual commitment Esther had made or they chose to believe that even in middle age, she was just expressing an extended form of adolescent rebellion. The Ursuline annals record that after Esther took her final vows, the family had congratulated their daughter, sending a messenger from Boston "charged with letters and gifts."[45] This seems unlikely, however, given John's poignant reference to the daughter "whom I have not heard of for this many years." Mary Snell's letter seems to have been the first overture from the Wheelwrights since Esther's profession. Even then, she felt compelled to placate her mother, smoothing over a painful history and insurmountable religious rift in what amounted to the Wheelwright family's very own counter-reformation. She wrote: "I am greatly affected with the news of the death of my father, whom I loved so tenderly, and whom I shall never forget, and I shall always share with you in the trouble of so grievous a separation."

Although Esther said she was grateful to Mary Snell for "honoring me with one of your letters," she offered to pray daily "that we shall have one day the happiness of meeting together in a *blessed and glorious Eternity*. This is what I wish from the bottom of my heart." While Mary Snell wished for Esther's return to the Congregationalist fold, her daughter hoped for her mother's Catholic conversion. "Oh what joy, what pleasure, what consolation would it give me, my dear Mother, if you had the happiness of knowing this holy religion which a kind providence hath made me embrace since I left you." Only five generations earlier, their English ancestors were Catholics who, Esther wrote, "professed for a long time with much heed and fervor."

Aside from the spiritual concerns, Mary Snell fretted over the state of her daughter's comfort in that unimaginable place, the cloister. Esther reassured her that "as Providence over-rules and governs all things . . . and assisted me in all my ways, this is what ought to lessen your cares and concerns for me." Bound by her vows, Esther would not be persuaded even by her mother's pleas to abandon her community. "Thus you see, my lovely Mother, the impossibility there is of complying with the desire you have of my return to you. It hath been always an infinite trouble to me to resist the desire that you and my Dear Father have so often repeated in times past."[46]

The wording suggests that Esther had, over the years, received other letters from her parents and still felt keenly "the infinite trouble . . . so often repeated" in their disappointment. But as a middle-aged woman, Esther had the cool maturity to reassure her mother that she lacked nothing "as to Temporals," and that her spiritual life was full of "continual favors." She sent love to her siblings, "whom I embrace a thousand times," along with her "tender attachments." Underneath this gentility, Esther hinted at a rapprochement with her mother, promising to write "more largely" and closing with "all love and possible respect," a humble and obedient daughter and servant. She signed as Esther Wheelwright, the name her parents had given her, rather than as Mother Esther Marie-Joseph Wheelwright de l'Enfant Jésus.

After the death of Esther's parents, it fell to her siblings to maintain this fragile contact with Québec, which would play a decisive role in Wheelwright history. Esther's brother John and, in turn, his son Nathaniel realized the powerful place she held within French colonial society. The Wheelwrights, now important merchants in Boston, appreciated that a useful family connection in Québec could help them build up their business, since the colonial system of credit and barter depended on a high degree of trust. By the time a Wheelwright visitor finally appeared at the cloister gates, John had long been trading with Esther's Abenaki kin and had much to gain from expanding into New France. The fates of brother and sister were thus intertwined.

CHAPTER 17

The Search for Esther's Child

*T*HIS MORNING, HUNGOVER, I DRAG MYSELF OUT OF bed at sunrise because I'm running out of time and I'm consumed with following up my lead on the possibility of Esther's having a child. John Demos believes the sequence of events leading up to Esther's entry into the novitiate was especially suggestive. Why, he wonders, was she "staying with the governor (which seems very unusual for a captive girl)"? He asks, "Was she 'lying-in' there till the baby came?"

From the centre of the city, I take a bus to Université Laval, in the suburb of Ste. Foy, which houses the Québec provincial archives. The library may have baptismal records for the St. Lawrence missions and the city covering the period when Esther lived there as a young woman.

The night before, I had asked Denys, an authority on seventeenth- and eighteenth-century Abenakis, to speculate on Esther Williams's rumour that my ancestor had been a mother before she entered the convent.

"It is possible that she had a child with an Abenaki," he agreed. "She would then be about eleven or twelve—that's quite young but not impossible, because Indian women had their children quite early. But it would be surprising if she had a child and left without it. Very seldom would that happen." Perhaps the child did not survive the smallpox epidemic that, according to the historian R. S. Bray, "entered every wigwam" in 1708.

There are endless possibilities, but only two scenarios seem even remotely imaginable: either Esther had a child before she left Odanak, or she was pregnant when Father Bigot negotiated her ransom or soon afterwards and gave birth in Québec or even Montréal.

When the city bus pulls up to the campus, I cross a vast expanse of summer-yellowed grass and roads roughened with frost to the Bibliothèque et archives nationale, a modern glass building. Compared to the campuses of London universities, it looks alarmingly empty and spacious.

Inside the hushed and air-conditioned space, the staff are patient with my French, now slowed by last night's festivities. I am directed to the online PISTARD database and find there a single "Wheelwright" entry, a photograph of the portrait of Esther Wheelwright "*dite* Mère de l'Enfant Jésus." But nothing comes up in a keyword search that would lead me to Esther's child.

I look online at the records of the Institut généalogique Drouin but discover that under the heading "Saint-François-de-Sales Mission Abenakis, Québec Vital and Church Records," the data begin only in 1854. I think again. Esther left Odanak in 1708, when she was twelve, and by 1710 she had been living with the Ursulines for more than a year, which means she could have fallen pregnant while living at the château in 1709. If Esther's child lived in Québec as a "*sauvage*," then he or she would be untraceable, since the earliest city census I can find dates from 1744, and even then, Native people are listed only by their first names, with no clan or family surnames.

A search through the Notre Dame parish records reveals that illegitimate children were occasionally baptized. An entry for April 20, 1705, records the baptism of Jean-Michel, "*fils de* Marguerite Barbeau" and "*d'un père inconnu.*" There is another intriguing reference, to a "Pierre Sanders, *nègre,*" baptized on September 17, 1705, and the son of "Marie *née à* Corlac" and working in service for the Marquis de Vaudreuil. On April 20, 1707, a twelve-year-old boy named Joseph, "*un sauvage de la nation,*" is baptized by Father Meriel, and in May 1711, "*une sauvages[se] de la nation des* Panis *nommée* Marie" has her baptism. Although there are records of the baptisms of English captives, African slaves and Native children, there is nothing of Esther's child here.

Since Abenaki visitors were entertained at the governor's residence, it's possible that Esther became pregnant while at the château. Even though there is no record in the Ursuline annals of the Abenaki families who visited their daughters and took part in services at the chapel, the Ursulines and Patrick Côte at the Musée des Abenakis told me that they were certainly there.

If Father Bigot was so determined to save Esther's soul from the heretical Wheelwrights that he found a home for her child, then he was involved in a coverup worthy of a Dan Brown novel. But it would have been easier for a French couple to adopt a mixed-race child and raise that child as their own. There are many recorded cases of other captive children being informally adopted by French families who went to great lengths to keep them. If such a private arrangement had been made, Esther could still have been presented at her novitiate as a young woman worthy of entering the Ursuline order, despite this misadventure.

Maybe this is the root of Esther's two years of anguish and her longing to be sent back to the convent or to her family in Odanak, rather than to the Wheelwrights, who would never have accepted an Indian grandchild or forgiven a sexual relationship outside of marriage. There would have been every reason for her to stay in Québec, even within the Ursuline cloister, if she was tied there through her own flesh and blood.

CHAPTER 18

The Wheelwrights of Boston

*W*HEN ESTHER WHEELWRIGHT'S MOTHER WROTE TO
her daughter of her father's death in 1747, another major
conflict between France and Great Britain was drawing to a close.
King George's War had broken out between the two powers in 1744,
sparking in the colonies a series of border conflicts, kidnappings
and the English siege of the French port of Louisbourg. Before the
conflict ended, a new generation of captive girls had appeared at
the Ursuline convent school, and ambassadors were once again dispatched from Boston to negotiate the release of English citizens
held in French territory.[1]

When New England's governor, William Phipps, asked the
Massachusetts Assembly for ambassadors for a mission to Québec
in 1752, Esther's brother John offered the services of his eldest son,
Nathaniel. John had the governor's ear because he was commissary
general of the colony and a private banker whose notes were valued at par with sterling in London and Boston.[2] Small merchants,
shopowners, wealthy widows and artisans all deposited their money

with John, who issued interest-bearing personal notes in return for their cash.[3] His French-speaking son Nathaniel, known in Boston as a "good-natured friendly fellow" and apprenticed to the merchant Thomas Hancock (father of John Hancock), was an obvious choice for Phipps's ambassadorial mission to New France.[4]

Captain Phineas Stevens, a veteran negotiator, led the party north to Québec, where Nathaniel would meet "the lady abbess" at the Ursuline convent, the first member of the Wheelwright family ever to do so. The ambassadors stopped in Montréal before riding farther north to seek out captives held at Trois-Rivières and Québec, where they met with the acting colonial governor, Charles le Moyne, Baron de Longueuil.[5] On Nathaniel's first visit to the Ursuline convent in 1752, he requested an interview with his aunt, Mother Esther Marie-Joseph Wheelwright de l'Enfant Jésus. He waited patiently in the parlour until he heard her footsteps moving across the flagstones, her black robe sweeping the ground, her long rosary swinging from the leather cincture at her waist.

Was it a shock for Nathaniel to see his English aunt dressed as a *religieuse?* If there was any initial awkwardness it soon dissipated, as Nathaniel noted in his journal how they quickly came to regard each other as "close relations" and even friends. During the summer of 1752, they met several times, with Nathaniel recording in his journal an astonishing conversation he had with Esther on June 13:

> *She gave me a particular account of her being detained in Canada, after she got out of the hands of the Indians, and the reasons why she was not returned according to the desire of her father and the promise of Monsieur La Marquis de Vaudruille [sic] . . . who received her as a present from the Indians and I always understood he was at the expense of her education, and*

of putting her into the nunnery, as they are obliged to give a sum of money with everyone. He had the credit of this but my aunt gave me to understand the contrary. She said she lived some time with Mons. De Vaudreuille, and as he had given his promise, was or appeared willing to return her, but finding an opportunity to reimburse himself, or rather get money . . . and at the same time have the credit of doing a charitable action, he forfeited his word, and sold her to a priest [Father Bigot] who had a sum of money given him by a lady in France to make a nun, and who paid Mons. de Vaudreuille 1400 livres for the expen[s]es he had been at as he said for her ransom and during her stay with him, as he produced an account which he made amount to that extravagant sum. Thus she was put into the convent without the least obligation to Mons. de Vaudreuille or his family.[6]

This journal entry is the only occasion when Esther gave her version (albeit mediated through Nathaniel) of how she became an Ursuline nun and why she had not returned to New England. Unlike Father Bigot's version, which was delivered as a public event, this was part of a private conversation where details were disclosed to a "close relation."

Nathaniel's grandparents and father had always understood that the Marquis de Vaudreuil had agreed to return Esther and so had removed her from the Ursuline school when the nuns set a date for her entry into the novitiate. But according to Esther, Vaudreuil changed his mind when he was offered a deal by Father Bigot. The patron's fund for Esther's religious education had also been used to reimburse the Vaudreuils for outfitting the English captive and for her upkeep at the Château St. Louis. Esther's entry into the novitiate provided Vaudreuil with "the credit of doing a charitable action," even if it meant betraying his agreement with the Wheelwrights and the New England government. The most enduring consequence of this transaction for Esther, however, was that she remained in debt to the community throughout her life. Perhaps this was a subtle hint that Nathaniel could right this ancient injustice.

Esther might have been attempting to persuade her wealthy nephew—and her brother John—that he was obliged to balance her books at the convent. She was a powerful contact for Nathaniel, who was negotiating for the release of English captives with her own Abenaki kin at the St. Lawrence missions and with the Ursulines of Trois-Rivières. Esther knew the villages, spoke Abenaki, was once an adopted daughter of an Abenaki clan and might even have known the captors or their families. Moreover, she had followed her own botched negotiations for release almost fifty years before, and if Nathaniel wanted to succeed, she was the perfect go-between and adviser.

But whatever assistance Esther gave her nephew in 1752, the ambassadors returned to Boston without the two captives they sought: four-year-old Fanny Noble and her brother, ten-year-old Joseph, taken from Swan's Island, Maine. Brother and sister had been adopted into Abenaki families at Bécancour, a few miles north of Trois-Rivières. Before they returned home, though, the ambassadors secured promises of redemption from the French and Indian captors. En route, Nathaniel, who was developing a knack for espionage, procured a set of maps of strategic locations in New France for the government and was reappointed an ambassador in 1754.[7] Governor William Shirley (who had recently replaced Phipps) was particularly concerned about the Noble children and another boy, Solomon Mitchell, still living with the Indians. Governor Shirley wrote to the Marquis Duquesne, the new French governor, demanding that he "deliver up those Children and whatever other Captives, appertaining to this Government, might be found in Canada, to Mr. Nathaniel Wheelwright, who I have commissioned to deliver my letter to him ... and to demand restitution of the said Children."[8]

On this second trip to Québec, Nathaniel contacted his aunt again before he began the delicate negotiations for the release of Fanny, who was staying with the Ursulines at Trois-Rivières, where Esther had stayed briefly in 1711. Governor Duquesne had given Nathaniel permission to return Fanny to her parents from the school at Trois-Rivières. But when Nathaniel arrived there, he discovered that Fanny's adoptive mother, "a Bécancour squaw," had taken the girl back to her village. Nathaniel was warned by his friend Louis Charly St. Ange that if he attempted to remove Fanny from her Indian parents by force, "they would take an opportunity to murder me on the Road at my return to New England."[9] With the stakes so high, he badly needed his aunt's help.

Nathaniel arrived at the gate of the Ursuline convent in Québec on January 26, 1754, for a visit with Mother Esther Marie-Joseph, having ten days earlier sought the bishop's permission. The bishop had granted the request with the vain hope that the meetings "might result in [Nathaniel's] conversion."[10] In the depths of a January morning, when the temperature dipped to -16 degrees Celsius, aunt and nephew met over a table laid with "a variety of wines and sweetmeats." Nathaniel then presented his aunt with a set of "fine linen," a *couvert d'argent* (a large silver spoon and four-tined fork) and a silver flask expertly engraved with the Wheelwright family's coat of arms (this affectation was typical of John Wheelwright, who used the coat of arms to reflect his elevated status). These were items a nun usually received from her parents on the eve of her profession (although the cutlery would be kept for her personal use).[11]

The flask and the cutlery, both made from fine French silver, implied Esther's membership in the nobility.[12] She may have subtly suggested to her nephew in 1752 that these were appropriate gifts, since they could be shared communally and created a tangible material link between the Ursulines and the Wheelwrights. This might even have been John's attempt to compensate Esther for her portion of her father's estate, which had been divided among her surviving siblings.

The Ursulines gratefully received the gifts, whatever Nathaniel's motives, and he was granted the rare privilege of touring Esther's cell. "The [nuns] are conveniently lodged; each hath her separate apartment, with a small bed, a table and one chair, nothing but what is necessary," he observed. He marvelled at the Ursuline chapel, appreciating its fine gilt work, embroidered altar cloths and paintings. The young English officer had clearly impressed his hosts, who sent him the next morning a "very Genteel deseart," a common compliment for noble visitors. "I was very politely received and Genteely entertained with a variety of sweetmeats," Nathaniel wrote in his diary on January 26, 1754.[13]

An ambitious merchant and politician, Nathaniel undoubtedly asked the advice of his "close relation" before travelling south to Bécancour for further negotiations over Fanny Noble's release. And within the Ursuline cloister lived Catherine de Ramezay, who was related to Fanny's French guardians and was someone to whom he (or Esther) might have made discreet inquiries. Although only a few English child captives remained in New France by the 1750s, it was just as difficult to get them back, especially if they had converted to Catholicism or been adopted into a family. But the consequences of leaving the children in the colony were equally devastating, as suggested by Esther's comments about being sold to a priest and the reference to Vaudreuil's betrayal of the Wheelwrights over her redemption.

The Noble case was especially complicated because both the Abenakis and the French made claims on Fanny, who had lived at Bécancour before her French guardian paid for her education with the Ursulines.[14] Baptized there as Marie Ursule Elaine on March 11, 1753, Fanny was described as "belonging to" a French couple, and her biological parents were disingenuously recorded as unknown. Governor Duquesne, however, appeared to make genuine efforts to push forward the negotiations for Fanny's release, giving Nathaniel permission to visit the Abenaki village with his "particular friend," Luc de la Corne, an accomplished linguist and wealthy fur trader.[15] In early March, Nathaniel finally got a break in the stalemate over Fanny when he learned that her Abenaki guardian was open to negotiations. In clear but bitterly cold weather, Nathaniel and Chaptes de La Corne left by sleigh for a meeting in Trois-Rivières with the regional governor, Monsieur Rigaud de Vaudreuil, son of Esther's host at the château; the mayor, Monsieur Denoielle; and Monsieur Louis-Joseph Godefroy Tonnacour, brother of Fanny's French guardian, Madame Ursule Charly St. Ange, and husband of Mary Scammon, a former captive. Among them was also Fanny's adoptive Abenaki mother.

Nathaniel was an outsider in the negotiations that followed. If Esther had patiently explained to her nephew how such negotiations were conducted, he apparently did not listen. Fanny's adoptive mother began by seeking compensation, since she had nursed Fanny as an infant and, saddled with her care, had missed hunting trips and was forced to rely on her family for food. "As the child was not accustomed to their way of living," the Abenaki woman had even paid for French provisions to feed her charge. The haggling had begun. The woman asked for three thousand *livres,* then quickly dropped to two thousand at Nathaniel's shocked response. Although the Massachusetts government and Fanny's parents had hoped to redeem their child without payment, Nathaniel was prepared to offer a ransom of eight hundred *livres.*[16] The Abenaki woman refused and said she would return to Bécancour with Fanny.

Eventually, Nathaniel agreed to another two hundred *livres,* for a total of a thousand, but he instructed his interpreter to "take the child and make as though he was going to carry [her] away with him" if the Abenaki woman resisted. Tonnacour persuaded Nathaniel that snatching the child was a bad idea, since "they never knew an Indian who had made a bargain and receive[d] the money, forfeit his word." Instead, Nathaniel gave the woman food parcels and paid for a sleigh to take her back to Bécancour. The next morning, the woman sent a message that she would rather keep the child and return Nathaniel's money.[17]

When Nathaniel learned that the poor condition of the roads had in fact kept the woman in Trois-Rivières, he asked Governor de Rigaud to intervene. "Although I was an English man and stranger, I hoped to have at least equal justice with an Indian in his government and under his protection," he wrote indignantly. The governor replied, "What will you do[?] You see she is obstinate, and she is an Indian." Nathaniel was furious that the woman's claims were recognized as legitimate, and he was forced to leave for Boston without the children, his mission incomplete.[18] He might well have poured out his frustrations to Madame Lestage (herself the owner of several enslaved Native children) when he stayed with her family at Berthier in late April. The advice from his relatives made little difference, however, and Fanny remained in Québec for another eight years.[19]

The breach with Esther had been mended. But with the Boston Wheelwrights, business was always paramount, and they saw the value of having a close relation, an Abenaki-speaker and a former captive in the French colony. Although it was treasonable for English merchants to trade with the French during the war, the Wheelwrights had clearly found ways to avoid these inconvenient restrictions.[20] John Wheelwright was known to have purchased flour from a French officer at Louisbourg, and he was in contact with François Bigot, the financial commissary of Île Royale and later the Intendant (administrator) of New France.[21]

On Nathaniel's return journey to Boston in August 1754, he stopped in Louisbourg, where he visited the notary G. Bacquerisse and transferred his power of attorney in the colony from François-Marie de Couagne, listed as a Canadian, to Antoine Pacaud, a Louisbourg resident. By cementing his trade ties with Chaptes de La Corne Saint-Luc, an important fur trader among the Six Nations, Nathaniel hedged his bets against a French military victory in North America. The diplomatic mission, paid for by the British Crown, had served its purpose, and Esther's position as her nephew's informal go-between was secure as war loomed once again. When the Seven Years' War began in 1756, Esther's English contacts and her family background would prove vital to the Ursulines' survival.[22]

Back in New England, Nathaniel travelled to Wells on August 22, 1754, where he spent a few days with his Wheelwright relatives. It would be the last time his grandmother Mary Snell had news of her daughter, but she "seemed to be quite consoled for her separation from her daughter by the ample evidence she received of the happiness which [Esther] enjoyed at the Monastery."[23] Since published extracts of Nathaniel's journal were circulated to the Massachusetts Assembly, Mrs. Wheelwright might have read his account of Esther's "cheerful nature" and his description of the "handsomely adorned" Ursuline chapel, with its "magic, mystical atmosphere of the altarpiece," and the "very curious embroidery, all of their own work."[24] Nathaniel related the story of Vaudreuil's treachery, and until her death in 1755, Mary Snell clung to a fading hope that "her beloved daughter Esther" would return.

Mary Snell, "advancing in years and labouring under great bodily infirmities," remembered Esther in her will. Having out-lived two of her adult daughters, Hannah Plaisted and Elizabeth Newmarch, she provided for her six surviving children (including Nathaniel and Sarah, born after Esther's abduction) and numerous grandchildren. If within a year of her death, Esther, "who has been many years in Canada, is yet living and Should by the Wonder working Providence of God be returned to her Native Land and tarry and dwell in it," she was to receive an equal portion of the Wheelwright estate. But the share came with the impossible demand that Esther reconvert, a plea she had repeatedly rejected.[25]

Despite Nathaniel's dubious accomplishments as an ambassador, he had at least successfully reopened relations between Esther and the Wheelwrights. This friendship extended to Nathaniel's father, John, who began corresponding with his sister. When Esther met a New Hampshire captive named Susannah Johnson a year after Nathaniel's second visit, she confidently recommended her brother, now sitting in the Governor's Council, as a useful contact. Mrs. Johnson was at the Ursuline school visiting two English captive girls, Polly and Submit Phipps, who were taken from Hinsdale, New Hampshire, in 1755. The sisters, ransomed by Monsieur de Vaudreuil, were, according to Mrs. Johnson, "beautiful girls, cheerful and well-taught," with "every attention paid to their education." Esther Wheelwright mentioned that she "had a brother in Boston, on whom she requested me to call, if ever I went to that place; I complied with her request and received many civilities from her brother." John met Mrs. Johnson after her release from captivity in Plymouth, England, in late 1757, when Nathaniel's father-in-law, John Apthorp, who was an agent for the province of New Hampshire, negotiated her ransom with the French.[26]

Nathaniel's friendship with Mother Esther Marie-Joseph did, however, have one unintended consequence. His report to the Massachusetts Assembly openly acknowledged his relationship with his aunt Esther, and with several prominent French merchants and politicians. Soon after his return to Boston, as the fragile peace between the colonies began to break down, Nathaniel Wheelwright became the subject of rumours that he was operating as a spy for the French. Most damning was the charge by a French prisoner of war that during the British attack on Louisbourg in 1744, John and Nathaniel had continued shipping flour to the enemy. Fortunately, the Boston authorities refused to believe these claims, since "the people concerned [the Wheelwrights] were of such station and spotless character that accusations by a Frenchman were meaningless."[27]

The Wheelwrights' reputation was virtually untouchable by this time. John supplied half of Boston's cash, and was a longstanding government member and a prominent member of the First Church of Boston. Before his death in 1760, he began to hand over business operations to his son, who expanded the banking services.[28] Nathaniel's wealth attracted a good marriage to Anne Apthorp, the twenty-year-old daughter of the merchant John Apthorp, known as the richest man in Boston. He was also the fourth generation of Wheelwrights to serve the colony; he was a warden of the poor, a member of a volunteer fire department and a fire warden.[29] He counted among his close friends William Palfrey, George

Washington's future aide-de-camp; the Anglican minister Reverend Henry Caner; and Sir William Pepperrell, under whom he served as an officer at Louisbourg.

But despite his marriage, his wealth, his prestigious pew at church and the family coat of arms, the rumours continued. On November 8, 1759, Captain Arthur Loftus, an officer just returned from the conquest of Québec, told his friends over a few pints at Mr. Grayston's Inn at Roxbury that "the French very well know [our] numbers and everything that passed and that a correspondence was carried on with the French from this town by a *person of consequence*" (emphasis added). The captain believed that since "Mr. Wheelwright had been [to Canada] in a public character and had a relation there, his name might be spoken of more familiarly by the French and from thence a suspicion might arise." Captain Loftus said he would not be surprised if General Jeffrey Amherst, commander-in-chief of the British army in North America, ordered the traitor to be hanged. A second officer, Captain Thomas Smelt, corroborated the charges, saying they "really gave him great surprise . . . Wheelwright was a man of reputation in the town till the fullest evidence appeared, he begged leave to disbelieve it."[30]

When the rumours reached Nathaniel, he sued both Captain Loftus and Captain Smelt for "being brought into great trouble and disgrace and danger." Nathaniel won the case in 1760, with Smelt paying damages of five hundred pounds and Loftus two thousand, huge charges for recently discharged officers. According to the historian E. P. Hamilton, however, "it is obvious that Wheelwright had either a reputation of the very highest or . . . connections that could assure him of securing a friendly jury."[31] Nathaniel's journal reveals that among his associates in New France were known spies, and according to Hamilton, he was "on very friendly terms" with the colonial governor, the Marquis Duquesne, with whom he often dined. If Nathaniel had been acting for the French, as the evidence suggests, this may explain why Québec's bishop granted him the rare privilege of touring the convent and visiting his aunt Esther so frequently.

In Esther's story it often seems impossible to fully understand the motives of its key players. Were John and Nathaniel simply using Esther's position to gain access to lucrative deals with the French? Or were the elaborate gifts of silverware and linens meant to atone for years of separation, an expression of a family's grief at the loss of their daughter? Whatever brought Nathaniel so often to the Ursuline convent in the years just before the British conquered New France, he had opened the lines of communication with Esther. This contact with the Wheelwrights would prove vital to her survival, and the survival of the Ursulines, over the next decade. Drawing on her English heritage and powerful relations, Esther would help guide her community through the most challenging years of its long history.

PART 3
The Fight for Survival

CHAPTER 19

Esther's Missing Dowry

*T*HE URSULINES HAVE GENEROUSLY GRANTED MY request to look at the silver *couvert d'argent* that Nathaniel Wheelwright brought Esther from Boston in 1754. A rectangular polished wooden box is waiting for me on the archive table when I arrive this morning.

The gifts are curious because they starkly embody the different universes of thought that separated the Abenakis from the Wheelwrights. In Abenaki society, every child was welcomed into a family and clan. There was no concept of illegitimacy, no notion of private property and no link between descendants and the transmission of goods and land.

The Wheelwrights' perspective was very different. Property descended through the male line, but female family members also received a share of their parents' estate. Even after fifty years, Esther's English relatives remembered they owed her a debt because she had never claimed her inheritance. The *couvert d'argent*, made from expensive French silver, probably purchased in London and engraved by Boston's finest silversmith, might have represented the Wheelwrights' first attempt at reparations.

I open the box and gently handle a large spoon, gleaming from a recent polish. Esther was allowed to use the cutlery, despite the prohibition against personal possessions. According to the Ursulines, the silverware was not a thing that they would deprive her of, since it was so precious, not only because of its value—the silver— but because it was something very meaningful to her.

I turn over the spoon (it's the size of a serving utensil) and see, for the first time, the Wheelwright coat of arms, a legal property that passed down the line from father to sons. I am holding an object that travelled from London to Boston with my distant ancestor Nathaniel, who passed it directly to Esther a few feet from where I am standing. Like a talisman, the object brings all three of us together.

Of course Esther—as a woman, and a childless one at that— could never claim official use of the arms, but the gift acknowledged her status as a person of rank and her entitlement to a share of the family property. Her siblings had materially benefited from her absence, since her portion of the considerable Wheelwright estate went to them. John, who had failed to bring Esther home from Montréal in 1710, had grown rich on government contracts that depended on the labour and skills of the Abenakis and other Native peoples, who supplied snowshoes, moccasins, scouts and food. Esther's captors had become useful business contacts to the Wheelwrights.

The archivist has pointed out various hallmarks on the fork, including a fleur-de-lys, a helmet, rondels and three wolves' heads. The coat of arms is divided into parts: wheels, referring to the Wheelwrights—the wheel, the chariot; [then] you have the heads of the animals—wolf and dog. She tells me that this was special for the family. Esther must have understood its importance because she later sent a silk painting of the Wheelwright arms back to her relatives in Boston.

I weigh the silver in my white-gloved hands and am amazed that this material connection has been preserved when so much has been lost. John and Esther, who had not met since they were children, corresponded regularly after 1752, communicating through such potent symbols and gestures. But once again, forces beyond Esther's control severed the contact with her family when the British began bombarding her city, abruptly ending the dream of a French nation in North America.

I place the spoon back into its nest of tissue paper in the polished box and shut the lid. Nathaniel was my great-grandfather's great-grandfather, and I wonder if I will be the last generation to pay homage to Esther.

CHAPTER 20

The Fall of New France

*W*HEN BRITISH FORCES BEGAN BOMBARDING THE city of Québec in 1759, Esther Wheelwright was in late middle age and had lived within the Ursuline cloister for more than half a century. Instead of easing into gentle retirement after her long years of service, she was about to face the greatest challenge of her career.

The British attacks against New France began that spring, when more than three hundred French merchant ships were picked off by Royal Navy cannonfire while crossing the Atlantic. Supplies in the French colony dwindled to dangerously low levels, and unusually bitter weather brought snow in June, fuelling fears of starvation. Observing the bare convent grounds that summer, an Ursuline sister wrote, "Nothing is growing. The flowers of the fruit-trees have been blighted by the frost and what is worse the wheat-fields have been frozen. There is every prospect there will be no harvest."[1] As farmers joined the militia to defend the capital, fresh meat, eggs and milk became increasingly scarce and bread ("black as their robes") was rationed to four ounces per day. Esther and her sisters learned to live without their usual supplies from the Mother House, which included everything from the bombazine (worsted cotton) used to make and mend their habits to winter slippers, notepaper, paintbrushes, vegetable salt, quinine and fine flour.[2] No longer able to guarantee their students' safety, the nuns reluctantly closed the boarding school, sending home thirty young girls. They kept only those without family or friends, sixteen-year-old Helen Vero and four-year-old Marie Madelene Billy, who endured the siege with them.[3]

Esther's worst fear was that the British military, already blasting the city, would defeat the French and install a foreign government that would force the colonists into exile.[4] Québec residents had heard terrible reports of the more than six thousand Acadians who had been expelled from their Maritime homes after refusing to swear allegiance to the English Crown in 1755. As the Ursuline historian recorded, "Catholicity was at that time by the legislation of England, a crime. The penal laws were in full force."[5] Although the siege cut off communication with Boston, Esther surely calculated that her family contacts might afford the nuns some degree of protection if a British victory became a reality.

That spring, Esther joined her sisters in praying for the French forces as they watched Québec turning into a military camp from their monastery windows. In the Upper Town, only one gate remained open, and the French soldiers mounted 106 cannons along the city's ramparts and a floating battery of gunboats, fire ships and fire rafts on the St. Lawrence.[6] The city became a river of human traffic; able-bodied men and boys rushed from the countryside to join the five battalions of French soldiers and one thousand Indian warriors, while the women, children and elderly were evacuated into rural villages.[7]

The Ursulines joined the other religious communities in preparing their buildings against looters should the battle breach the city limits. They hurried to remove all their fragile sacred objects and stained-glass windows from the chapel and packed them securely in the monastery cellar.[8] The monastic routine that had dominated Esther's life for more than half a century was shattered when bombs fired across the river from Pointe-Lévy broke through the convent walls on July 12. The Lower Town was already deserted, and the Upper Town's remaining residents began to panic. Esther prayed beside the forty-four members of her community as bombs set houses alight and reduced them to piles of rubble throughout that first night of unimaginable terror.[9]

During a lull in the attack the next morning, the seventy-four-year-old Mother Superior, Marie-Anne Migeon de Branssat de la Nativité, gathered the community together. The nuns had complete confidence in their spiritual leader, who had proven a tough and competent negotiator since her election in 1735. She had bought, sold and leased properties for the convent, and supervised the building of mills and storehouses. A consummate diplomat, she had interceded with high-handed ecclesiastical authorities, wresting back control of convent elections from the local bishop. Now that action was needed, Mother Migeon wasted no time. The narrow underground vault where their sacred objects were stored could hold only a few people, but the nuns at the Hôpital Général offered the women refuge. After a quick consultation with Esther and her senior council, the Mother Superior sent the nuns to their cells to pack "a little parcel, such as [each sister] could carry." Mother Migeon had kept an emergency bag packed.[10]

Meanwhile, two of the younger sisters, Mother Davanne de St. Louis de Gonzague and Mother Marie-Antoinette Poulin de St.

François, offered to stay behind with a lay sister, Racine de la Resurrection, and four others. The Ursulines' chaplain, Canon Pierre-Joseph Resche, and Fathers Charles-Ange Collet and Barbell joined them to guard the artworks and holy relics, extinguish fires and pray for a French victory.[11] The historian C. Alice Baker assumes that Esther was among those who stayed, since she had "the fervor of a devotee . . . [and] the force and fearlessness of the Wheelwrights."[12] But if she did, the Ursuline history does not record this. More likely, Mother Migeon needed Esther's considerable organizational skills at the Hôpital Général. Esther had endured many cross-border conflicts as a child in New England, and thus was battle-hardened and understood the need for calm. The younger nuns were left behind to make their heroic act.

Thirty-six Ursulines then swiftly departed their convent, hurrying out the gates and across the city in single file. For women who expected to die within the monastery walls, this trip was both unimaginable and unavoidable. Instead of sewing in recreation that afternoon, they pulled up their heavy robes, "sorrowful and trembling," and picked their way down the slope and through the Palace Gate, across a shattered landscape of blasted buildings, towards the Hôpital Général's elegant spire, rising like a beacon above the riverbank.[13] When they arrived, Mother Superior Marie Charlotte de Ramezay de St. Claude de la Croix greeted her guests with "tenderness and affection." Mother St. Claude was a former Ursuline pupil, and her sister Catherine was among the arriving nuns. The ties among these women ran close and deep. Esther also had a close relation here: her cousin Hannah Parsons' twenty-nine-year-old daughter, now known as Mother Marie-Catherine de St. Joseph, who was a hospital nun and a former Ursuline pupil.[14] Many Ursulines had relatives among the eight hundred refugees crammed into rooms, sheds and barns with their few salvaged possessions. Since the Hôpital Général nuns never turned anyone away from their doors, the refugees had to share space with a resident population of disabled, abandoned, mentally ill, wounded or dying patients.[15]

The only remaining vacant space was the choir, and this was where nuns from all three of Québec's religious orders—the Augustine Sisters from the Hôpital Général and the Hôtel-Dieu and the Ursulines—took short breaks from their nursing rotas to recite the Hours together.[16] The British bombardment was relentless; nightly they destroyed houses in Québec's neighbouring parishes, and in a single day, they wrecked more than fifty buildings in the Lower Town.[17] The Ursulines even watched helplessly as a building at their convent was bombed and the resulting fire spread through their outbuildings, burning their chapel and ravaging neighbouring houses.[18]

There was little time for grieving, however, as the first wounded British soldiers were carried into the Hôpital Général from a battle at the outlying village of Montmorency on July 31. Although every nun had brothers and fathers among the French forces, they set aside their feelings, dispensing "the same charity" to each man in their care. The nuns even donated their personal linen (the long chemises worn next to the skin in lieu of underwear) for bandages when supplies ran short. Moving among them, performing last rites for the dying and offering spiritual comfort to the wounded, was Canon Jean-Olivier Briand. (The bishop, Henri-Marie Dubreil de Pontbriand, had retired on July 1 to nearby Charlesbourg.)[19]

But feeding, clothing and sheltering this huge influx of visitors soon took its toll on the Hôpital Général's resources. As the Ursuline historian wrote, "Famine, always inseparable from war, threatened to reduce us to extremity."[20] Esther was among the Ursulines nursing the soldiers over long hours in quarters so cramped there was barely space to wash the daily mountains of sheets and bandages. The nuns, however, still managed to impress the British officers with their nursing standards and their exquisite diplomacy. Captain John Knox recalled how they simultaneously cared for three or more soldiers in rooms that were swept each morning and sprinkled with vinegar to cut the smell of wounded flesh. The officers were quartered in apartments separate from their men and had the privilege of being tended by the younger sisters.[21]

As Esther worked round the clock to save the wounded soldiers, news reports from the French encampment grew worse. Although the French held the strategic advantage, with a "numerous body of armed men," there were rumours that the Canadian troops—local Frenchmen and Indian warriors—were deserting en masse, with up to two hundred men leaving their quarters on a bad night.[22] As the siege continued into August, the rumours grew wilder every day, building to a climax on the sixtieth day, when the British mounted a surprise assault.

Before dawn on September 13, a straggling file of five thousand red-coated, white-breeched soldiers, under the command of General James Wolfe, formed battle lines on the Plains of Abraham, a grazing pasture at the city's eastern end. When the French commander, General Louis-Joseph de Montcalm, finally reached the plains, he was staggered by the enemy's numbers. After a brief skirmish, Montcalm realized that his troops were hopelessly outnumbered and ordered them to run towards the enemy down a thicket-strewn slope. The British held their fire, advanced through the smoke and tore into the French ranks. The remaining soldiers fled back to the city, with Montcalm bringing up the rear on horseback before he was shot while in his saddle.

Montcalm kept upright long enough to ride through the Palace Gate, where a crowd had gathered, hungry for news. When one woman saw the bleeding general, she cried out, "Oh, my God! Oh, my God! The marquis is dead." In fact, he died the next morning, at the home of a local surgeon. In the Lower Town, the regimental commander, Captain McDonnell, went to the Hôpital Général to reassure the three Mothers Superior they were safe from attack.[23] Soon the stretcher bearers arrived, carrying men wounded with bayonets, grapeshot and small bullets. The women dragged extra beds from the stores, and when these were filled, patients were laid on every available surface, in barns and sheds. Among them were some of the 664 wounded British soldiers, a devastating number for one day of fighting.[24] "We had in our infirmaries 72 officers, of whom 33 died," recorded the Hôpital Général historian. "The amputation of legs and arms was going on everywhere." The colonial soldiers who fought but escaped injury that day included Esther's nephews Jeremiah Wheelwright, Daniel Wheelwright and Simon Jefferds.[25]

Over the next few hours, Esther and her sisters would read their future in every scrap of news, praying for the miracle of a French victory to restore the established order.[26] But the *religieuses* were now at the mercy of unknown forces. In a desperate bid to prevent the British from taking power, the Hôpital Général's Mother Superior tried to demoralize the wounded officers by spreading false rumours of a French victory.[27] Her plot failed, and the next day her brother, Lieutenant Jean-Baptiste-Nicolas-Roche de Ramezay, and his officers led Montcalm's funeral cortège through the streets to the Ursuline chapel, one of the few buildings left standing in the city.

Montcalm had died at 4 a.m. and was interred at eight that evening in a service hurriedly performed by torchlight under the bomb-damaged roof of the convent chapel.[28] The five Ursulines who had stayed to guard the convent throughout the battle gave the response as Fathers Resche, Collet and Barbell murmured the Latin Requiem. The sisters shook with emotion as the coffin, that potent symbol of their nation's loss of power, was lowered into a crater that a bomb had carved into the stone floor.[29] When the news of Montcalm's death reached the Hôpital Général, Bishop Pontbriand appointed Jean-Olivier Briand as his successor and left to join the French army retreating towards Montréal so he could remain in French territory. Briand, known as a man too shy to preach, continued giving last rites to soldiers, regardless of their race or religion.

Further losses drove home to the Ursulines the consequences of a British victory. Mother St. Louis reported to the Mother House that since September 13, the Ursulines had become prisoners; the siege had scarred the city, and the nuns feared severe food shortages as winter approached.[30] The British commanders, despite their polite and respectful manner, seemed oblivious to the pending crisis for the city's population. Esther may have accepted more easily than her sisters that if the Ursulines were to recover, they would need to befriend the invaders. Above the walls of Québec now flew the Royal Union.

As the fighting ceased, the Ursulines began to count their own casualties. Esther, who had spent her childhood as a prisoner of war, may have already been considering how her English family might help her community, but the other English nun, Dorothy Jordan, was deeply traumatized. Already in poor health and weakened by meagre rations, Dorothy had stayed at the Ursuline convent after learning that the French had lost, perhaps because she feared that her "compatriots would become prosecutors of her faith."[31] In the same room, during the battle on September 13, Mother Charlotte de Muy de St. Helen died, resigned "to go forth from this world, that she might not see her country ruled by a foreign power."[32] The lesson of Esther's childhood—that to survive one must adapt—had returned to shape the remainder of her life.

If the Ursulines needed in any lessons in how to woo the British, they had only to observe the actions of Mother St. Claude. Only a week after her brother had surrendered to the British, she sent General Jeffrey Amherst a basket of fruit preserves with a note expressing the nuns' eagerness "to present their respects to his Excellency, to express their deep appreciation for his protection [and] wishing him health."[33] Mother St. Claude even learned to brew tea for their British guests, whom she entertained regularly.

The Ursulines returned to their bombed-out cloister after an absence of seventy days. Esther and her sisters filed back up the slope to the Upper Town across a bleak landscape—skeletons of tangled masonry, children scavenging for fallen planks and timbers to play seesaw and their parents picking through the debris for anything with which to rebuild their homes. The Cathedral of Notre Dame was a burned-out shell, the Jesuit seminary pockmarked with cannonfire, and at the Récollet church, bombs had broken the pavement, exposing bones and skulls from the graves below. The commissary general, Benoît-François Bernier, reported, "Québec is nothing but a shapeless mass of ruins. English and French, all is chaos alike. The inhabitants, famished and destitute, escape to the country. Never was there seen such a sight."[34]

Back at the convent, Esther surveyed the extensive damage; the schoolhouse lay in ruins, and cannonfire had damaged the sacristy, the chapel and the church. Several cells in the dormitory were wrecked, and the roof had fallen in; chimneys were knocked down and the laundry was dilapidated. But despite the bombing, the nuns who'd stayed behind had safeguarded the stained-glass windows, statues, paintings, tabernacles, altar furniture and sacred vessels.[35] Since their cloister had withstood the worst of the shelling and was among the few buildings left standing, it would be requisitioned for the Crown by Brigadier-General James Murray, the hot-headed and impetuous Scottish officer left in charge of the four thousand British troops remaining in the colony.

The siege and battle had reduced the Ursulines to abject poverty, and Mother Migeon realized they could not afford to repair the buildings, let alone make them habitable, before the coming winter. Murray's offer to use the convent as a temporary military hospital would give them the money needed for the monastery repairs. Mother Migeon could hardly refuse. So soon after the nuns' arrival back at the convent, the classrooms, the pupils' canteen and several large rooms on the lower two floors became wards for the soldiers. The cloister's top floor was reserved for the sisters. Military discipline was enforced, and any soldier who strayed beyond the agreed internal boundaries would be severely punished. Although the Ursulines had spent several weeks nursing British soldiers, it was a different matter to share with them their home and most sacred space. But Mother Migeon realized the arrangement might serve the community well, and the Ursuline historian observed how artfully she exerted her influence "over strangers and Englishmen . . . who not only professed that religion hated and proscribed by their nation, but who was at the head of an establishment, the very name of which would, at that day, have raised a cry of horror in England."[36] The Ursulines had a reputation among the British as "the severest order in the Romish church."[37]

Still, Murray's men set aside their prejudices when they arrived to occupy the convent and its grounds in early November. Among the first were "*les gens sans culottes,*" the kilted soldiers of the

78th Fraser Highlanders, whom Mother Migeon presented with a set of St. Andrew's crosses. These gifts, made by the nuns, were wrought with an emblematic heart, "expressive of the attachment and affection which every good man bears to his native country."[38] Although the Ursulines were strictly barred from giving religious instruction or attempting to convert their patients, they provided the best, and often first, medical care these battle-weary soldiers had ever experienced.

Although Esther and her sisters were relieved to occupy their own space again, they were still expected to work under conditions so rudimentary that a "pestilent malady" had soon broken out in one of the wards, killing many patients.[39] To stop its spread, soldiers from the 63rd Regiment of Foot—"scorbutic men, many of whom were totally unfit for service by age and infirmity"—were sent into the countryside.[40] The tireless work took its toll as well, with two Ursuline lay sisters dying of exhaustion in early 1760. The monastery's already limited resources were stretched even further to make room for some of the city's twenty-six hundred refugees—mainly women and children returning from the countryside. A British officer turned artist, Richard Short, sketched an illustration he titled *A View of the Orphans' or Ursulines' Nunnery*, which suggests the convent gained a reputation for accommodating these destitute children.[41] Several, however, did not survive the winter and were buried in the convent's schoolyard.[42]

Esther would have observed how Mother Migeon took every opportunity to ingratiate the nuns with the officers and soldiers, who in turn expressed their appreciation for the excellent care they received. The nuns responded quickly when the Scottish soldiers, and even Murray—who apologized to one correspondent for writing in a sloppy hand due to frostbite—suffered after the first heavy snowfalls.[43] When the Highlanders found the Côte de la Montagne, the steep hill between the Upper and Lower towns, impossible to navigate, they tried sliding down—only to discover that their kilts were "a sorry defence against the Canadian winter." The nuns spent their recreation hours knitting the soldiers long tartan stockings and woollen vests to wear beneath their kilts and jackets.[44] In thanks, the Scottish soldiers scraped away the powdery drifts that covered the convent garden paths, chopped wood and carried water and daily provisions from the commissariat or the bakery. After Murray forbade the men to strip buildings for firewood, the soldiers harnessed themselves to giant sleighs and searched the countryside for wood to heat the convent's ovens.[45]

Murray rewarded the Ursulines' services by keeping them on army rations long after their nursing duties had ended in June 1760, for which the nuns were extremely grateful.[46] As the Ursuline historian wrote, "Our conquerors assisted us in everything . . . with a kindness we did not look for."[47] Despite this support, Mother Migeon shared with Esther, who would soon assume this enormous responsibility, the knowledge that the community faced a mountain of debt. During the siege, the convent's farmlands along the Saint-Charles River had been set alight, the cattle driven off and the harvest left to rot in the fields. The Ursulines had no prospect of replenishing their exhausted supplies from the Mother House; there was no income from the boarding school or the novitiate, both of which remained closed; and their traditional patrons had either fled to France or lost their wealth in the *fortunes de guerre.*

Debts, a military regime and a hostile Protestant population were all problems that Esther would inherit when she stepped into Mother Migeon's shoes as Superior. The transition began in December 1759, when Esther was elected as *assistante supérieure* above three more senior nuns.[48] This was the third time in her career that an exception had been made for her (after her shortened novitiate and her incomplete dowry). But Esther's English family connections and background were more important than disgruntled feelings within the ranks during this time of crisis. The vote to elect Esther was unanimous.

The Mother Superior and her assistant were kept busy balancing the order's need for morale and their own need to appease the British. It was a tough act that required great humility, especially when Murray informed the nuns that the Anglican chaplain, Reverend John Brooke, would conduct twice-weekly services in their chapel. Four days after it was made usable again, on September 27, 1759, the British officers and soldiers were given leave to attend their first Divine Service, where a thanksgiving was heard.[49] Captain John Knox was impressed by the chapel's exquisite beauty, which he described as "ostentatiously glittering and [as] captivating as possible," as he listened to a sermon on the destruction of Québec, a city now "among the richest jewels that adorn the British crown." The irony that Montcalm's grave lay beneath the pulpit was not lost on the congregation, the minister or the Ursulines.[50]

Because Esther was the only convert from the Protestant religion, she was able to fully understand the liturgy Reverend Brooke offered in his Sunday and Wednesday services.[51] Whatever ambiguous emotions it provoked in Esther, she understood her community's "secret sorrow—if a stronger word would not better express the sentiment," at sharing their chapel with outsiders who, they felt, "professed no respect" for their religion.[52] Despite his efforts at diplomacy, Murray was forced to encroach further on the Ursulines' space when he needed a council chamber and requisitioned their *salle de communauté*. Twice a week, the nuns' recreation room was given over to Murray's military tribunal, at which he deliberated on local crimes, ordering three hangings and several public whippings that winter.[53]

But when Mother Migeon and her assistant believed that Murray had overstepped his authority, they protested. The nuns were horrified, for example, to learn that a young British soldier posted in the monastery had been sentenced to hang after he slipped into the choir to see the procession of nuns. Mother Migeon wrote a strongly worded letter to Murray, reminding him that "the conquerors of the French" had a reputation for compassion. When the message arrived at Murray's quarters, he turned to the fellow officers at his dining table and asked, "What do you think, gentlemen? You judge; can I refuse a demand made with such grace?" Despite his patronizing attitude to Mother Migeon's protest, he respected her request and the soldier was pardoned.[54]

The British occupation of the monastery would last only another few months. The French made one last-ditch effort to retake the city under the leadership of François de Gaston, Chevalier de Lévis, on April 28, 1760, when his forces met British troops for a second battle on the Plains of Abraham. After only three hours of fighting, the convent's wards filled again with wounded soldiers, the stretcher bearers arriving hour after hour.[55] Esther wrote to the Mother House that the Ursulines were praying for a miraculous French victory. "It has just been announced to us that peace is made and that this poor country is restored to the French," she wrote. "I hope it may be true and that we can send you this news by the first ship that leaves for France."[56] But Lévis was soundly defeated at Québec, and the French army capitulated to the British on September 8, 1760.

By June, a new hospital on the Île d'Orléans was finished, and Murray left with his British soldiers, grateful for the Ursulines' services. Still, Mother Migeon realized that however much he appreciated their generosity, Murray answered to the English king, and therefore the Ursulines' position remained precarious. That spring, the Jesuits had been expelled from Québec and their seminary turned into a military warehouse.[57] In March, Murray had ordered troops to destroy mills and tenements belonging to the Hôtel-Dieu in the nearby village of Calvaire after the inhabitants were charged with "transmitting intelligence to the enemy." Murray told the Mother Superior that if the inhabitants "should presume to correspond with our enemies, directly or indirectly, or in any respect contrary to that good faith . . . which they owe to the King of Great Britain," the Hôtel-Dieu would be converted into a barracks.[58] In the countryside, farmers and artisans avoided contact with the occupiers, who, the Ursulines observed, "monopolize whatever trade and commerce that can be carried on . . . and consider themselves, in all respects, and wish to be treated, as lords of the land."[59]

When Mother Migeon ended her extended third term as Superior, it would become Esther's responsibility to ensure that the Ursulines survived a transition fraught with treachery. All the skills Esther had nurtured during her tenure as principal of the boarding school and head of the novitiate's boot camp would be tested when she was handed the keys to the convent. As the Ursulines made plans for their election in 1760, Anglican Church leaders in London had already agreed that French citizens in Québec should swear allegiance to the British Crown, a demand that had spectacularly failed in Acadia.[60] Even more worrying for the nuns was the English belief that convents, by creaming off a generation of young, marriageable women, would limit the colony's number of potential mothers. One British official declared that convents did more harm than good, "inasmuch as they bury before it is time many young women who might be useful in producing subjects to the king."[61]

As Mother Superior, Esther would need to convince the British that the Ursuline order was indispensable to the new colony by offering badly needed services. The incomers were determined to establish such modern institutions as the Anglican Church, a newspaper, English civil and criminal law and representative government, and perhaps there was an opportunity for the Ursulines in educating their daughters.[62] And who better than Esther Wheelwright, a former child captive and relation of Boston's famous banking family, to understand what these English families needed? From behind the grille, Esther was about to carry out a mission of quiet and effective diplomacy that would ensure her order's survival to Canada's founding.

Back in Wells, the Wheelwrights celebrated the British victory over the French with their sons all delivered back unharmed from the battlefields. One local soldier described in song the citizenry's relief that the conflicts over the borderlands had finally ended:

> Brother soldiers, did you hear the nuse,
> It is peace by land and by sea,
> The soldiers to be no more used;
> They all disbanded will be.[63]

CHAPTER 21

Esther's Eight Namesakes

*I*F MY DAUGHTERS WERE HERE, I'D STAY FOR A WHILE longer and show them Esther's city. This morning, after phoning London, I feel impatient to reach the end of the story brewing in my head so I can go home. When I head downstairs to my hotel lobby, I feel a rush of envy as the Spanish firefighters line up to check out, their rectangular bags forming an obstacle course in the cramped space.

There's a schizophrenic state induced when you try to live in the eighteenth and twenty-first centuries simultaneously. But I'm clinging on with only two precious days left to understand Esther's final years, when she emerges from the anonymity of the Ursulines' documents as their Mother Superior.

The news of Esther's election must have reached New England, because several Wheelwright relations appeared at the convent gates after 1759, requesting interviews with Aunt Esther. Mother Esther Marie-Joseph Wheelwright de l'Enfant Jésus still prayed that the French military would rise like Lazarus and put the colony back together again, even while she greeted her curious English guests with immense courtesy. It was her version of my mid-Atlantic dance.

I realize now that the story handed down through the generations in my family is of a lost child who made good in French Canada, saving the Ursuline convent from closure and the nuns from exile by the British conquerors. She stands out among the unwritten lives of wives and daughters, a rare female descendant of Reverend John Wheelwright's Puritan stock who was venerated for her own accomplishments.

Along with the story, succeeding generations of Wheelwrights inherited Esther's portrait, the one I saw in Boston at the start of this journey. Today in the Wheelwright file, I come across an 1896 letter from C. Alice Baker to Ned Wheelwright discussing the portrait's possible meaning. "The original has been handed down in the Wheelwright family through those named Esther," wrote Baker, "and is now owned by the eighth Esther in descent from the niece to whom your Esther sent it." She saw the portrait as "almost like another embassy between the family and the convent."[1]

Baker regarded Esther's story as a "romance," an idea supported by Agnes Repplier, who wrote in a 1931 biography of Marie de l'Incarnation: "There was always this natural affinity between adventure and the Ursulines. In what other convent could little girls have had the felicity of being taught and scolded by a *religieuse* who had enjoyed such terrifying experiences?"[2]

I am discovering that this painting has played an almost mystical role in my family's history. Baker was right when she said that it formed a durable bond between the Wheelwrights—who were Yankees, Protestants and British Americans—and the Ursulines of Québec. As Ned wrote on January 2, 1898, "It is a strange circumstance that the story of my Yankee family should be so much connected with that of the Québec Ursulines."[3]

As I hunt through the file out falls a small brown envelope containing a sepia photograph of two young girls wearing crisp dresses, their hair curled in delicate blonde wisps, their eyes large and tender. They are not smiling but wear guarded expressions, perhaps wary of the photographer, one Orso B. Brand of Highland Park, Illinois. In faded blue ink are scrawled the names: "Esther Wheelwright" below the younger girl, and "Margaret Davis" below the other, who looks to be about four.

I flick through the correspondence file and find a letter to the Ursulines from one of the grown-up girls. Margaret Stewart Davis, the niece of William Bond Wheelwright, wrote on May 2, 1943, that "a copy of your picture of Mary Snell Wheelwright" was her son Christopher's most treasured possession.[4]

I've seen this photograph, or a copy of it, of the now vanished portrait of Mary Snell Wheelwright, which Esther's nephew Joshua Moody brought from Maine to Québec after 1759, and which a Hester Wheelwright copied as a miniature in the nineteenth century. As if the portrait and the photograph were sufficient proof of a bond, Margaret Davis wrote again in 1943 to ask the Ursulines to pray for Christopher, who had enlisted as a lieutenant in the U.S. army.

The other little girl in the photograph, now Mrs. Esther Wheelwright West, wrote the following summer from Norfolk, Virginia. "I am Esther Wheelwright's namesake and you have my picture from childhood in your cloister. Therefore I am making bold to ask if the convent will help me now." Mrs. West wanted the nuns to say a perpetual novena for her husband, Colonel George Brooks West, a doctor in the U.S. medical corps. Both requests were granted, even though neither of the women was Catholic.

I lay the photographs of Esther Wheelwright West and of Mary Snell Wheelwright's and Esther Wheelwright's portraits side by side, looking for something the women share—a curve of the mouth, a jawline or cheekbone. I wonder what message each namesake was given, what version of Esther's story moved Mrs. West to ask the Ursulines to pray for her man.

I am thrilled to learn that the tradition of passing on Esther's name carried on for at least eight generations, the story kept alive through carefully documented histories written by Alice Baker and her protegé, Emma Coleman, as well as through John Heard's biography of Reverend John Wheelwright. Some of my relations were inspired to write to and even visit the convent—Mary Wheelwright sent a Christmas card in 1898; Ned Wheelwright proffered a list of all his "kinfolks" who were Catholic converts; a Mrs. Lloyd Vernon Briggs (née Wheelwright) and the French countess Eleanor Beaufort-Spontin visited in 1932; and the Goodwin sisters paid their respects in 1948 as "kin women of Mother Wheelwright."

Despite their oppositional faith, these relations seemed to regard Esther as possessing some special spiritual power to heal and protect. If she intended to permanently bind her family to the Ursulines, she could not have done it more effectively if she had sailed down the Atlantic to Boston herself in her full habit and mantle.

Several generations of Wheelwrights dutifully passed Esther's story on to future daughters and nieces, seeing in it mystery, romance and an exotic kind of female presence. If they knew of her struggles within the convent, her parents' anguish at their daughter's conversion, the questions about her vocation or her possible child, they go unmentioned in their letters. Instead, Esther's story has been smoothed over, rubbed and polished with the telling, simplified.

I found at the Massachusetts Historical Society a poignant letter from a Mrs. Jenks to the historian Gerald Kelly about Esther's fading contact with the Wheelwrights in her old age. It refers to an exquisitely embroidered pincushion that Esther sent to a namesake in 1766. This was her last contact with the Wheelwrights. "During the remaining 18 years of her life," writes Mrs. Jenks, "she heard no more from them, nor they from her."

CHAPTER 22

The Mother Superior's Gift

FTER THREE DAYS OF INTENSIVE PRAYER, THE
senior nuns of the Ursuline assembly gathered to vote
for Mother Migeon's replacement on December 15, 1760. After hearing the Mass, the nuns formed two neat lines, each sister holding
her secret ballot beneath her sleeve as she approached the ballot box.
The assistant superior, Mother Esther Marie-Joseph Wheelwright
de l'Enfant Jésus, was the first to kneel and slip her vote into the
box. Since extraordinary times called for extraordinary measures, the
nuns agreed that Esther should become their Mother Superior. According to one Québec historian, the election was "a very deliberate
and diplomatic move to consolidate the relations of the Community
with the English."[1] Bishop Jean-Olivier Briand confirmed her appointment by placing the keys to the monastery gate directly into
Esther's hands before the assembled nuns began to chant the *Te
Deum.*[2]

Mother Migeon—who had led the Ursulines through the siege
and established an effective working relationship with Murray, who

was appointed the military governor of Québec in October 1760—was always going to be a hard act to follow. Bishop Pontbriand had authorized the Ursulines to elect her for an extra year, even though this constituted a breach of the Rules. But by December 1760, the elderly Superior was exhausted and ready to step down. Esther was her obvious replacement.

There were huge demands on the new Mother Superior as the convent struggled to overcome its vast debts, its loss of traditional patrons and the lingering fear of expulsion. The Ursulines ran the largest of Québec's three convents, which made them a target for the Anglican authorities.[3] Inside the cloister, Esther faced the daunting task of reopening the boarding and day schools and the novitiate—all of which the English Church actively opposed. She would also have to appoint, from her list of aging and worn-out nuns, the convent's administrators: the sub-prioress, who safeguarded religious observance and internal discipline; the procurator and her assistant, who found and distributed the household supplies; the refectorians, who ran the kitchen; the sacristan, who was responsible for bell-ringing; vestrians for mending and distributing habits; and an infirmarian, who ran the hospital wing under the supervision of the city's physician.[4]

For the next nine years, Esther would manage this large community, where her duties included entertaining important English guests, running a charity for the poor and supervising the convent's extensive gardens, grounds and landholdings. Her immediate priority, however, was to ensure the convent's financial and political survival. The Ursulines had traditionally found support among the wives and daughters of the French nobility; Esther realized now the importance of forging relationships with the English wives of merchants, officers and clergymen. The sisters needed this support if they were to impress upon the British the quality of their educational services and find new patrons for their charitable work.

A week after Esther's election as Mother Superior, Murray appointed Reverend John Brooke chaplain to the town of Québec and parish priest to its British subjects. So among the most influential patrons Esther would win over was Reverend Brooke's wife, Frances Moore Brooke, who is credited with writing the first Canadian novel, *The History of Emily Montague*, during her five years living in the colony. Frances arrived from England in 1763 with her seven-year-old son, John, and her sister Sarah. She already had a reputation as an established writer whose London circle included James Boswell, Dr. Samuel Johnson, Samuel Richardson, David Garrick, Fanny Burney and Oliver Goldsmith. She had even once edited a weekly magazine on theatre, politics and religion entitled *Ye Old Maid.*[5]

A friendship between the Ursuline Mother Superior and Mrs. Brooke seemed, on the surface, unlikely, given Frances's outspoken views on French Catholic assimilation into English Protestant culture. She openly criticized Murray for allowing Catholic public festivals and letting local priests convert British soldiers so they could marry Frenchwomen. She feared that the Anglican Church offered the colonists few attractions, arguing that they "dislike our Church principally for want of Music & Shew" and suggesting an organ would draw larger congregations.[6]

Even more worrying for Esther, Frances had attacked the reputation of Father Resche, the Ursulines' parish priest, after he said he resented sharing the chapel with Reverend Brooke. Calling Resche the "most bigoted priest in Canada," Frances claimed he had leased out an English Protestant cemetery within Notre Dame's churchyard and wanted to use the land to build new houses. She believed reports that the priest was having Protestant corpses exhumed and callously thrown into the river.[7] Frances reported these incidents to the ecclesiastical authorities in London, fuelling their concern about the power the Catholic priests still held in Canada.

But if Frances had her reservations about Resche, this did not prevent her growing fascination with the Ursulines and the other communities of religious women in Québec. "The Canadians are very attached to their Convents, [more] than any other part of their Religion, as they educate & provide for their Daughters cheaply," she wrote. The Ursulines, she believed, were "the best nuns" because of their Mother Superior, "an Englishwoman, 60, very moderate."[8] Esther so impressed Frances, in fact, that she appears as a thinly disguised character in *The History of Emily Montague*.[9] Like many novelists, Frances used her fiction to explore a very real and troubling issue, her anti-Catholic prejudices. Through her eponymous heroine, Emily Montague, she describes a visit to the Ursuline convent, whose inhabitants carried an "air of gloominess with which the black habit, and the livid paleness of the nuns, extremely corresponds."[10] But if Emily found the nuns disturbing, she admired their chapel, which Frances described as a spiritual space, "ornamented and lively to the last degree," and a sharp contrast with the nuns' bare living quarters.

In *The History of Emily Montague*, Frances painted a vivid portrait of Esther, whom she had met several times in the Ursuline parlour. "The Superior is an English woman of good family who was taken prisoner by the savages when a child and plac'd here by the generosity of a French officer," she wrote. That Esther was of a "good family" gives the women an equal status, bridging their differences, and suggests that Frances knew something of the Boston Wheelwrights. "[The Superior] is one of the most amiable women I ever knew, with a benevolence in her countenance which inspires all who see her with affection: I am very fond of her conversation tho' sixty and a nun."[11] Their shared heritage and class helped them to overcome their religious and political differences, to the point that Frances could call Esther "my good old country-woman."

Frances may have been disinclined to trust Catholic kindness, but the Ursulines believed that God had miraculously turned her heart towards them, and they welcomed her into their chapel.[12] Frances even attended one of the five veiling ceremonies held before 1766, when she returned to England.[13] She used this experience to write a scene in which Emily Montague observes the young women's happiness at entering the religious life that Frances considered so abhorrent:

> *Her form was elegance itself; her air and motion animated and graceful; the glow of pleasure was on her cheeks, the fire of enthusiasm in her eyes, which are the finest I ever saw: never did I see joy so lively painted on the countenance of the happiest bride; she seem'd to walk in air; her whole person looked more human.*[14]

Through Emily, Frances expressed her concern that a novice was "an amiable victim" who was innocent of the hard life that lay ahead of her. She wrote,

> *The ceremony, form'd to strike the imagination and seduce the heart of unguarded youth, is extremely solemn and affecting; the procession of the nuns, the sweetness of their voices in the choir, the dignified devotion with which the charming enthusiast received the veil, and took the cruel vow which shut her*

from the world for ever, struck my heart in spite of my reason, and I felt myself touch'd even to tears by a superstition I equally pity and despise.

Frances, however, believed that the novice's joy and excitement were merely transient. Like many Anglicans, she was reluctant to accept the idea that religious women could find contentment in such a regimented and austere life. Her heroine spoke of the "air of chagrin which [the Ursuline sisters] in vain endeavour to conceal; and the general eagerness with which they tell you unask'd they are happy," and said this "is a strong proof to the contrary."[15] Frances did not confine her concerns to fiction but in 1765 wrote to a London bishop asking, "What must be done, if Nuns desire to leave the Convent, as it is said some do?"[16]

The ecclesiastical authorities in London shared these concerns, and they drew up plans to let the religious communities die out by stopping all "new professions, engagements or admissions." The existing nuns would be required, "upon pain of deprivation," to swear their allegiance to the English king and to sever their ties to France. But Frances's fictionalized portrait of Mother Esther and the veiling ceremony at least humanized these Catholics and their rituals, and may have influenced the British public, if not the church leaders. Adam Mabane, an eighteenth-century Québec physician and judge, described the novelist's influence, which extended from Québec to London: "Particular attention is paid to Mrs. Brooke [by the English,] either from fear of her bad Tongue or from Gratitude for the good offices." Those who met with her disapproval, he said, paid the price, with their reputations dissected "at the Tea Tables of London."[17]

Whatever Reverend and Mrs. Brooke's reservations about the Ursulines, they did not prevent them from enrolling a five-year-old girl named Frances Lucy Johnson (whether she was a relation or a ward is unknown) at the boarding school in February 1766.[18] Reverend Brooke's endorsement was critical to the convent because of the family's influence, and when Frances left Québec at the end of Esther's first term as Superior in 1768, she hinted at the intimacy that had grown up between them:

> *I have just come from visiting the nuns; they expressed great concern at my leaving Canada, and promised their prayers on my voyages; for which proof of affection, though a good Protestant, I thanked them very sincerely. I was no less pleased with the affection the late superior, my good old country woman, expressed for me, and her regret at seeing me for the last time.*[19]

Brooke's cherished image of a serene Mother Esther belied the harsh reality of running the convent under a military regime. But *The History of Emily Montague* sold well and was often used as a travel guide to Québec, even prompting visits to the convent.

While the Anglican authorities were considering how to rid the colony of its religious communities, newly arrived merchants and civil servants were demanding that the Church provide a governess as an alternative to the Catholic schools.[20] By 1765, Hector Theophilus Cramahé, a Swiss-born British army officer, was lobbying the government to build a free school where the colony's children could learn English.[21] The Ursulines were suddenly faced with competition, not only from the English governesses but from within their own ranks. An Anglican Church report from Québec suggested that while the

Ursuline teachers were well respected, many English parents preferred the Congrégation de Notre Dame school in Montréal.[22]

The Ursulines weathered the storm, however, and another seven English girls enrolled as boarders in 1763. Over the next two decades, more than a quarter of the school's students were Scottish, Irish or English.[23] Like the Brookes, many influential officers and merchants enrolled their daughters and granddaughters, including Lieutenant Colonel Paulus Irving, a member of the military council and quartermaster, and James Brooke, a tavernkeeper.[24] By 1776, even Cramahé was won over; he paid the fees at the Ursuline school for a Catherine Botte, aged nine. If the English worried that religious conversion lay at the core of the Ursulines' pedagogy, their fears were unfounded. The nuns regarded their English students as "naturally very gentle and docile," but they respected their parents' prohibition against instructing them "in our Holy faith."

Keeping the British parents happy and the boarding school full was critical to the Ursulines' survival as Esther struggled to settle its debts. Despite the generosity of "our illustrious General [Murray]," a large bill arrived from the British army's commissary general for supplies provided from October 1759 to May 1761. To Esther's astonishment, this included the months when the Ursulines had nursed Murray's soldiers and officers. The $1,352 in silver dollars demanded was impossible for the Ursulines to repay, since they had ended the previous year in debt. Esther wrote directly to Murray and offered the English king, in lieu of payment, "some fields which we have been accustomed to sow and which are now in very bad condition." But she also asked Murray to plead the Ursulines' case so that King George would "be unable to refuse to cancel this sum for us."[25]

Esther's subtle diplomacy worked. After an anxious interval, Murray finally received word from England that "payment will not be demanded . . . until [the Ursulines] are able to satisfy it." Murray added, "I think too well of your community to believe that it might ever give any occasion for dissatisfaction."²⁶ Relieved, Esther turned her energies to new money-making enterprises. Among her first moves was to take in paying lodgers, since space was at a huge premium in battle-scarred Québec. This followed the French Ursulines' tradition of renting a suite of rooms within the cloister to "some lady of high degree."²⁷ Claude-Godefroy Coquart, a homeless Jesuit missionary; Marie-Josephte de la Fontaine, the eighteen-year-old wife of Judge François-Joseph Cugnet; and Madame Marie-Anne Chasle Perthius, a wealthy widow whose relatives had boarded at the Ursuline school—all became temporary paying boarders.²⁸

Esther found other equally inventive ways to recoup the community's costs. Since the parishioners of Notre Dame used the Ursuline chapel over five successive winters while their church was being repaired, they were charged for keeping fires in the sacristy, for the hosts made in the convent kitchens and even for the burial of three parishioners. Under Esther's authority, the Ursulines used their workshops to manufacture holy objects—religious medallions, altar decorations, gilding, chandeliers, altar cloths, artificial flowers and oil paintings—for sale to churches whose own relics had been lost or damaged. Their kitchens produced communion hosts and candles, secular *eau de vie* (used in medicines), syrups and tarts, while their biscuits became a British army staple.²⁹ When Québec's seminary reopened, the Ursulines supplied the priests with jams and desserts, earning them almost eighty-four *livres* in 1763. They sold fresh fruit, vegetables, eggs, butter, milk, meat and flour harvested from their gardens and outlying lands to the locals.³⁰ Their extensive landholdings provided supplies of firewood, so they no longer needed to buy charcoal or other fuels.

Esther found labourers to replant their fields along the Saint-Charles River with wheat from the forty bushels that were a gift from Montréal's Saint-Sulpice Seminary in June 1762.[31]

But Esther's biggest financial success was in promoting the convent's art to the tourists newly arrived in the city. A speciality was embroidered birchbark boxes, an art form the Ursulines had taught to their Native *séminaristes,* who in turn passed on these skills to their mothers and sisters in the mission villages.[32] Esther saw the commercial potential of these works, and soon baskets, pocketbooks, dressing boxes and even miniature Indian canoes were being sold through the convent's turnstile. They became instantly popular with the English ladies and gentlemen, who, she observed wryly, "had not come over to Canada with empty purses."[33] As Esther explained in a May 1761 letter to the Jesuit procurator, who administered the Ursuline's affairs in Paris, "We sell at a high price to the English gentlemen, yet they seem to consider it a privilege to buy, so eager are they for our work. It is really impossible for us notwithstanding our industry to supply the demand."

These sales alone provided a revenue stream of twenty-one thousand *livres* a year—three times the convent's total income in 1759. It was, Murray agreed, "very ingenious, fashionable work."[34]

Among the ladies and gentlemen crowding through the convent gate was one of the Boston Wheelwrights, who brought news for his aunt Esther. Captain Daniel Wheelwright, the twenty-five-year-old son of her brother Samuel, dropped anchor in Québec after depositing a cargo of colonial troops from the West Indies in 1761. Wheelwright had previously sailed to Québec under Murray's orders, and there the officers discussed matters at his office in the Ursuline convent. Daniel was the first to meet Esther in her role as Mother Superior. Over tarts and *eau de vie* from the convent's kitchen, he told her of Mary Snell's death and the conditions of her mother's will.[35] Esther's brother John had passed away the year before in Boston, leaving "a very considerable fortune" to Nathaniel, his third son by his second wife.[36]

This next generation of Wheelwrights knew much about their long-absent aunt. Daniel reported that his brother Job and his wife, Abigail, had named their second daughter in her honour. It seems understandable that Esther would relish this renewed contact with her English family, especially since Nathaniel, who had close ties to the old French regime, was now a leading Boston banker. Before Daniel weighed anchor, Esther put together a parcel of gifts for her namesake, including rich silk dresses, an exquisitely embroidered pincushion and a sample of the famous birchbark boxes. A convent artist was commissioned to paint a silk square with the Wheelwright coat of arms for baby Esther's parents.[37] These gifts represented the best of the Ursulines' artistry. She also enclosed a letter to her surviving brother, Samuel Wheelwright, still farming in Wells.

The exchange of gifts—"specimens of the nuns' work," according to a Wheelwright relative—had a language of its own. The birchbark boxes and embroidery Esther offered as symbols of her affection. But there was another layer of meaning here, since her primary responsibility was to ensure her community's survival under the English regime. With these gifts, sent to a family of wealthy and powerful merchants, Esther may have been trying to gauge her chances of selling the nuns' art in New England. After all, Bostonians "took their Money by the thousands from the treasury to trust it to [Nathaniel Wheelwright]," who had often called upon her assistance during his missions to ransom the captives held at Odanak.[38]

The next Wheelwright relation to pay homage was Joshua Moody, whose late mother, Mary, had been Esther's younger sister.

In 1762, Moody presented Esther with a miniature oil portrait of her own mother, Mary Snell.[39] For Esther to be able to keep this personal possession within the convent, it had to be turned into a Madonna. A convent artist painted a golden veil across the head and draped a royal blue shawl around the neck, and then the retouched portrait was set in a gilt frame and displayed among other cherished images of the Virgin Mary along the chapel wall.[40] This resolved the contradiction of having the Protestant Mary Snell's presence in the Ursulines' sacred space, and it also enabled Esther to keep her souvenir. Before Moody returned to Maine, the Mother Superior had her own portrait painted, which was considered highly unusual.[41] She gave this to her nephew, who, once back in Boston, presented the portrait to Job and Abigail Wheelwright in trust for their daughter.

As the boarding school was attracting increasing numbers of English girls, Esther also offered a place to her little namesake in the *pensionnat*. However, it seems that for Job and Abigail, this request was a step too far, and they politely turned it down. According to a later namesake, Esther Mitchell Morse, "Of course the Puritan parents were not disposed to gratify her this request."[42]

These contacts with the Wheelwrights were vital to Esther's vision of cultivating new patrons and clients among the English colonists, especially as the Ursulines were rapidly losing theirs in France. Since there was a restricted postal service and prohibitions on French imports, the old system of relying on the Mother House in Paris for annual supplies had to change. The nuns struggled to adhere to the Rules and were reduced to using *petites ruses* with the military officials to obtain material for their habits and other religious items from England. As Esther explained in a letter to the Mother House in Paris:

We shall very soon be in a condition not to be able to dress ourselves according to the Rules. Since the war, we are especially in need of bombazine for our veils. Indeed, the need is so pressing that soon we shall not be able to appear decently, having nothing but rags to cover our heads. We cannot buy these things of the English. They do not know how to [dress] the nuns. I think, my dear Mother, you might send us a few pieces of bombazine by some of our Canadians, who might return to their poor country.[43]

Among the Ursulines' Canadian supporters was René-Ovide Hertel de Rouville, who evaded the postal restrictions to deliver their letters to Paris. (Ironically, he was a relation of the officer who had raided Wells in 1703.) Esther explained to her superiors that while Rouville was happy to bring bombazine to Québec, the Ursulines were hard pressed to pay for it. "Everything is very dear," she lamented. For those who depended upon the sisters' charity, however, things were far worse. The alms traditionally supplied by Québec's wealthy Catholics and the French Crown had dwindled. The homeless, and widows and orphans who depended on their charity were left empty-handed.[44]

Esther maintained her composure throughout these trials, but her resentment towards the conquerors is evident in a letter she wrote to the Mother House about a rumour that "this poor country" might be delivered back to French rule.[45] Murray privately acknowledged tensions in the colony, admitting that Britain "had not a friend in the country, all were enemies, both within and without the walls, all were interested in our Destruction, all bound in duty or obligation to contribute towards it."[46] But as she had throughout her life, Esther managed the internal contradiction of praying for a French victory to remove "the foreign element of language, custom and religion" while also nurturing genuinely affectionate relationships with Murray, Frances Brooke and her Wheelwright kin.[47]

Towards the end of Esther's first term as Mother Superior, her diplomatic skills were challenged when a murder was tried in the Ursuline convent under Murray's direction. Before Esther was consulted, Murray's secretary, Hector Theophilus Cramahé, had sought Bishop Briand's permission to use the monastery for a public criminal trial. Briand had little choice but to agree, as Cramahé advised, "I think you are too judicious and too reasonable to disapprove."[48]

The following day, Lieutenant Colonel Roger Morris presided over a military tribunal of a dozen British officers and heard evidence on the murder of Louis Dodier, a local farmer. When Dodier's bloody corpse was found in his Saint-Vallier stable on a morning in late January 1763, the villagers attempted to disguise his murder as an accident. They had hoped to avoid involving government authorities, but Major James Abercrombie, the commanding British officer, immediately suspected Dodier's father-in-law, Joseph Corriveau, of the crime. The men had been quarrelling for months about money and property, and Dodier's wife, Marie-Josephte, had once asked Major Abercrombie's permission to leave her husband because of his violent abuse.

Father and daughter were arrested and placed on trial for murder. A succession of witnesses testified that the Corriveaus had told them Dodier died after being kicked in the head by his horse. But a stableboy swore that since the horses were unshod, such a kick could not have killed Dodier. A regimental surgeon examined the body and agreed. Joseph was found guilty and sentenced to hang for murdering his son-in-law, while Marie-Josephte was charged as an accessory and sentenced to sixty lashes in a public place. Murray ratified the proceedings, and a carpenter was hired to build the gallows and prepare the floggings.

The night before the execution, Joseph confessed to Father Augustin-Louis de Glapion that he was protecting the real culprit, Marie-Josephte, and offered to make Murray a deal. When challenged, Marie-Josephte quickly admitted the truth: she had stabbed her abusive husband to death while he lay sleeping in bed. When the court martial reconvened, Marie-Josephte was found guilty and sentenced to be hanged and gibbeted (her corpse hung in an iron cage and put on public display). One witness recalled her last morning, on April 18, 1763, when this small woman was taken in a cart through the convent's big doors towards the gallows on the Plains of Abraham. That she was condemned to gibbeting, a uniquely English punishment and one never before used on a woman, aroused the Mother Superior's protective instincts.[49] According to Ursuline oral history, Esther expressed her concerns about the severity of Marie-Josephte's punishment, since gibbeting was unheard of among the French.[50] Nevertheless, the corpse was displayed in a cage at Pointe-Lévy and removed five weeks later.

A few weeks after Marie-Josephte's hanging, on May 24, 1763, a peace treaty was signed, ending the Seven Years' War. An Ursuline sister wrote to the Mother House of her community's reluctant acceptance:

> We have felt the disappointment the more acutely from having flattered ourselves for so long that the final arrangements would be very different; for we could not persuade ourselves that Canada would be so easily given up. Nothing is left but for us to adore with submission the impenetrable decrees of the Almighty.

Whatever private reservations Esther Wheelwright harboured, she joined her sisters on June 14, 1763, in a public festival of "joy and thanksgiving" in the Ursuline chapel for the treaty's passage. The community gave thanks "for the continuation of the Catholic and Roman religion," accepting that the French were finally and irrevocably defeated.[51]

CHAPTER 23

The Virtues of Tolerance

I CAN'T LEAVE QUÉBEC WITHOUT VISITING THE CHAPELLE
des Ursulines, which was built between 1724 and 1726 but filled
with objects created by the artist Pierre-Noël Levasseur from 1726 to
1736. The original chapel was where Father Bigot gave his sermon
in 1712 as Esther took her white veil, where Nathaniel Wheelwright
was dazzled by opulent splendour on his visits in the 1750s, where
Esther first sang the *Te Deum,* prayed out the Hours and was buried
in 1780 to await the Resurrection.

This is my final day at the convent. Even after all my reading
and research, I'm still soaking up what's left of the past, feeling that
Esther lingers here. It seems an appropriate place to bid Esther fare-
well, but then I remember that her mortal remains were transferred
from the monastery's mausoleum in 1996, along with those of the
other sisters buried here between 1723 and 1792.

Back in the archives, the archivist flicks through a narrow
drawer of file cards and plucks one out triumphantly. *"C'est ici,"* she
says and copies out an address. It is a cemetery where, like a family,

the nuns go to pray for their sisters in heaven. The archivist tells me that it's a must.

I tuck the scrap of paper into my bag and walk back along the corridor, stopping at the plaque that Edith F. Wheelwright of Westwood, Massachusetts, paid to have erected in my ancestor's memory in 1931. After the dedication, Mrs. Wheelwright wrote to Mother des Anges, the Ursuline secretary, "Mother Esther was wonderful, of course, and I can assure you that the Wheelwright family are maintaining her standards of goodness for Mr. Wheelwright is a wonderful man."

Ah, standards of goodness. I'll try to live up to that. But if that's what the Wheelwrights of the 1930s were honouring, how would the Ursulines like Esther to be remembered?

The nuns I've spoken to tell me that after 1759 their order endured a time of suffering and poverty when they feared a future where the British conquerors would forbid them to use their language and religion. Esther's greatest achievement, the nuns believe, was her ability to negotiate with General Murray. As one Ursuline sister tells me, "We had to be obedient." Esther was by then thoroughly French, but still regarded as a "Daughter of Albion," a perfect go-between, translator and diplomat.

Esther had to cope with "two mentalities" while running the convent and negotiating with an alien government. The Ursulines believe that she had to be wise, and that she was a good superior because she was open to people, she possessed a sharp political intelligence and she felt obvious compassion.

Yes, I want to shout, better than goodness! How about a model of religious and ethnic tolerance, of the virtues of negotiation and forgiveness, of the power of kindness?

Then the archivist shakes my hand and sums it all up with an elegant simplicity: "Just write something good for our mother."

Back at the hotel, I book a taxi for Jean-Lesage International Airport and pull the scrap of paper from my bag. The time's tight, but before I leave for London, I must pay my final respects to Esther.

CHAPTER 24

A Troubled Peace

*I*F MOTHER ESTHER MARIE-JOSEPH IS REMEMBERED BY
the Ursulines as a saviour who successfully negotiated with
the British conquerors to save the community from extinction, the
reality of her last years was far more complicated. The cloister was
fraught with internal dissent, the fallout of adjusting to so much
upheaval and uncertainty under the military regime. Esther and
her sisters had endured famine, sieges, warfare, epidemics, the loss
of family members and their French identity. They faced a faction
of hostile British merchants and civil servants who favoured their
expulsion from Canada. These tensions took their toll, and during
Mother Esther's final two terms, from 1769 to 1772, she struggled to
contain bitter feuds erupting within her ranks.

The problem began with numbers. The Ursulines were slow
to replace the sisters who had died of illness and old age after 1759,
when the novitiate was forced to close. By 1770, their population had
fallen to just eighteen choir nuns and eight lay sisters. The terrible
aftermath of the war and uncertain prospects had kept potential

novices from coming, and without new recruits, the future looked bleak. The novitiate had finally reopened in March 1764, the year of Esther's golden jubilee as a professed nun.[1] Esther used her celebration, which was attended "by the elite of Québec," to promote religious tolerance, illustrating with her own history how the "two races" could live together in harmony.[2] The monastery remained profoundly French, but its sisters appreciated "the worth of the daughters of Albion," including their Mother Superior and the English girls now filling the boarding school.[3]

But while Mother Esther preached tolerance, the older nuns were growing increasingly concerned about their loss of influence over the colony's young women. They feared their city had become a British military garrison, peopled by soldiers who drank in newly opened pubs and visited dancehalls and theatres that catered to their tastes. The change was troubling, as one choir nun lamented:

> *Some of our pupils, soon after their [F]irst Communion, are taken from us, and before the age of fourteen, they are introduced into society and allowed to go to the theatre. You may easily imagine the sad results of these dangerous amusements . . . We hear many complaints of the vanity and luxury which are becoming prevalent in society.*

Equally disturbing was the trend of Catholic women, even former Ursuline pupils, changing their religion to marry Anglicans, further shrinking the pool of potential postulants and those who could pay the full dowry as choir nuns.[4] The girls who did express a desire for the novitiate often had dubious motives; Bishop Briand suspected that some recruits at the Hôpital Général were more attracted to the regular meals and warm beds than a life of spiritual enlightenment.[5]

In the Ursuline novitiate, many struggled to respect the Rules, and every departure sent an anxious ripple through the community. A decade after the novitiate reopened, eight of fourteen novices had left, all of them lacking the "necessary qualities" or having "lost the vocation."[6] Since each choir novice contributed a thousand to two thousand *livres*, every departure depleted the convent's vulnerable coffers.[7] Despite Esther's entrepreneurial achievements, the community's financial problems persisted; even the French Crown began demanding a 15 percent tax now that the convent was operating in a foreign country. Severe windstorms and heavy rains flooded the lowlands and decimated the harvest in 1768, exacerbating existing food shortages. A year later, wheat for seed and flour was so scarce that many people were reduced to feeding on grass and roots; unemployment was high, and according to the convent's annals, bankruptcies were "in style."[8] The colony seemed to teeter on the brink.

The Ursulines' collective insecurity was made worse by the administrative vacuum left after the conquest, when all the religious communities were unsure whether the British would allow the appointment of a bishop, and if so, how far his authority would extend. Even Esther's election as Mother Superior proved problematic, since Bishop Briand was forced to bend a French law forbidding a foreigner from assuming the post.[9] Monsignor Étienne Montgolfier, the vicar general of Montréal, fudged the issue by assuring Briand that the Ursulines were no longer subject to French law. To demand that Mother Esther step down, he argued, would only cause unhappiness in the convent and would undermine the Ursulines' autonomy.[10]

But the doubt over Esther's election lingered, and a letter to the Mother House, written days before her third re-election, in December 1769, reveals her loneliness. "We are not lacking in debts and some pretty large ones," she wrote. "Nobody but me, however, knows about them and I am in no hurry to acquaint the Community with the fact, for fear of distressing them."[11] Esther's strategy, however, may have been interpreted in the convent as personal weakness. The convent's historian, while emphasizing her quiet strength, her gentleness, her grace and her exquisite politeness, questions her authority during this last term. She lacked, the historian wrote, "a firmness which is sometimes necessary." This seemingly mild rebuke of the woman meant to embody Jesus Christ hints at a period of remarkable upheaval.[12]

Mother Esther was surely exhausted as she served this third term. The French *ancien régime* was fast disappearing and the colony of New England was ripe for revolution. In the convent, four elderly sisters died between March and April 1770, and the beloved former superior, Mother Migeon, now languished in the hospital, "quite infirm and helpless," unable even to attend daily Mass.[13] Esther felt her "burden [begin] to grow heavy," with the number of senior nuns shrinking further from illness and old age. That summer, a crisis erupted when the portress, the sister who managed the temporal affairs of the community, caught a young Ursuline nun with "a fickle imagination" entering the convent in the early dawn after "taking the air" along the city's streets. As a contemplative order, the Ursulines considered sacrosanct the vow of obedience to the Mother Superior and to the Rules. The young nun would have known that no *religieuse* was allowed to "follow her own inclinations in the disposal of her time."[14] It was an act of heresy.

The Ursulines were highly conscious of Protestant prejudices towards religious women, and a cloistered nun walking the streets at dawn was, at the very least, endangering her community's reputation. On July 18, Bishop Briand reprimanded Mother Esther

Marie-Joseph for allowing the convent's gate to be left open, comparing this sloppiness with the brisk efficiency of the Ursulines he had known as a schoolboy in Brittany. "I had seen the hem of the robes of two nuns who came to open the gate and to close it at once, each time that carriages entered and left . . . They were not afraid there, of hardship in observing the rule."

Briand warned that if the gate were ever left open again, the offending nun would be excommunicated. He then set a severe punishment for the miscreant. Esther had to ensure that the nun was confined to her room, banned from Divine Office and Mass, and barred from speaking with anyone but her. She would report to the Superior's office at 9 p.m. every evening, escorted by Father Glapion. As Briand explained, "Examples are needed to make us wise."[15]

Confined to her cell, the young nun refused to eat, even with Esther visiting her three times a day and tempting her with "everything . . . that is to her liking." The Mother Superior explained that her violation of the Rules was so serious that no lighter punishment was possible. But the woman was oblivious to her situation, and possibly mentally unbalanced, insisting that these walks were necessary. "She seems to be afflicted by this misfortune," Esther wrote to Briand. "She confided in me today, as something already decided, that she should go out sometimes to take the air when she needed to restore her health and that she would return afterwards. I did not discuss this with her." The episode badly affected the whole community. "Her presence is an object of so much pain," said Esther, "that it can only be hoped that she may ever cease to torment us."[16]

The young nun's fate is unknown, but if she left the convent, the Ursuline history does not record her departure. That she breached the Rules so seriously, however, reflected poorly on Esther's authority, which came under scrutiny again two years later. This time, criticism erupted after Mother Esther appointed a nineteen-year-old novice, Sister des Roches de Ste. Angèle, as class mistress, replacing a lay nun, Sister St. Olivier. The *maîtresse générale*, Mother Marie-Antoinette Poulin de St. François, was outraged that she was not consulted, even though Esther had few choices for the appointment. Among the eighteen choir nuns, three were still novices, five were too elderly to teach and several younger sisters were in poor health.

Mother Poulin went behind her Superior's back, an act of breathtaking subordination, writing to Bishop Briand with her complaint in February 1772. She humbly asked the bishop for advice on "a little difficulty" before launching into the details. Esther, she claimed, never accepted "any representation, however carefully considered, just and reasonable it may be." Mother Poulin admitted learning of the Superior's plans by "listening in secret" to a conversation, but she justified her behaviour by pointing out that neither she nor the assembly had been consulted about this unsuitable candidate. Then she explained her reservations about the new teacher:

> *The state of this poor child, whom I do not think is ready yet to guide others, touches me deeply, especially because of the make-up of the class, which would require a first rate mistress to put everything back on a sound footing. I beg your Excellency very humbly to grant me the grace of answering my prayer by allowing this young novice the advantage of completing her novitiate so that she may learn to obey before she controls others.*[7]

That Mother Poulin felt moved to subvert Esther's authority by appealing directly to the bishop speaks volumes about the breakdown within the community. The Superior was not required to justify her decisions to the nuns below her, and matters concerning the school were usually aired at the convent assembly. But rather than chastising Mother Poulin for criticizing her Superior, Briand wrote an open letter to the community and scheduled a visit in a bid to restore Esther's authority.

Mother Marie-Elizabeth Richard de St. Augustin also complained to Briand on March 7, 1772. Her first charge was that Esther had not allowed the community "time to savour the sweetness" of his letter. After it was read aloud, Mother St. Augustin was upset that "our Mother delivered a great rebuke to us, which in everyone's opinion was wholly out of place." The nuns had clearly discussed the matter at length behind Esther's back, another sign of their unhappiness.

The women were stung that Esther criticized displays of vanity and banned "footwear contrary to the Rule," which was regarded as a flagrant violation of their vow of poverty. Then, "with the sharpest zeal," Esther admonished a lay sister for swapping her own ragged bedspread for a brightly coloured one from the infirmary. According to Mother St. Augustin, the Superior had done a *volte-face*, publicly condemning the lay sister for an action she had earlier sanctioned. But such a petty theft ran contrary to the Ursulines' vow of obedience and indicated yet again that Esther's authority was not being properly respected. Mother St. Augustin felt that Esther had allowed the lay sister to get away with a boldly impudent act and had been slow to punish her. Speaking for the choir nuns, she wrote to Briand, "We are much disturbed."

The lay sister, however, bragged that she had Esther's permission to swap the bedspread. She returned the offending item to the infirmary, but, wrote Mother St. Augustin, it was "with a mocking air." One astonished choir nun pointed out to Esther that Bishop Briand would be very displeased if he knew a sister "had permission to keep something which she ought not, as she had boasted." All of this could have been avoided, Mother St. Augustin believed, if Esther had delivered an appropriate punishment in the first place.

Mother Esther was also criticized for ignoring the bishop's instructions on the day school's opening hours by allowing a class mistress, Sister St. François, to admit the children twice a day, instead of just once. Mother St. Augustin thought this poor practice and asked Briand to ban Sister St. François from teaching "because of her incompetence in every way," an opinion she claimed the majority of the nuns shared. She ended with a flourish: "Anything I could say to you would not express to what a point [Sister St. François] has demonstrated her arrogance."[18] Clearly, the hierarchy of the convent was breaking down.

By writing to Briand, the nuns were violating their sacred vows of obedience and the Rule that every Ursuline show the utmost respect towards her Mother Superior, who held "the place of Christ" within the monastery. The Ursuline historian, in a discreet nod to Esther's perceived shortcomings, wrote that her gentle nature and exquisite manners, which had served her so well in negotiating with Murray and befriending English visitors like Frances Moore Brooke, also rendered it difficult for her to be sufficiently tough with the younger nuns.[19]

Bishop Briand scheduled his visit for March 3. Before the assembled Ursuline community, he spoke of "little disorders" that could ruin a convent and praised the "good souls" who had reported their "alarm at the least appearance of evil." He moved swiftly to practical matters and lapses in the Rules. The nuns were leaving for choir at 5:15 a.m., much later than their usual practice, and with fewer nuns assisting at Divine Office. If this was a permanent change, the Mother Superior must ask his permission, and in the meantime, the

Ursulines must work together to prevent such breaches. "Mention was made to me of brightly coloured curtains, of counterpanes [bed-spreads] permitted only in the infirmary, of varied and fancy foot-wear," said the bishop. He scolded the Ursulines for buying "refined" shoes and condemned as a "dangerous liberty" the practice of using their own private money to buy gifts.[20]

Then Briand addressed Mother Poulin's concerns about the school's management. The headmistress, he said, had to keep her teachers informed about changes, and the teachers had to consult the Superior with their concerns. Should the school gate be opened to pupils twice a day? Briand suggested that it was appropriate to open it when necessary, since many girls travelled long distances to school, and they should not be left waiting outside in bad weather.

Having addressed all the complaints, he urged the Ursulines to be vigilant in respecting the Rules. "Love poverty," urged Briand. "It is a vow which is delicate and on which it is easy to delude one-self." Buying elegant shoes and coveting brightly coloured blankets opened the door to further abuses and to a false conscience. "Avoid everything which might make you possessive or wilful," he contin-ued. "Think that it is an exemption in a grave matter and that all exemptions should be narrowed down rather than extended." He added that it was disobedient to obtain Esther's permission for the things they wanted by extortion, by surprise, by lying or making false allegations. He demanded that the nuns restore their respect for the much-maligned Mother Superior.[21]

Four days later, Esther assured Briand that the community would "labour more than ever to make ourselves what you desire and what God demands of us." But she also defended her deci-sions on changing their routine. The nuns were leaving later for choir, she explained, because wood was so expensive that fires in their cells were lit only on Sundays and feast days. Esther promised, however, that the nuns could chant their Vespers in a freezing cold choir "without too much hardship." The Rules had also been bent to accommodate their busy chaplain, who preferred to say the Mass at 6:15 a.m., but this arrangement could also be changed.

Esther promised she would "with pleasure" crack down on signs of vanity, removing "anything superfluous," including the troublesome coloured bedspread. She confessed to Briand her sin of being too lenient with her nuns and students, "granting, perhaps often, permissions which I should not." She asked God's pardon for her faults. Her contrition acknowledged Briand's superior authority and let slip a glimpse of the strain she must have felt, nearing her ninth decade, in keeping the community from disintegrating.[22]

Esther's loneliness was made worse because letters containing support and advice from the Mother House in Paris were now so intermittent. She wrote to her superiors in September 1772, lamenting that there had been no correspondence from Paris in more than a year.[23] The next month, Esther was taken to the infirmary with a high fever, and she remained bedridden throughout the early winter. The convent's assembly was suspended while the nuns waited for the Mother Superior's recovery. She resumed her post just before the elections in mid-December.

"The illness of our venerable Mother Superior is becoming more and more serious," Joseph-François Perreault, the vicar general, wrote to Briand on November 3, 1772. "At the age of 76, there is everything to fear."[24] Esther survived, but she was so weak that the community decided against electing her for a fourth term. Instead, she assisted the new Mother Superior, Davanne de St. Louis de Gonzague, her signature growing more elastic as she laboured with her quill beneath her successor's clear and confident letters.[25]

A tumour now obscured her eyesight, distorting her handwriting and robbing her of the dexterity she needed to embroider on fine material. Instead, she spent her days in the exquisitely humble act of mending her sisters' linen.[26]

But Esther's diplomatic skills were not wasted in her twilight years, when influential Englishwomen began seeking her out after the London publication of *The History of Emily Montague* in 1769. Frances Brooke's novel was dedicated to the new governor, Guy Carleton, the 1st Baron of Dorchester, whose wife, Lady Maria Carleton, became a regular visitor to the Ursulines. Esther's carefully cultivated friendships with the colony's influential English ladies seem to have endured.

Educated at the Ursuline school in Versailles, Lady Carleton stopped by the cloister to ask the nuns for a blessing whenever travelling to and from the colony. She cut a striking figure. Small, fair-haired, with ramrod-straight posture and French court manners, she was fond of elaborate skirts, coiffed her hair with lace and red ribbons, and wore scarlet shoes with very high heels and gold buttons.[27] Although an English Protestant, Lady Carleton paid homage to the former Mother Superior, presenting the community with a set of silver candlesticks for their chapel. The annalist records the Ursulines' delight with the gift and says even a Catholic "could not have been more thoughtful and delicate in the choice of a parting souvenir."[28]

The nuns believed that Lady Carleton's "partiality for the French at Québec" helped to promote tolerance so "no one was molested on account of his religion."[29] The governor had been among the wounded officers cared for by the Ursulines in their convent hospital in 1759, and when he arrived in the colony to assume its highest post, they received him like "an old friend."[30] Lady Carleton's sister Anne also befriended the nuns, even moving into the convent as a "parlour-boarder" following the death of her husband, an officer and nephew of Guy Carleton's. Lady Anne Carleton occupied the apartment that was later used as the chaplain's rooms until 1778.[31] Having grown used to the convent's "secluded way of living," she asked to stay permanently, but Mother Superior St. Louis refused and she returned to London.[32]

Esther, being cared for in her old age within the cloister, had outlived her elder siblings in Wells and Boston, her parents, all the other captives from the 1703 raid and even the Massachusetts colony itself. In 1775, she was forced to endure one final military conflict when Colonel Benedict Arnold's American forces attempted to seize Québec from the British. Colonel Arnold's troops were raised to defend the colony against what his supporters saw as oppressive British government policies. After successful assaults on Fort Ticonderoga on Lake Champlain and Crown Point in New York, the forces pressed north via the Chaudière Valley.[33] From the convent windows, the Ursulines watched as American soldiers raised batteries and positioned cannons towards the city, preparing for yet another assault on its ramparts. Three weeks after reaching Québec, on November 11, they began blasting the city.

On December 15, 1775, Mother Esther Marie-Joseph was elected as assistant superior for a second term "in military style, to the sound of guns and cannon." This time the nuns, "like warriors," were better prepared to last out a siege; their thoughtful *dépositaire* had stocked up enough food for several weeks, and the teaching nuns had dismissed all but fifteen of their boarding students, with those remaining bedding down in the convent's most secure rooms.[34] The Ursulines recited the Hours in the safety of their vaults before heading back upstairs to teach and counsel "so many afflicted persons who came to ask for alms and a word of encouragement."[35]

The Continental army began its final assault on Québec in a drifting blizzard on New Year's Eve 1775. In freezing temperatures, the men sheltered wherever they could, warming their guns beneath the folds of their coats. Church bells rang throughout the city, and in the convent the older nuns recognized the sound of musket shot scattering like hailstones. A bomb fell close enough to rip away a nun's apron, another tore through the infirmary, while a third blasted through a window and fell onto an empty bed in the novitiate. The Ursulines removed their window sashes and the American soldiers lowered their guns, showing they intended the sisters no harm.[36] The Ursulines at Trois-Rivières demonstrated their humanity and their instinct for diplomacy, as they had done after the battle of 1759, by taking in twenty-one of Arnold's wounded soldiers when his troops were defeated there on June 8, 1776.[37]

This was last military conflict that Esther would witness, and it brought together all the splintered factions of her life. Jeremiah Wheelwright Jr., who had inherited the family position of commissary general of the army, was among the troops. Esther's nephew Captain Daniel Wheelwright also served in the conflict, and the following year Wheelwright men fought on both sides of the Revolutionary War.[38] Even Esther's former Abenaki kin were involved, operating as scouts from the St. Lawrence missions and serving as trackers to lead the American volunteers through the harsh winter wilderness from Massachusetts to Québec.[39]

For days, the Ursulines recited the Hours in their cellar and sang hymns while cannons pounded the buildings outside the convent walls. "All this," wrote Mother St. Louis with weary understatement, "was not pleasant."[40] The siege lasted until the American forces were soundly defeated in May 1776, extinguishing the hopes of Colonel Arnold and General George Washington that a Canadian invasion would bring the French-speaking colonists into the Revolutionary War. The British had triumphed and secured Québec once again.

Revolution had swept through Massachusetts, where the Wheelwrights were divided over their loyalty to the British Crown. At the same time, in Esther's adopted motherland of France, the Ursulines faced a growing threat from Republicans, who persecuted nuns at the Mother House in the rue St. Jacques. In Québec, meanwhile, the Ursulines, who considered themselves "as French as ever" prayed that their sisters would survive the revolution.[41] All their letters had stopped, and recently arrived visitors from Europe brought alarming rumours that the French Ursulines feared expulsion from their cloister and had been harassed by mobs.[42]

And what of Esther's Abenaki clan, now dispersed across two new borders and living under foreign rulers in both countries? The Abenaki boarders at the Ursuline school had long disappeared, and the tradition of educating girls from the St. Lawrence missions was over. When Mother Superior St. Louis put forward a potential sponsor for an aboriginal pupil, a Monsieur Lisotte, the assembly refused.[43] After the conquest, many Abenakis returned from the St. Lawrence region to Maine, where the British Crown decreed that "Nations or Tribes of Indians with whom we are connected and who live under Our Protection should not be molested or disturbed in the Possession of . . . their Hunting Grounds." Despite this assurance, the Abenakis were pushed to the margins of their land during the late eighteenth century as the New World filled with European settlers—English, German, Scottish, Irish and French Huguenots.[44]

As Esther's gnarled fingers pushed a needle through soft, worn cloth, where did her mind wander? Maybe to her parade of mothers: Mary Snell, who had sheltered her in the crook of her arm in Reverend John Wheelwright's farmhouse at Wells; her adoptive Abenaki mother, who fed, clothed and nurtured her in the wigwam at Norridgewock and St. François, teaching her about the virtues of reciprocity, the power of dreams and the possibilities of transformation; and Mother Migeon, the *maîtresse des pensionnaires,* who saw the potential and symbolic importance of this English captive girl hidden beneath her second-hand French gown.

These women had acted as guides, but it was Esther's personality, her talent for survival and her incredible life force that made her place at the very heart of Canada's early history. Father Rale's teachings, Father Bigot's calculated intervention, her Abenaki kin's generosity in releasing her and the Marquis de Vaudreuil's political ambitions all shaped her journey to the cloister. But it was Esther who chose to make her home among a people, no longer foreign, in a far-flung corner of a waning French empire. There she enjoyed a life unimaginable to her parents and siblings, rising to the most powerful religious position for a woman in eighteenth-century colonial life. She laboured to preserve the French Catholic community that had adopted her, negotiating with her fellow countrymen and -women to usher it through its darkest hours.

Esther's sisters record that through the turmoil of her last few years, she "lived like another Moses in the midst of her adoptive family . . . showered with the most precious graces."[45] She remained one of the "voices" of the convent's assembly, casting her vote on the suitability of the novices and offering her advice on the vital business of her community. She suffered no lingering illness and followed her spiritual routine before she died suddenly at 8 p.m. on October 29, 1780. The confessor to the community, Father Gravé, heard her final confession and performed the last rites.[46] "She died as she had lived," reported the convent's historian, "aspiring towards Heaven, repeating unceasingly some verses of the Psalms." She finally had the "happy death" for which she had so long prayed.[47]

Legacy and Reputations

*L*IKE MOST LIVES, ESTHER WHEELWRIGHT'S REFUSES
to cohere into a neat narrative; it is often contradictory
or incoherent, or the facts are simply absent. There is no simple for-
mula of heroic triumph over victimhood, with a former captive rising through the eighteenth-century Catholic hierarchy to save the
French language and her adopted religion from British interference.
I locate Esther's heroism elsewhere. Digging into documents in
archives across three countries and into the oral history passed down
through my family produces a lesson in tolerance.

To survive the trauma of her childhood, Esther learned to
adapt, and to keep on adapting throughout her life, to bewildering
circumstances. Ripped from her home, she endured the captive trail
to Norridgewock, where her Abenaki captors taught her to honour reciprocity and communal well-being over the Puritan ideals
of individual competition and respect for authority. A second time
Esther was forced to leave a loving family and change her identity,
completely, utterly and without explanation. As a French Catholic

she succeeded, even showing such intellectual promise, strength of character and spiritual depth that she was nominated for the Ursuline novitiate. It is this capacity for resilience that has guided me along my journey to find her.

If I can make any claim to Esther through my family, these are the qualities that make me proud of my association. Whatever pressure her Catholic mentors exerted on her to take her vows, she found a place within the Ursuline community and a purpose bigger than her own or her family's concerns. Without these accidents of history, I would never have known this ancestor of mine, the only Wheelwright woman from the eighteenth century whose life has been chronicled, who has left some vestige of her character, personality and beliefs. That her history knits together three disparate peoples, cultures and religions is quite literally awesome.

In the absence of documented evidence, I have tried to move Esther's story beyond the racism inherent in earlier readings of her life as a white girl rescued by Europeans from her "savage" captors. The purpose of many Wheelwright letters to the Ursuline convent in the early twentieth century was to thank the nuns for saving Esther from captivity. As Eugene Stevenson, a New Jersey politician, wrote in 1922, "My ancestress certainly owed a debt to the Ursuline nuns which she could never repay because *they rescued her from the savages* and brought her up and educated her and then in her mature years bestowed upon her the greatest honour in their gift" (emphasis added). A decade later, in June 1936, William Bond Wheelwright also wrote to thank the sisters, "whose predecessors instructed and cared for our kinswoman Esther Wheelwright whom God *protected among the Abenakis* in the wilderness" (emphasis added).

Another two decades later, in 1955, Edwin Newton Wheelwright from Illinois wrote to the historian Gerald Kelly, "Your mention of Esther Wheelwright pleases me for I am very fond of the story of the little puritan girl who was captured by the Indians, was rescued by the Jesuit priests, taken to Québec and finally became Mother Superior."[1] This version of Esther's story ignored what she gained from her Abenaki family and the beliefs they instilled within her.

Esther's separation from her family was violent, terrifying and a tragic loss for her parents. But while my relations display a natural concern and empathy for Esther, there is no mention among their letters of the Abenaki boy held captive by the Wheelwrights as a bargaining chip in their negotiations. Ned Wheelwright, writing in the nineteenth century, is the only relation to mention that the Wheelwrights' abhorrence of Esther's captivity sat uneasily alongside their ownership of African slaves. That John Wheelwright also sold contracts for white indentured servants brought from England in the 1720s seems to have been long forgotten.

Nor were my relatives aware that Esther's brother John profited from trading with her captors and employing their services. There is strong circumstantial evidence that Nathaniel, from whom I am also directly descended, traded illegally with the French and used his friendship with Aunt Esther to forge new business contacts. The Wheelwrights, the French Catholics and the Abenakis were bound together through mutual necessity and a shifting web of alliances, where each held political power.

But just as Esther renewed her relationships with John and Nathaniel, the tide shifted again. John passed away in October 1760, and six years later Nathaniel followed, after suffering a bout of yellow fever in Guadeloupe, where he was buried. Nathaniel was on the run from his creditors after causing the biggest financial scandal in eighteenth-century Boston. The merchant James

Otis wrote to friends in England on January 25, 1765, that the news was spreading through the city and people were panicking because Nathaniel could no longer honour his banknotes. "The failing of Mr. [W]heelwright . . . has given as great a shock to our credit as your South Sea Bubble did in England some years ago."[2] It was rumoured that Nathaniel lost more than £154,000 before he left Boston for London and the West Indies. Many Bostonians were devastated. "Widows and Orphans are ruined [and] can only bewail their fate," wrote Otis.

With John dead, Nathaniel disgraced and the family indebted, it's no wonder that the relatives with whom she had been most intimate failed to contact Esther. By 1776, according to family accounts, the Wheelwrights had been torn asunder, with some fighting for independence from Britain and others declaring themselves Loyalists. The truth was more complex. Nathaniel's only surviving children, Charles Apthorp and Joseph, were sent to live with Reverend Henry Caner and were part of the evacuation of British Loyalists from Boston to Halifax. From there, the orphaned boys returned to England, not because of their political beliefs but because of financial and domestic necessity.

Whether Esther knew any of this or not, she still hoped the Wheelwrights would clear the debt she owed to the convent from her entry into the novitiate in 1714. In 1789, the Ursulines sent a Dr. Le Terrière to Salem to inspect a copy of John Wheelwright's will. The accompanying letter seemed to confirm that despite Esther's status as Mother Superior and half a century of service to the community, she was still troubled by her inability to pay her full dowry all those years ago. It read that Esther had "always in her lifetime hoped that her father would do something in her favour, having promised it himself when he came to Canada, knowing that her dowry or portion of his Daughter's never had been paid to the Community as [is] usual by the Constitutional rules of the order and that she was indebted still at her death."[3]

Since there is no evidence that either of the John Wheelwrights visited Esther in Québec, the letter had most likely confused Nathaniel with his grandfather. Regardless, the review of the will went no further, and the convent seems to have lost contact with the Wheelwrights until the late nineteenth century, when Ned Wheelwright and C. Alice Baker began making inquiries into Esther's story. Although Ned's book *A Frontier Family* devoted only a few lines to Esther's story, he visited the convent in 1907 and pondered the connections between his "Yankee family" and the Québec Ursulines.

My great-uncle Arthur in Australia, who obtained a copy of Ned's book, became "keenly interested in our family genealogy" and only then, in the 1960s, traced our family's roots back to Reverend John and Esther Wheelwright. The story had come full circle by the time my uncle Peter handed it down to me and my siblings in the 1970s. The final piece of the puzzle fell into place in London, when I began investigating the origins of the coat of arms that Nathaniel and John had engraved on Esther's expensive French silverware in 1754. The gift had confirmed Esther's aristocratic background to the Ursulines; their historian wrote after her death in 1780, "Her ancestors were noble, as the arms of her family bear witness, but she needed not the illustration of birth or title to win from all who knew her a willing tribute of love or admiration."

Timothy Duke, Chester Herald, researched the arms at the College of Arms in London and found that they were an invention of the eighteenth-century. He wrote in 2008, "It is clear from the results of these searches that the arms and crest used by the Wheelwrights in America, and displayed on silver, bookplates and at least one memorial [John Wheelwright's], were not on official record for the family." So the Wheelwrights' engraved silverware and the silk painting of the arms that Esther sent to her family perpetuated a myth of the Wheelwrights. They were gentlemen but not nobles, and the arms were used without the stamp of authority.

My English and American relatives have remembered Esther as a lost child, but in Québec, she has been honoured for her role in shaping Canadian history. During the four-hundredth anniversary of Québec's founding, in 2008, Esther's biography was told as part of a Radio-Canada program, *De remarquables oubliés* (Forgotten heroes). The Québec historian Jean-Marc Phaneuf, whose ancestor Matthias Farnsworth III was taken captive in 1704, commented on Esther's historical significance. "If Esther had not been a victim of the captivity wars, she would certainly have become an important woman in New England, but as a wife, married to a military man and giving him many children," he explained. "But she married another cause and became a religious woman. I believe that Mère de l'Enfant Jésus did a lot for humanity in her life. She changed history and proved that when love enters, people can be stronger than war."

The show's producer, Lise Maynard, says that when it aired in July 2008, it sparked an excellent reaction with listeners in the province. Many people, including a former Ursuline and several relations of former captives, phoned in or sent emails, eager for more information. The CBC English-language station in Québec also produced a program on Esther to coincide with the anniversary, and she has been featured as a Canadian woman of achievement.

Among those of my relatives who have done much to recover Esther's life is my sister Penny, who in 2004 made *Captive!*, a documentary about her for a Canadian broadcaster. The interviewees in that film included one with Dominique Deslandres, a professor of history at the Université de Montréal, who suggested that we are "revealing Esther" to a new generation of Canadians by writing her story. Across the border, when Penny's film was shown at the Old York Museum, just south of Wells, the historian Richard Bowden said, "The story of Esther Wheelwright offers insights into the origins of some 20th-century prejudices, fears and conflicts between Catholics and Maine."

Bowden further suggested that readers over the age of fifty of either French-Canadian or English heritage would remember the bad old days in Maine before the "cultural revolution," when conversion to Catholicism was still considered a heresy. "Then, inter-faith dating was frowned upon and ecumenical events were practically non-existent," he wrote. "Then, 'Frenchman' jokes were brazenly told and schoolground taunts of 'You're not going to heaven because Protestants aren't real Christians' were common." In the face of Esther's story—which exposes the intimate connections between French Canadians, English Americans and the Abenakis—these prejudices melt away.

My research into Esther's life has opened my eyes and my ears to another way of understanding the past. Now I can see better what lies beneath official documents and obscuring institutional histories, can see better how to interpret the subtle, symbolic meaning of silver spoons, false family crests and painful silences. There is always a subtext that suggests the enduring power of a story, our yearning to know what came before us and our desire to understand where the past might lead us.

It would take another trip to Québec, another year later, before I realized that I had been on a wild goose chase that day with Ahmed at the Bellmont Cemetery. It was a misunderstanding, a combination of language confusion and pressure on me to get home. Esther's remains had been transferred to the Cimetière Notre-Dame de Belmont, on the Avenue Chapdelaine in the city suburbs. It was late summer when I finally found her and her sisters, on the rue St. Nazaire.

"I've come to say goodbye," I said to the stone with Esther's name on it. "Adieu."

Another taxi driver fired up his car, and we sped off down the tarmac and onto the main road. I felt my pulse decrease as I became consumed with the pain of leaving my home in Canada, where my past lay, for my home in London, where my heart and my future awaited.

ACKNOWLEDGMENTS

*I*N A WRITING PROJECT THAT HAS TAKEN SUCH A VERY long time to complete, I have been extremely grateful for the support of colleagues, fellow historians and authors, archivists, friends and family members. All have taken an interest and played a vital part in enabling me to see this book through from a vague idea to a fully fledged manuscript. Everyone was intrigued by Esther Wheelwright's story, but their support in my ambition to weave the wisps of documentary evidence into a whole was invaluable. Without this support, Esther would never have been re-animated in these pages.

In certain knowledge that I am forgetting people whose help was critical, I would particularly like to thank the following:

My first debt goes to my agent, Anne McDermid, for suggesting that I turn Esther's story into a book. Equally, my editors, Jim Gifford and Iris Tupholme, were champions of the project from the beginning, took the risk of commissioning it and were paragons of patience through its many drafts. With the generous financial support of the

Canada Council for the Arts, I was able to undertake the primary research in Québec and New England that this project required. Vic Sage, Ali Smith, Sharon Toliani-Sage and the Lorna Sage Memorial Fund are owed a huge debt for their moral and financial support. I'd especially like to thank Vic Sage for giving me the opportunity to test drive an early version of Esther's story at a workshop in the Life Writing Department at the University of East Anglia.

Among the friends and family members who have offered their support and insight, I owe a special thanks to my sister Penny Wheelwright, with whom I worked on a docudrama based on Esther's life for Vision TV. Ariane Koek gave me a chance to explore Esther's story by producing a piece for BBC Radio 4; Lise Maynard at Radio-Canada and Peter Black at the CBC also interviewed me for programs about Esther to coincide with the four-hundredth anniversary of Québec's founding. I owe a big debt of thanks to the historian Ann M. Little, whose own version of Esther's story will be published soon. She provided me with references, chewed the fat over the challenges my ancestor's life has presented and was a terrific companion in the archives. The historians Bruce Bourque, Denys Dêlage, John Demos, Dominique Deslandres, William Henry Foster, Ken Hamilton, Eve LaPlante, Jean-Marc Phaneuf and Michael Winship all gave generously of their time. Thanks also to Allegra Robinson, Janice Weaver and Noelle Zitzer at HarperCollins for their skill and patience.

I would like to thank my relations, especially Peter Wheelwright, for allowing me to quote from his family history; Nathaniel Wheelwright, for putting me in touch with him; and Tony and the late Nick Wheelwright, for sharing their family stories and research. My mother, Tish, shared our family's genealogical research and showed a constant interest in the incremental progress of the book.

There is a long list of friends on both sides of the Atlantic who provided help en route: Jeremy Jones and Helen Roberts, Margot Livesay, George Robb, William Penniston, Andrea Stuart, David Smith, Neil McKenna, Jeffrey Moore, Peter Moore, William Henry Foster, Julian Putkowski, Andrew Holgate, Isabelle Marcoul and Andy Patterson. Thank you for your unfailing enthusiasm and for reading my chapters, putting me up on trips and sharing research and references.

Among the archivists, I must thank Barbara Rimkunas of the Exeter Historical Society; Marie-Andrée Fortier and Sister Marie Marchand (OSU) of the Monastère des Ursulines; Dani Fazio of the Maine Historical Society; the staff of the Massachusetts Historical Society; Jane Shapecomb, Hope Shelley and the artist Chris Cloutier of the Historical Society of Wells and Ogunquit; Greg and Michael at the Ogunquit Beach Inn; Lucille Greer of the Norridgewock Historical Society; Michelle Bélanger at the Musée des Abénakis; the Sisters of the Ursuline Convent, Grosvenor Road, London; and Timothy Duke at the College of Heralds, London.

Finally, I need to thank my lovely daughters, Thames and Isis, who have had endured my absences and put up with my grumpiness as I neared my deadlines. Always and forever, they've made everything worthwhile, and they are the true inheritors of Esther's story.

Reverend John Wheelwright = Mary Hutchinson
(1592–1679)   (1605–?)

Colonel Samuel Wheelwright = Esther Houchin
(1634–1700)   (?–?)

Colonel John Wheelwright = Mary Snell
(1664–1745)   (?–1755)

Esther Wheelwright   John Wheelwright = Elizabeth Green
(1696–1780   (1689–1760)   (1694–1744)

Nathaniel Wheelwright = Ann Apthorp
(1721–1766)   (1734–1764)

Joseph Wheelwright = Frances Hadwen
(1764–1832)   (1778–1840)

John Hadwen Wheelwright = Sarah Catherine Hanley
(1807–1874)   (?–1845)

John Joseph Hanley Wheelwright = Alice Anne Gawthorp
(1834–1888)   (1841–1930)

John Sylvester Wheelwright = Beatrice Ella Syme
(1885–1962)   (1884–1985)

David Anthony Wheelwright = Tish Doreen Ball
(1925–)   (1932–)

Walter Stuart Menteth = Julie Diana Wheelwright
(1957–)   (1960–)

Thames Menteth-Wheelwright
(1994–)

Isis Menteth-Wheelwright
(1997–)

NOTES

Archive collections frequently cited in the notes have been identified by the following abbreviations:

AAQ: Archives de l'Archidiocèse de Québec

AMUQ: Archives du Monastére des Ursulines de Québec

APQ: Archives de la Province de Québec

CO: Colonial Office, National Archives, London

GKRM: Gerald M. Kelly Research Materials, Massachusetts Historical Society, Boston

HMC: Haldimand Manuscript Collection, The British Library, London

HSWO: Historical Society of Wells and Ogunquit

LAC: Library and Archives Canada, Ottawa

LPL: Lambeth Palace Library, London

MAC: Massachusetts Archives Collection, Massachusetts State Archives, Boston

MHS: Massachusetts Historical Society, Boston

PCRM: Province and Court Records of Maine, Alfriston

SPG: Society for the Propagation of the Gospel Papers, Lambeth Palace Library, London

WHS: Wisconsin Historical Society, Madison

WO: War Office, National Archives, London

CHAPTER 2: THE WHEELWRIGHTS OF WELLS

1. Peter M. Wheelwright, A Frontier Family, Part 2: The Wheelwrights of Maine (privately published manuscript, 2008), 3.

2. John Heard Jr., John Wheelwright: 1592–1679 (Cambridge, MA: The Riverside Press, 1930), 10–11.

3. Ibid., 10, quoting Cotton Mather's letter to George Vaughan.

4. Ibid., 12.

5. For a detailed account of the Wheelwright/Hutchinson controversy, see Michael P. Winship, *The Times and Trials of Anne Hutchinson: Puritans Divided* (Lawrence, KS: University of Kansas Press, 2005).

6. Heard, *John Wheelwright*, 67.

7. Edward E. Bourne, *History of Wells and Kennebunk, Maine* (Bowie, MD: Heritage Books, 2002), 5.

8. Jeremiah Hubbard and Jonathan Greenleaf, "An Account of Wells," *Collections of the Maine Historical Society* 1 (1865), 336–92.

9. Edmund March Wheelwright, *A Frontier Family, Part 1* (Cambridge, MA: The Colonial Society of Massachusetts, 1894), 13.

10. P. Wheelwright, *The Wheelwrights of Maine*, 6.

11. Alan Taylor, *American Colonies: The Settling of North America* (London, UK: Penguin Books, 2001), 109.

12. Paul Johnson, *A History of the American People* (London, UK: HarperPerennial, 1997), 79; Taylor, *American Colonies*, 199.

13. Taylor, *American Colonies*, 202. King William's War began in 1689 and the Seven Years' War, also known as the French and Indian War, ended in 1763.

14. Bourne, *History of Wells and Kennebunk*, 390.

15. Ibid.

16. Emma Lewis Coleman, *New England Captives Carried to Canada Between 1677 and 1760 During the French and Indian Wars*, vol. 1 (Westminster, MD: Heritage Books, 2004), 223; MAC, vol. 37 (Jan. 27, 1691–92), 359.

17. MAC, vol. 37 (Jan. 29, 1691–92), 258. Mary Plaisted was the daughter of John Wheelwright's aunt, Susanna Rishworth *née* Wheelwright.

18. William Henry Foster, *The Captor's Narrative: Catholic Women and Their Puritan Men on the Early American Frontier* (Ithaca, NY: Cornell University Press, 2003), 66.

19. John Barnard, "The Autobiography of the Reverend John Barnard," *Collections of the Massachusetts Historical Society*, vol. 5, 3rd ser. (1836), 232.

20. Bruce Bourque, *Twelve Thousand Years: American Indians in Maine* (Lincoln, NE: University of Nebraska Press, 2001), 166–67; Evan Haefeli and Kevin Sweeney, *Captors and Captives: The 1704 French and Indian Raid on Deerfield* (Boston, MA: University of Massachusetts Press, 2003), 37.

21. M. Halsey Thomas, ed., *The Diary of Samuel Sewall, 1674–1729*, vol. 1 (New York, NY: Farrar, Straus and Giroux, 1973), entry for May 15, 1700.

22. Records of the First Church of Wells (Congregational), Wells, Maine, *Proceedings of the New England Historical and Genealogical Society*, vol. 17 (Jan. 1921): 42–56, HSWO.

23. Wheelwright family tree (private collection), Inferior Court of Common Pleas, Jan. 7, 1706–1707, vol. 4, 205, PCRM.

24. Alice Morse Earle, *The Sabbath in Puritan New England* (London, UK: Hodder and Stoughton, 1892), 66; Hubbard and Greenleaf, "An Account of Wells," 340.

25. Winship, *Anne Hutchinson*, 9.

CHAPTER 4: TAKEN CAPTIVE

1. Bourne, *History of Wells and Kennebunk*, 247.

2. Ibid., 276.

3. Inferior Court of Common Pleas, Jan. 7, 1706–1707, vol. 4, 205, PCRM.

4. Samuel Wheelwright's will, dated May 13, 1700, *Maine Probate Records*, vol. 1, PCRM.

5. Bourne, *History of Wells and Kennebunk*, 390.

6. Alice Morse Earle, *Home Life in the Colonial Days* (London, UK: Macmillan, 1898), 128, 144.

7. Bourne, *History of Wells and Kennebunk*, 242.

8. Earle, *Home Life*, 262, 282.

9. Bourne, *History of Wells and Kennebunk*, 232.

10. Kelly, "Thy Hand Shall Lead Me," 12, GKRM, carton 4, MHS.

11. Ann M. Little, *Abraham in Arms: War and Gender in Colonial New England* (Philadelphia, PA: University of Pennsylvania Press, 2007), 129–30.

12. Bourne, *History of Wells and Kennebunk*, 246.

13. C. Alice Baker, *True Stories of New England Captives Carried to Canada During the Old French and Indian Wars* (Bowie, MD: Heritage Books, 1990), 43.

14. Mary Calvert, *Black Robe on the Kennebec* (Monmouth, NJ: Monmouth Press, 1991), 137.

15. Baker, *True Stories of New England Captives*, 43; Bourne, *History of Wells and Kennebunk*, 245.

16. Foster, *The Captor's Narrative*, 67.

17. *New England Historical and Genealogical Society Register*, vol. 18 (Apr. 1864), 234; Coleman, *New England Captives*, vol. 1, 172.

18. Bourne, *History of Wells and Kennebunk*, 276.

19. Haefeli and Sweeney, *Captors and Captives*, 112.

20. Coleman, *New England Captives*, vol. 2, 144.

21. Hope Moody Shelley, *My Name Is Wells, I Am the Town: A History of the Town of Wells, Maine, on the Occasion of Its 350th Anniversary of Incorporation* (Wells, ME: Penobscot Press, 2002), 21.

22. Dorothy Slavin, "Situation of Defensible Houses, 1676–1723," HSWO.

23. Haefeli and Sweeney, *Captors and Captives*, 99; Bourque, *Twelve Thousand Years*, 176. Pierre Daviault, *Le Baron de Saint-Castin, chef Abénaquis* (Montréal,

QC: Royal Society of Canada, 1939), puts the number of warriors assembled at five hundred.

24. Daviault, *Le Baron de Saint-Castin,* 152.

25. John Gyles, *Memoirs of Odd Adventures, Strange Deliverances* (Boston, MA: Massachusetts Historical Society, 1936), 28. There is a Wheelwright connection here, as Esther's brother John Wheelwright was the truck master at Fort St. George while Gyles was commander of the local garrison.

26. Also spelled Rasle, I have used Rale throughout. Calvert, *Black Robe on the Kennebec,* 75.

27. Gyles, *Memoirs,* 3.

28. Ken Hamilton, interview with author, July 2005. That John Wheelwright commanded the largest local militia is suggested in Jeremiah Powell's "A Map of Coastal Maine Forts, 1723," MHS, coll. 7, box 1/1, which puts his military personnel at one hundred. Vintage Maine Images, www.vintagemaineimages.com, item 28982.

29. Reuben Gold Thwaites, ed., "Father Sebastien Rasles . . . to Monsieur His Brother," *The Jesuit Relations and Allied Documents:* Travels and Explorations of the Jesuit Missionaries in New France, 1610–1791, vol. 67 (Cleveland, OH: Burrow Brothers, 1896–1907), 202.

30. Gyles, *Memoirs,* 3.

31. Ibid., 28; Haefeli and Sweeney, *Captors and Captives,* 286.

32. Kelly, "Thy Hand Shall Lead Me," 37, GKRM, MHS.

33. "Sermon du P. Vincent Bigot," op cit., GKRM, MHS.

34. Coleman, *New England Captives,* vol. 1, 400.

35. Bourne, *History of Wells and Kennebunk,* 246–53.

36. *The Calendar of State Papers Colonial,* vol. 1 (London, UK: Public Record Office, 1860), 641.

37. Ibid.

38. Thomas, *The Diary of Samuel Sewall,* vol. 1, Aug. 12, 1703.

1. Coleman, *New England Captives,* vol. 1, 400.

2. Ibid., 410. Coleman quotes Bourne's record that one of the Parsons daughter was taken on August 10 and a second was taken in October, along with her mother, during a raid on the house of Arthur Bragon in York.

3. Haefeli and Sweeney, *Captors and Captives,* 130–31 and appendix E, 286.

4. Ibid., 132.

5. "Sermon du P. Vincent Bigot," AMUQ, GKRM, MHS.

6. James Axtell, *Natives and Newcomers: The Cultural Origins of North America* (Oxford, UK: Oxford University Press, 2001), 197–98.

7. "Sermon du P. Vincent Bigot," AMUQ, GKRM, MHS.

8. James Axtell, interview with author; Convers Francis, *The Life of Sebastian Rale* (Boston, MA: Little Brown, 1849), 168.

9. John Demos, *The Unredeemed Captive: A Family Story from Early America* (New York, NY: Knopf, 1994), 5.

10. *The Calendar of State Papers Colonial,* vol. 1, 641.

11. Bourne, *History of Wells and Kennebunk,* 255.

12. Thomas, *The Diary of Samuel Sewall,* vol. 1, 491.

13. Coleman, *New England Captives,* vol. 1, p. 410; *The Calendar of State Papers Colonial,* vol. 1, 641.

14. *The Calendar of State Papers Colonial,* vol. 1, 647.

15. Pierre-François-Xavier de Charlevoix, ed., and John Gilray Shea, trans., *History and General Description of New France* , vol. 2 (Chicago, IL: Loyola University Press, 1962), vol. 2, 289.

16. Calvert, *Black Robe on the Kennebec,* 120.

17. Francis Parkman, *A Half Century of Conflict* (Boston, MA: Little Brown, 1893), 206; "Report of a Raid on Norridgewock by Joseph Heath and Joseph Harmon to Col. Gosse," Maine Historical Society, coll. 365, box 1, file 9.

18. Stuart Trueman, ed., *The Ordeal of John Gyles: Being an Account of His Odd Adventures, Strange Deliverances, etc., as a Slave of the Maliseets* (Toronto, ON: McClelland and Stewart, 1969), 5.

19. Ken Hamilton, interview with author, July 29, 2004.

20. Axtell, *Natives and Newcomers,* 199–201.

21. Frank G. Speck, *Penobscot Man: The Life History of a Forest Tribe in Maine* (Philadelphia, PA: University of Pennsylvania Press, 1940), 21.

22. Axtell, *Natives and Newcomers,* 199, 201.

23. I am grateful to the historian Denys Dêlage for this observation.

24. Frank G. Speck, "Cultural Problems in Northeast North America," *Proceedings of the American Philosophical Society* 64 (1925): 283.

25. Axtell, *Natives and Newcomers,* 203.

26. Ibid., 199.

27. Alice Nash, "The Abiding Frontier: Family, Gender and Religion in Wabanakis History, 1600–1763" (Ph.D. diss, Columbia University, 1997), 76–77, 83–84.

28. Coleman, *New England Captives,* 2, 254.

29. Ken Hamilton interview.

30. Barbara Austen, "'Captured . . . Never Came Back': Social Networks Among New England Female Captives," in *New England/New France,* Annual Proceedings of the Dublin Seminar for New England Folklife, (Boston, MA, July 15–16, 1989), 28–38.

31. "Sermon du P. Vincent Bigot," AMUQ, GKRM, MHS.

32. Denys Dêlage, *Bitter Feast: Amerindians and Europeans in Northeastern North America, 1600–64* (Vancouver, BC: UBC Press, 1994) 314–15; Bunny McBride, *Women of the Dawn* (Lincoln, NE: University of Nebraska Press, 1999), 16. I am also grateful to the historian Ann M. Little for the insight into the pronunciation of "Molly."

33. Earle, *Home Life,* 103.

34. "Sermon du P. Vincent Bigot," AMUQ, GKRM, MHS.

35. Little, *Abraham in Arms,* 114–15.

36. *Les Ursulines de Québec depuis leur établissement jusqu'à nos jours,* vol. 2 (Québec : Des Presses de C. Daneau, 1878), 90–91, AMUQ.

37. Speck, *Penobscot Man,* 253.

38. Calvert, *Black Robe on the Kennebec,* 126; Colin G. Calloway, ed., *North Country Captives: Selected Narratives of Indian Captivity from Vermont and New Hampshire* (Hanover, NH: University Press of New England, 1992), 68.

39. Patrick Côte, "Creation," Musée des Abénakis, Odanak, Québec.

40. Francis, *Life of Sebastian Rale,* 186–87.

41. Axtell, *Natives and Newcomers,* 209.

42. "Sermon du P. Vincent Bigot," AMUQ, GKRM, MHS. "[Esther] demonstrated a wonderful facility in understanding the barbarian tongue."

43. Frederick Matthew Wiseman, *The Voice of the Dawn: An Autohistory of the Abenaki Nation* (Hanover, NH: University Press of New England, 2001), 39; Alice Nash, "Mary Accept This Wampum Forever: Gender and Wabanakis Catholicism" (paper presented at the annual conference of the Institute of Early American History and Culture First, Ann Arbor, MI, June 4, 1995); Edward J. Lenkin, *Picture Rocks: American Indian Rock Art in the Northeast Woodlands* (Lebanon, NH: University Press of New England, 2002), 102.

44. Calvert, *Black Robe on the Kennebec,* 121

45. Ibid.,132

46. Kenneth M. Morrison, *The Solidarity of Kin: Ethnohistory, Religious Studies and the Algonkian–French Religious Encounter* (New York, NY: State University of New York, 2002), 98.

47. McBride, *Women of the Dawn,* 16.

48. "Sermon du P. Vincent Bigot," AMUQ, GKRM, MHS; Coleman, *New England Captives,* vol. 2, 389.

49. Esther's brother Joseph and his wife, Mary, according to parish records, presented two "Mulattos" for baptism in their local church. *New England Historical and Genealogical Society Register* (July 1922), 190. I am grateful to Hope M. Shelley for this reference.

50. Francis, *Life of Sebastian Rale*, 168.

51. Calvert, *Black Robe on the Kennebec*, 124.

52. Wiseman, *The Voice of the Dawn*, 98–99.

53. Gyles, *Memoirs*, 104.

54. Wiseman, *The Voice of the Dawn*, 99.

55. Calvert, *Black Robe on the Kennebec*, 127.

56. Parkman, *A Half Century of Conflict*, 211; Wiseman, *The Voice of the Dawn*, 37.

57. *Boston Newsletter*, May 15, 1704.

58. Cotton Mather, *A Modest Inquiry into the Grounds and Occasions of a Late Pamphlet Entitled "A Memorial of the Present Deplorable State of New-England"* (London, UK: S. Phipps, 1707), 28.

59. "Sermon du P. Vincent Bigot," AMUQ, GKRM, MHS.

CHAPTER 8: THE CRYING BLOOD

1. Thomas Charland, "Rale, Sébastien," *Dictionary of Canadian Biography Online* [hereafter referred to as DCBO], www.biographi.ca; Baker, *True Stories of New England Captives*, 43.

2. *The Calendar of State Papers Colonial*, vol. 116.

3. *Boston Newsletter*, Feb. 19, 1705, and Mar. 5, 1705.

4. Charland, "Rale, Sébastien."

5. Calvert, *Black Robe on the Kennebec*, 150.

6. Ibid., 119.

7. Raymond Douville and Jacques Casanova, trans. Carola Congreve, *Daily Life in Early Canada*, in *Daily Life Series* no. 12 (London, UK: Allen and Unwin, 1968), 71.

8. Bourque, *Twelve Thousand Years*, 173.

9. "Plan du village des Abénakis levé en l'année 1704," LAC, National Map Collection, NMC 000–4901.

10. Calvert, *Black Robe on the Kennebec*, 155.

11. Charland, "Rale, Sébastien."

12. Thwaites, *Jesuit Relations*, vol. 72, 263; ibid., vol. 69, 73.

13. *Fêtes des professions et des scriptures, 1688 à 1780* (Celebrations of professions and burials), 70, AMUQ.

14. Calvert, *Black Robe on the Kennebec*, 154. Between 1705 and 1708, Father Rale broke his thigh and relocated to the Jesuit seminary hospital in Québec.

15. "Sermon du P. Vincent Bigot," AMUQ, GKRM, MHS.

16. Thwaites, *Jesuit Relations*, vol. 65, 91.

17. John Williams, *The Redeemed Captive: Returning to Zion* (Bedford, MA: Applewood Books, 1853), 27.

18. Ibid., 150.

19. "Sermon du P. Vincent Bigot," AMUQ, GKRM, MHS.

20. Ibid.

21. Thwaites, *Jesuit Relations*, vol. 7, 7.

22. R. S. Bray, *Armies of Pestilence: The Effects of Pandemics in History* (Cambridge, UK: James Clarke and Co., 1996), 131.

23. "Sermon du P. Vincent Bigot," AMUQ.

24. *Glimpses of the Monastery: Scenes from the History of the Ursulines of Québec During Two Hundred Years* (Québec, QC: L. J. Demers et Frère, 1897), vol. 11, 179. The unnamed author was Mother Josephine Holmes de St. Croix.

25. Reverend Henry Schuyler, "The Apostle of the Abenakis," *The Catholic Historical Review*, ser. 1 (1910): 164–74.

26. "Sermon du P. Vincent Bigot," AMUQ, GKRM, MHS.

27. Christopher J. Bilodeau, "Policing Wabankis Missions in the Seventeenth Century," in *Ethnographies and Exchanges: Native Americans, Moravians, and Catholics in Early North America*, ed. A. G. Roeber (University Park, PA: Pennsylvania State University Press, 2008), 98–99.

28. "Sermon du P. Vincent Bigot," AMUQ, GKRM, MHS.

29. Mather, *A Modest Inquiry*, 22.

30. Coleman, *New England Captives*, vol. 1, 400, 410.

31. Trueman, *The Ordeal of John Gyles*, 11.

32. Bourne, *History of Wells and Kennebunk*, 261.

33. Haefeli and Sweeney, *Captors and Captives*, 286.

34. Coleman, *New England Captives*, vol. 1, 270; Foster, *The Captor's Narrative*, 77–79.

35. Coleman, *New England Captives*, vol. 1, 270; Foster, *The Captor's Narrative*, 82, 186 (note 62).

36. Sister St. Dominic Kelly, trans., *Marie of the Incarnation (1599–1672)* (Solesmes, France: Abbé St. Pierre, 1971), 35.

37. Calvert, *Black Robe on the Kennebec*, 152.

38. Morrison, *The Solidarity of Kin*, 95.

39. Ibid., 96.

40. Nash, "Mary Accept This Wampum Belt"; Thwaites, *Jesuit Relations*, vol. 65, 89–90.

41. Thwaites, *Jesuit Relations*, vol. 116, 17.

42. *Les Ursulines de Québec*, vols. 3–4, 363, AQUM; Austen, "Captured . . . Never Came Back," 34; Coleman, *New England Captives*, vol. 2, 148.

43. Bourne, *History of Wells and Kennebunk*, 267–8.

44. Baker, *True Stories of New England Captives*, 51.

45. *Council Records of Massachusetts under the administration of Joseph Dudley*, Robert N. Toppan, ed., (Boston, MA: Proceedings of the Massachusetts Historical Society, 1900), second series, vol. 8, 393.

46. Coleman, *New England Captives*, vol. 1, 426; *Annales des Ursulines de Québec*, vol. 1, 1639–1822, 127, AMUQ. "At length . . . by virtue of some small presents, she was recovered and they were given another slave in her place." Bilodeau, "Policing Wabankis Missions," 98.

47. "Sermon du P. Vincent Bigot," AMUQ, GKRM, MHS.

1. Nicholas Greudeville Lahontan, *Dialogues de Monsieur le Baron de Lahontan et d'un sauvage dans l'Amérique* (London, UK: A. Amsterdam, 1704), 51, 52, 258.

2. James MacPherson Le Moine, *Maple Leaves: Canadian History and Québec Scenery*, (Québec City, QC: Hunter, Rose and Co., 1865), 67.

3. François Boucher, *2000 Years of Fashion: The History of Costume and Personal Adornment* (New York, NY: H. M. Abrams, 1965), 294; Jan Noel, "Women of the New France Noblesse," in *Women and Freedom in Early America*, ed. Larry D. Eldridge, (New York, NY: New York University Press, 1997), 31.

4. Yves F. Zoltvany, "Joybert de Soulanges et de Marson, Louise-Élisabeth de (Rigaud, Marquise de Vaudreuil)," and "Rigaud de Vaudreuil, Philippe de, Marquis de Vaudreuil," DCBO, www.biographi.ca; Baker, *True Stories of New England Captives*, 43.

5. Le Moine, *Maple Leaves*, 67.

6. Noel, "Women of the New France Noblesse," 30–31.

7. Zoltvany, "Rigaud de Vaudreuil," DCBO; Allan Everett Marble, *Surgeons, Smallpox and the Poor: A History of Medicine and Social Conditions in Nova Scotia, 1749–1799* (Montréal, QC: McGill University Press, 1993), 8; Bray, *Armies of Pestilence*, 131.

8. *Glimpses of the Monastery*, 246.

9. Jan Noel, "Besieged but Connected: Survival Strategies at a Québec Convent," *Historical Studies* 65 (2001): 37.

10. *Fêtes de professions et des scriptures*, 70, AMUQ.

11. Claire Gourdeau, *Les Délices de nos coeurs: Marie de l'Incarnation et ses pensionnaires amérindiennes, 1639–1672* (Sillery, France: Éditions du Septentrion, 1994), 78.

12. 'Registre des entrées et sorties des petites filles françaises et sauvages de 1641," *Pensionat*, 1/NG, 1, 1.1, AMUQ.

13. Sister Catherine Frances, *The Convent School of French Origin in the United States, 1727–1843* (Philadelphia, PA: Sisters of St. Joseph, 1936), 25.

14. *Glimpses of the Monastery*, 211.

15. *Pensionat*, 1/NG, 1, 1.1, AMUQ.

16. *Annales des Ursulines de Québec*, vol. 1, 116, AMUQ.

17. Kelly, *Marie of the Incarnation*, 32.

18. Roger Magnuson, *Éducation in New France* (Montréal, QC: McGill-Queen's University Press, 1992), 96.

19. *Glimpses of the Monastery*, 116, 120–21; Kelly, *Marie of the Incarnation*, 303.

20. *Glimpses of the Monastery*, 90.

21. *Les Ursulines de Québec*, vol. 2, 228, AMUQ; Nancy Lusignan Schultz, *Fire and Roses: The Burning of the Charlestown Convent, 1834* (New York, NY: The Free Press, 2000), 79.

22. *Les Ursulines: 350 ans d'education au Québec* (Québec City, QC: Ursulines de Québec, 1989), 46.

23. *Les Ursulines de Québec*, vol. 1, 123–24, 134, AMUQ.

24. Frances, *The Convent School of French Origin*, 27.

25. Ibid., 38.

26. Ibid., 47.

27. *Glimpses of the Monastery*, 210–12.

28. *Reminiscences of the Last Fifty Years, 1839–1889* (Québec City, QC: L. J. Demers et Frère, 1897), 173. (This is a supplement to *Glimpses of the Monastery*.) Schultz, *Fire and Roses*, 71.

29. Frances, *The Convent School of French Origin*, 45.

30. *Les Ursulines de Québec*, vols. 3–4, 360, AMUQ.

31. Kelly, "Thy Hand Shall Lead Me," 75, GKRM, MHS.

32. *Pensionat* 1/NG, 1, 1.1, AMUQ. Twenty to twenty-five captive English girls were pupils with the Ursulines between 1690 and 1760.

33. Coleman, *New England Captives*, vol. 1, 269; *Pensionat*, 1/NG, 1, 1.1, AMUQ.

34. *Pensionat*, N/1,1.1, AMUQ.

35. "Sermon du P. Vincent Bigot," AMUQ, GKRM, MHS.

36. *Glimpses of the Monastery*, 180.

37. Zoltvany, "Joybert de Soulanges et de Marson, Louise-Élisabeth de (Rigaurd, Marquise de Vaudreuil)"; Karen Anderson, *Chain Her by One Foot: The Subjugation of Women in Seventeeth-Century New France* (London, UK: Routledge, 1991), 87.

38. "Lettre circulaire du P. Vincent Bigot le 10e septembre 1720," *Canada Letters*, vol. 15, no. 6, GKRM, MHS, carton 4; Thomas Charland, "Bigot, Vincent," DCBO, www.biographi.ca; *Conclusions des assemblées des disertes de 1687 à 1865*, vol. 2, 1/e, 2, 3, 1, 1, 0, 1687–1865, AMUQ.

39. Madame de Vaudreuil au Ministre (1709), LAC, CIIA, vol. 30, 422–30; APQ, 1942–1943, 416; Madame de Vaudreuil à Paris (1712), LAC, CIIA, vol. 33, 249–253; APQ, 1947–1948, 187; APQ, 1947–1948, 187.

40. Kelly, "Thy Hand Shall Lead Me," 89.

41. *Les Ursulines de Québec*, vol. 2, 92, AMUQ; Pensionat, 1710, 1/NG, 1, 1.1, AMUQ.

CHAPTER 12: YEARS OF ANGUISH

1. *Glimpses of the Monastery*, 207.

2. "Sermon du P. Vincent Bigot," AMUQ, GKRM, MHS.

3. *Conclusions des assemblées des disertes de 1687 à 1865*, vol. 2, 1/e, 2, 3, 1, 1, 0, 1687–1865, AMUQ.

4. *Les Ursulines de Québec*, vol. 2, 29, AMUQ.

5. Ibid., 70.

6. "Sermon du P. Vincent Bigot," AMUQ, GKRM, MHS.

7. Ibid.

8. Vaudreuil to Dudley, Québec, Jan. 14, 1711, LAC, CIIA, vol. 31, 110–16; Vaudreuil au Ministre, Québec, Oct. 25, 1711, LAC, CIIA, vol. 32, 41–64 ; APQ, 1946–1947, 427–37.

9. Kelly, *Marie of the Incarnation*, 229; *Council Records of Massachusetts under the administration of Joseph Dudley*, Robert N. Toppan, ed. (Boston, MA: Proceedings of the Massachusetts Historical Society, 1900), second series, vol. 5, 380.

10. *Glimpses of the Monastery,* 193; *Les Ursulines de Québec depuis leur établissement jusqu'à nos jours,* vols. 3–4, 360.

11. Elizabeth Rapley, *A Social History of the Cloister: Daily Life in the Teaching Monasteries of the Old Regime* (Montréal, QC: McGill-Queen's University Press, 2001), 166.

12. Kelly, *Marie of the Incarnation,* 224.

13. Kelly, "Thy Hand Shall Lead Me," 95, GKRM, MHS.

14. Nicolson to Vaudreuil, Annapolis Royal, Oct. 11, 1710, LAC, C11A, vol. 31, 117–20; *Collection des Manuscrits, Contenant Lettres, Mémoires, et Autres* Documents *Historique Relatifs à la Nouvelle-France, etc.* (Québec City, QC: 1883–1885), vol. 2, 524–25 [published source].

15. "Sermon du P. Vincent Bigot," AMUQ, GKRM, MHS.

16. Ibid.

17. MAC, vol. 69:159a, 18 May 1960; Coleman, *New England Captives,* vol. 1, 249.

18. "Sermon du P. Vincent Bigot," AMUQ.

19. Coleman, *New England Captives,* vol. 1, 427; Vaudreuil to Dudley, June 16, 1711, LAC, C11A, vol. 32, 119–23.

20. Edward P. Hamilton, "Robert Hewes and the Frenchman: A Case of Treason?" *American Antiquarian Society* (Oct. 1958): 195–210; *The Boston Gazette,* Apr. 24 1721, Feb. 13 and Feb. 20, 1727.

21. Haefeli and Sweeney, *Captors and Captives,* 204.

22. Foster, *The Captor's Narrative,* 65.

23. Coleman, *New England Captives,* vol. 1, 356; Foster, *The Captor's Narrative,* 64, 70.

24. Foster, *The Captor's Narrative,* 75.

25. Coleman, *New England Captives,* vol. 1, 414; Records of the First Church of Wells (Congregational), Wells, ME, *Proceedings of the New England Historical and Genealogical Society* (Ser. 17, January 1921), 45.

26. Coleman, *New England Captives,* vol. 1, 411–12.

27. Ibid., vol. 2, 122, GKRM, MHS, carton 4.

28. Coleman, *New England Captives,* vol. 1, 422.

29. Williams, *The Redeemed Captive*, 83.

30. Coleman, *New England Captives*, vol. 1, 414. Mary Storer Papers, Cat. 6/74, MHS.

31. Emily Clark, *Masterless Mistresses: The New Orleans Ursulines and the Development of a New World Society, 1727–1834* (Chapel Hill, NC: University of North Carolina Press, 2007), 259.

32. Saliha Belmessous, "Assimilation and Racialism in Seventeenth-Century and Eighteenth-Century French Colonial Policy," *The American Historical Review* 110 (2005): 323.

33. Noel, "Women of the New France Noblesse," 37.

34. Coleman, *New England Captives*, vol. 1, 249.

35. Henry J. Morgan, *Sketches of Celebrated Canadians and Persons Connected with Canada* (Montréal, QC: R. Worthington, 1865), 34–35.

36. Haefeli and Sweeney, *Captors and Captives*, 212.

37. *Boston News-Letter*, Sept. 15–22, 1712.

38. MAC, vol. 71, 739–740 (July 13, 1713).

39. *Boston News-Letter*, July 25, 1712.

40. *Les Ursulines de Québec*, vol. 2, 92, AMUQ.

41. *Fêtes des professions et des scriptures*, 70, AMUQ.

42. The Reverend John Williams and Family, Gratz Collection, Historical Society of Pennsylvania, case 8, box 28. Quoted in Haefeli and Sweeney, *Captors and Captives*, 160.

43. *Annales des Ursulines de Québec*, vol. 1, 128, AMUQ; Rapley, *A Social History of the Cloister*, 166.

CHAPTER 14: AN URSULINE NOVICE

1. Dale Miquelon, *New France, 1701–1744* (Toronto, ON: McClelland and Stewart, 1987), 234.

2. The Ursuline community to Dr. Penn, Aug. 22, 1789, GKRM, MHS, carton 4.

3. *Les Ursulines de Québec*, vol. 2, 242, AMUQ; ibid., vol. 2, 49; *Annales des Ursulines de Québec*, vo1.1,128, AMUQ; *Fêtes des professions et des scriptures*, 70, AMUQ; "Régulations des entrées, 1647–1783 "; "Régulations des entrées 1647–1861," *Régulations du Monastère*, 4, AMUQ.

4. Noel, "Women of the New France Noblesse," 34.

5. *Cérémonial des vêtures et des professions pour les religieuses de la congrégation des Ursulines de Québec* (Paris, Seconde edition revue et corrigee, 1860).

6. *Glimpses of the Monastery*, 194.

7. *Les Ursulines de Québec*, vols. 3–4, 360, AMUQ.

8. Ibid., 358.

9. *Glimpses of the Monastery*, 199.

10. Monica Baldwin, *I Leap over the Wall: Contrasts and Impressions After 28 Years in a Convent* (New York, NY: Rinehart and Co., 1951), 173.

11. Schultz, *Fire and Roses*, 58–59.

12. *Les Ursulines de Québec*, vol. 2, 93–95, AMUQ.

13. Ibid., 96–97.

14. Ibid., 99–100.

15. Ibid.

16. Ibid., vols. 3–4, 339.

17. *Cérémonial*, 14–16.

18. Baldwin, *I Leap over the Wall*, 6, and display at the Musée des Ursulines, Québec City.

19. *Les Ursulines de Québec*, vols. 3–4, 341, AMUQ; *Cérémonial*, 37–38.

20. *Les Ursulines de Québec*, vols. 3 to 4, 341, AMUQ; *Cérémonial*, 39–40.

21. Rapley, *A Social History of the Cloister*, 168.

22. Karen Armstrong, *Through the Narrow Gate: A Nun's Story* (London, UK: Flamingo, 1997), 136; Rapley, *A Social History of the Cloister*, 160.

23. Douville and Casanova, *Daily Life in Early Canada*, 136; the Musée des Ursulines, Québec City; Kelly, *Marie of the Incarnation*, 111.

24. Elizabeth Kuhns, *The Habit: A History of the Clothing of Catholic Nuns* (New York, NY: Doubleday, 2003), 84.

25. Baldwin, *I Leap over the Wall*, 74.

26. Kelly, *Marie of the Incarnation*, 181.

27. Katheleen Elgin, *Nun: A Gallery of Sisters* (New York, NY: Random House, 1964), 135.

28. *Les Ursulines de Québec*, vols. 3–4, 663, n. 1, AMUQ.

29. Baldwin, *I Leap over the Wall*, 72.

30. *Glimpses of the Monastery*, 200.

31. Kelly, *Marie of the Incarnation*, 193; *Glimpses of the Monastery*, 190.

32. Edward P. Hamilton, ed., "Nathaniel Wheelwright's Canadian Journey, 1753–4," *The Bulletin of the Fort Ticonderoga Museum* 4 (February 1960): 30.

33. Rapley, *A Social History of the Cloister*, 131.

34. Ibid, 136.

35. Baldwin, *I Leap over the Wall*, 11–12.

36. Ibid, 13.

37. Rapley, *A Social History of the Cloister*, 136. Monica Baldwin believed that without such friendships, women in monastic communities were deprived of "new words, new ideas, new ways of looking at things" that foster emotional growth. She wrote, "A large part of one's being never really develops. One remains rather like a child, with the same outlook and vocabulary as when one first 'went in.'" Baldwin, *I Leap over the Wall*, 112.

38. Kelly, *A Social History of the Cloister*, 116.

39. Moshe Sluhovsky, "The Devil in the Convent," *The American Historical Review* 107, no. 5 (Dec. 2002): 1–52.

40. Kelly, *A Social History of the Cloister*, 275.

41. Baldwin, *I Leap over the Wall*, 199; Kelly, *A Social History of the Cloister*, 362; Silvia Evangelisti, *Nuns: A History of Convent Life* (Oxford, UK: Oxford University Press, 2007), 38, 185.

42. William Kirby, *The Golden Dog: A Legend of Québec* (Montréal, QC: Lovell, Adam, Wesson, 1877), 651.

43. Clark, *Masterless Mistresses*, 104–105.

44. Baldwin, *I Leap over the Wall*, 199.

45. Ibid, 199.

46. *Les Ursulines de Québec*, vol. 2, 414–15, AMUQ.

47. Hafeli and Sweeney, *Captors and Captives*, 212.

48. *Les Ursulines de Québec*, vol. 2, 98, AMUQ.

49. Copie d'une lettre de Soeur Wheelwright de l'Énfant Jésus, Religieuse Ursuline de Québec ; Kelly, Thy Hand Shall Lead Me, 157–159, GKRM, MHS.

50. *Les Ursulines de Québec*, vol. 2, 86, AMUQ.

51. Auguste Gosselin, *L'Église . . . jusqu'à la Conquête*, vol. 1, *Québec, 1911–1913* (Québec City, QC: Laflamme et Proulx, 1911), 254.

52. .*Entrées, vêtures, professions et décédées*, 1/G1, 1, 1.6, AMUQ; *Fêtes des professions et des scriptures*, 70, AMUQ.

53. "A Journal of the Negotiation Between the Marquis de Vaudreuil, etc.," *New England Historical and Genealogical Register* 5 (1848): 21–42, 29.

54. *Fêtes des professions et des scriptures*, 70; *Annales des Ursulines de Québec*, vol. 1, 128, AMUQ.

55. *Les Ursulines de Québec*, vol. 2, 93, AMUQ.

56. Alfred Rambaud, "La Croix de Chevrières de Saint-Vallier, Jean-Baptiste de," DCBO, www.biographi.ca; *Entrées, vêtures, professions et décédées*, 1/NG1, 1, 1.6, AMUQ, *Glimpses of the Monastery*, 180–81.

57. *Les Ursulines de Québec*, vol. 2, 93, AMUQ.

58. Ibid., vols. 3–4, 546.

59. Ibid., 67, 73, 74.

60. Evangelisti, *A History of Convent Life*, 30.

CHAPTER 16: SISTER ESTHER MARIE-JOSEPH WHEELWRIGHT DE L'ENFANT JESUS

1. Zoltvany, "Joybert de Soulanges et de Marson, Louise-Élisabeth de (Rigaud,

Marquise de Vaudreuil)"; "Lettre circulaire du P. Vincent Bigot," GKRM, MHS, carton 4.

2. Haefeli and Sweeney, *Captors and Captives*, 227, 229–30.

3. Bourque, *Twelve Thousand Years*, 192–94; Parkman, *A Half Century of Conflict*, 236–38.

4. *Les Ursulines de Québec*, vol. 2, 174–76, AMUQ; Coleman, *New England Captives*, vol. 2, 390.

5. *Glimpses of the Monastery*, 220.

6. *Les Ursulines de Québec*, vol. 2, 38–39.

7. Frances, *The Convent School of French Origin*, 56. The description of Esther's daily life in the classroom is drawn from the *Règlements* drawn up by the Mother House in Paris in 1705.

8. Ibid., 54.

9. *Glimpses of the Monastery*, 299.

10. Frances, *The Convent School of French Origin*, 31, 56.

11. Ibid., 32.

12. Ibid., 31.

13. Ibid., 35.

14. Claire G. Reid and Micheline V. Demers, "Les Ursulines et la musique," *Cap-aux-Diamants* (1989), 21–22.

15. Frances, *The Convent School of French Origin*, 48.

16. *Glimpses of the Monastery*, 214.

17. Frances, *The Convent School of French Origin*, 36–37.

18. Kelly, *Marie of the Incarnation*, 302.

19. *Les Ursulines de Québec*, vols. 3–4, 363, AMUQ.

20. *Glimpses of the Monastery*, 207.

21. Frances, *The Convent School of French Origin*, 38.

22. *Glimpses of the Monastery*, 213.

23. *Pensionat*, 1/NG, 1, 1.1, AMUQ.

24. Magnuson, *Éducation in New France*, 96; Frances, *The Convent School of French Origin*, 34.

25. Clark, *Masterless Mistresses*, 33.

26. Gabrielle Lapointe, "Daneau de Muy, Charlotte *dite* de Sainte-Hélène," DCBO, www.biographi.ca; *Glimpses of the Monastery*, 191–97.

27. Noel, "Women of the New France Noblesse," 36.

28. Barbara Austen, "Captured . . . Never Came Back," 28–38.

29. Theodore Atkinson, "The Diary of Honorable Theodore Atkinson, Commissioner, from the Governor of New Hampshire to Canada, 1724–25," in *Register of the Society of Colonial Wars in the State of New Hampshire* (Boston, 1907), 64; Coleman, *New England Captives*, vol. 1, 102.

30. Foster, *The Captor's Narrative*, 166.

31. Hamilton, "Nathaniel Wheelwright's Canadian Journey," 283; Coleman, *New England Captives*, vol. 2, 242, 243; Atkinson, "The Diary of Honorable Theodore Atkinson"; *Les Ursulines de Québec*, vol. 2, 103, AMUQ.

32. *Fêtes des professions et des scriptures*, 71, AMUQ; Baldwin, *I Leap over the Wall*, 95; Frances, *The Convent School of French Origin*, 37.

33. Marcel Trudel, *L'Église Canadienne sous le régime militaire, 1759–1764* (Québec, QC: Les Presses de l'Université Laval, 1957), 32.

34. *Glimpses of the Monastery*, 187.

35. *Les Ursulines de Québec*, vol. 2, 274, AMUQ.

36. Trudel, *L'Église Canadienne*, 32.

37. Marie-Emmanuel Chabot, "Guyart, Marie, *dite* Marie de L'Incarnation," DCBO, www.biographi.ca.

38. Trudel, *L'Église Canadienne*, 32.

39. Evangelisti, *A History of Convent Life*, 43.

40. Kirby, *The Golden Dog*, 549.

41. Coleman, *New England Captives*, vol. 1, 429.

42. *Boston Weekly News-Letter*, Aug. 29, 1745.

43. John Wheelwright's will, dated 1745, *Maine Probate Records*, vol. 1, PCRM.

44. Bourne, *History of Wells and Kennebunk*, 254.

45. Ibid., 254.

46. "Copie d'une letter de Soeur Wheelwright de l'Enfant Jésus," AMUQ.

CHAPTER 18: THE WHEELWRIGHTS OF BOSTON

1. Austen, "Captured . . . Never Came Back," 32. Between 1747 and 1757, five Eng-lish girls were registered as boarders at the Ursuline school.

2. James Otis, "Diary of James Otis," *Proceedings of the Massashcusetts Historical Society*, 2nd ser., vol. 43 (1909–1910), 254.

3. John Huxtable Elliott, *Empires of the World: Britain and Spain in America, 1492–1830* (New Haven, CN: Yale University Press, 2006), 314; Fred Anderson, *Crucible of War: The Seven Years' War and the Fate of Empire in British North America, 1754–1766* (New York, NY: Knopf, 2000), 668.

4. *The Letterbook of Reverend Henry Caner, 1728–1778* (Bristol, UK: Special Collections Department, Bristol University Library, Microform Academic Publishers, n.d.), x.

5. Coleman, *New England Captives*, vol. 1, 115; Baker, *True Stories of New England Captives*, 340.

6. Hamilton, "Nathaniel Wheelwright's Canadian Journey," 292.

7. *Journals of the House of Representatives of Massachusetts* (Boston, MA: Massachu-setts Historical Society), 1753–1754, vol. 30, June 13, 1753.

8. Ibid.

9. Coleman, *New England Captives*, vol. 2, 254.

10. *Annales des Ursulines de Québec*, vol. 1, 216, AMUQ.

11. *Les Ursulines de Québec*, vol. 1, 144, AMUQ.

12. E. Wheelwright, *Frontier Family*, 34.

13. Hamilton, "Nathaniel Wheelwright's Canadian Journey," 292.

14. Coleman, *New England Captives*, vol. 2, 254.

15. Tousignant and Madeleine Dionne-Tousignant, "La Corne, Luc de, known as Chaptes (Chap, Chapt) de La Corne or as La Corne Saint-Luc," DCBO, www.biographi.ca.

16. Coleman, *New England Captives*, vol. 2, 155.

17. Hamilton, "Nathaniel Wheelwright's Canadian Journey," 282.

18. Ibid., 283.

19. Coleman, *New England Captives*, vol. 2, 255. For information about Madame Lestage's child slaves, see Foster, *The Captor's Narrative*, 164–65.

20. Haefeli and Sweeney, *Captors and Captives*, 173.

21. Suffolk County, Superior Court of Judicature, Record Book, vol. 1, 1760–1762, 11, Massachusetts Archive Collection, Boston, MA.

22. Anderson, *Crucible of War*, 668. In the coming years, Nathaniel would prosper by simultaneously acting as a British military contractor and trading with the French.

23. Hamilton, "Nathaniel Wheelwright's Canadian Journey," 292; *Les Ursulines de Québec*, vol. 2, 103, AMUQ.

24. Hamilton, "Nathaniel Wheelwright's Canadian Journey," 282.

25. Mary Wheelwright's will, *Maine Probate Records*, vol. 1, PCRM; *Les Ursulines de Québec*, vol. 2, 103, AMUQ.

26. Susannah Willard Johnson, *A Narrative of the Captivity of Mrs. Johnson* (Windsor, VT: Alden Spooner, 1807), 89–90.

27. Suffolk County, Superior Court of Judicature, Record Book, vol. 1, 1760–1762, 288, Massachusetts Archive Collection, Boston, MA.

28. Otis, "Diary of James Otis." Otis's letter provides evidence of Nathaniel's wealth, describing his clients' trust in his credit as "madness."

29. Jared Sparks, *Lives of John Ribault, Sebastian Rale and William Palfrey* (Boston, MA: Charles C. Little and James Brown, 1845), 341; "Boston, August 24," *American Weekly Mercury*, September 10, 1724.

30. Hamilton, "Robert Hewes and the Frenchman," 10.

31. Ibid, 11.

CHAPTER 20: THE FALL OF NEW FRANCE

1. *Glimpses of the Monastery*, 266.

2. *Affaires du Canada*, 1/N2, 3, 1/N2, 5, vol. 5, AMUQ.

3. *Pensionat*, 1/NG, 1, 1.2, AMUQ; *Livre des entrées et décédées*, 1/G1, 1, 1.1, AMUQ.

4. *Glimpses of the Monastery*, 267.

5. Ibid.

6. Francis Parkman, *Montcalm and Wolfe: The Riveting Story of the Heroes of the French and Indian War* (New York, NY: Random House, 1999), 359.

7. Ibid., 355, 357.

8. *Glimpses of the Monastery*, 268.

9. Ibid., 270.

10. Gabrielle Lapointe, "Migeon de Branssat (Bransac) Marie-Anne *dite* de la Nativité," DCBO, www.biographi.ca.

11. Ibid.

12. Baker, *True Stories of New England Captives*, 61.

13. *Glimpses of the Monastery*, 270–71.

14. Anon., "Relation du siege de Québec en 1759," in *Memoires sur le Canada: Études sur l'instruction publique chez les Canadiens-français*, ser. 1, vol. 4, ed. D. P. Myrand (Québec City, QC: J. T. Brousseau, 1873), 4; Coleman, *New England Captives*, vol. 1, 413.

15. *Les Ursulines de Québec*, vol. 2, 381–82, AMUQ; Noel, "Besieged but Connected," 28–29.

16. *Les Ursulines de Québec*, vol. 2, 384, AMUQ; Trudel, *L'Église Canadienne*, vol. 2, 222.

17. Parkman, *Montcalm and Wolfe*, 371; Anon., "Relation du siege de Québec," 6.

18. *Glimpses of the Monastery*, 272–73.

19. *Les Ursulines de Québec*, vol. 2, 384, AMUQ; Noel, "Besieged but Connected," 39.

20. *Les Ursulines de Québec*, vol. 2, 384, AMUQ.

21. Captain John Knox, *An Historical Journal of the Campaigns in North-America, for the Years 1757, 1758, 1759, and 1760: Containing the Most Remarkable Occurrences of That Period, Particularly the Two Sieges of Québec, etc., etc.*, vol. 1 (Toronto, ON: The Champlain Society, 1914), 212.

22. Parkman, *Montcalm and Wolfe*, 394.

23. Ibid., 406; *Glimpses of the Monastery,* 274.

24. Parkman, *Montcalm and Wolfe,* 406.

25. E. Wheelwright, *Frontier Family,* 33; Bourne, *History of Wells and Kennebunk,* 436.

26. *Glimpses of the Monastery,* 276.

27. Noel, "Besieged but Connected," 34.

28. Parkman, *Montcalm and Wolfe,* 479.

29. *Glimpses of the Monastery,* 275–76; Baker, *True Stories of New England Captives,* 62; *Les Ursulines de Québec,* vol. 3, 10, AMUQ.

30. *Affaires du Canada,* AMUQ, 1/N2, 3, 1/N2,5, vol. 5, Sept. 29, 1759, AMUQ.

31. Coleman, *New England Captives,* vol. 2, 390.

32. *Glimpses of the Monastery,* 277; Gabrielle Lapointe, "Daneau de Muy, Charlotte *dite* de Sainte-Hélène," DCBO, www.biographi.ca.

33. Noel, "Besieged but Connected," 40.

34. Parkman, *Montcalm and Wolfe,* 422; *Glimpses of the Monastery,* 278–79.

35. *Glimpses of the Monastery,* 278.

36. Ibid., 300.

37. Frances Moore Brooke, *The History of Emily Montague* (Ottawa, ON: Graphic Publishers, 1931), 19.

38. Knox, *An Historical Journal of the Campaigns in North-America,* vol. 2, 156, 158.

39. Hilda Neatby, *Québec: The Revolutionary Age, 1760–1791* (Toronto, ON: McClelland and Stewart, 1966), 19; *Glimpses of the Monastery,* 282.

40. WO 34/78, National Archives, London.

41. Richard Short, *A View of the Orphans' or Ursulines' Nunnery (Québec), 1761,* LAC, C-000354.

42. *Glimpses of the Monastery,* 278–79.

43. *The Boston Post Boy,* Dec. 8, 1760.

44. Parkman, *A Half Century of Conflict,* 425; Louisa Blair, *The Anglos: The Hidden Face of Québec City,* vol. 1, *1608–1850* (Québec City, QC: Commission de la capitale nationale du Québec, 2005), 21; *Glimpses of the Monastery,* 282.

45. Blair, *The Anglos,* 20.

46. Neatby, *Québec: The Revolutionary Age,* 19.

47. Peter Doll, *Revolution, Religion and National Identity: Imperial Anglicanism in British North America* (London, UK: Associated University Press, 2000), 83.

48. *Annales des Ursulines de Québec,* vol. 1, 252, AMUQ.

49. Knox, *An Historical Journal of the Campaigns in North-America,* vol. 2, 229.

50. Ibid., 223.

51. Ibid., 277, 279; SPG Papers, Vol. 11, ff. 25–26. Mrs. Brooke to Bishpo Terrick of London, Jan 24, 1765, Lambeth Palace Library; Reverend John Brooke, Fulham Papers Colonial, 1:ff:1. 110–112/ 1:f, LPL.

52. *Glimpses of the Monastery,* 283.

53. Frederick Bernays Wiesner, *Civilians Under Military Justice: The British Practice Since 1689, Especially in North America* (Chicago, IL: University of Chicago Press, 1967), 39.

54. *Les Ursulines de Québec,* vol. 3, 19–21, AMUQ; Trudel, *L'Église Canadienne,* vol. 2, 290; Alfred Leroy Burt, *The Old Province of Québec* (Toronto, ON: Ryerson Press, 1933), 19; Knox, *An Historical Journal of the Campaigns in North-America,* vol. 2, 120.

55. *Glimpses of the Monastery,* 285

56. *Affaires du Canada,* AMUQ, 1/N2,3, 1/N2,5, vol. 6.

57. *The New London Summary,* Mar. 7, 1760.

58. Knox, *An Historical Journal of the Campaigns in North-America,* vol. 2, 464.

59. *Glimpses of the Monastery,* 287.

60. Extracts from Mrs. Brooke's letters to Bishop Terrick of London, 24 January 1765, SPG Papers, vol. 2, ff. 25–26, LPL.

61. Records of the Executive and Legislative Councils, supplemented by the S series (internal correspondence of the Province of Québec) in the Colonial Office correspondence in the PRO, CO 42/18, 11, LAC.

62. Blair, *The Anglos,* 23.

63. Bourne, *History of Wells and Kennebunk,* 459.

CHAPTER 21: ESTHER'S EIGHT NAMESAKES

1. *Esther Wheelwright et sa famille*, s.d. 1713–1986, AMUQ.
2. Agnes Repplier, *Mère Marie of the Ursulines, a Study in Adventure*, (Garden City, NJ: Literary Guild of America, 1931), 76.
3. GKRM, carton 4, MHS.
4. *Glimpses of the Monastery*, op cit., 289.

CHAPTER 22: THE MOTHER SUPERIOR'S GIFT

1. Trudel, *L'Église Canadienne*, 230.
2. *Livres contenant les actés d'élection des supérieures du monastère*, 1iE2, 1,1.1, AMUQ.
3. "Continental Colonies," vol. 1, f. 114, Fulham Papers, LPL.
4. *Fêtes des professions et des scriptures*, 71, AMUQ; Baldwin, *I Leap over the Wall*, 95; Frances, *The Convent School of French Origin*, 37.
5. Lorraine McMullen, *An Odd Attempt in a Woman: The Literary Life of Frances Brooke* (Vancouver, BC: University of British Columbia Press, 1983), 63.
6. Brooke Fulham Papers, vol. 1, f. 1, LPL.
7. Society for the Proclamation of the Gospel, vol. 11, LPL.
8. Ibid.
9. Frances Moore Brooke, *The History of Emily Montague* (Montréal, QC: Centre for Editing Early Canadian Texts, McGill-Queen's University Press, 1985), xli.
10. Brooke, *The History of Emily Montague* (1931), 19.
11. Ibid.
12. Mrs. Brooke to B. P. Terrick, Jan. 24, 1765, SPG, vol. 2, ff. 25–26, LPL. "Some of the Nuns say that Hereticks could not naturally be good to the People as the English are, but that God hath miraculously turned their Harts."
13. *Livre des entrées et décédées*, 1/G1, 1, 1.1, AMUQ.

14. Brooke, *The History of Emily Montague* (1985), 21.

15. Ibid., 20.

16. Mrs. Brookes to B. P. Terrick, Jan. 24, 1765, SPG, vol. 2, ff. 25–26, LPL.

17. *Glimpses of the Monastery*, x.

18. James H. Lambert, "Brooke, John," DCBO, www.biographi.ca; McMullen, *An Odd Attempt in a Woman*, 74.

19. Brooke, *The History of Emily Montague* (1985), 241.

20. *SPG Journal*, vol. 15, 163–64, Meeting of Jan. 8, 1762, LPL.

21. Doll, *Revolution, Religion and National Identity*, 134.

22. Fulham Papers, vol. 1, f. 198, LPL.

23. A total of 398 girls passed through the Ursuline boarding school between its reopening in 1761 and 1780; 108 are listed as *Angloises. Pensionat*, 1/NG, 1, 1.2, AMUQ.

24. Ibid.; Trudel, *L'Église Canadienne*, 230; Fulham Papers, vol. 1, f. 108, LPL.

25. *Les Ursulines de Québec*, vols. 3–4, 40–41, AMUQ.

26. Ibid., 42–43.

27. Frances, *The Convent School of French Origin*, 38.

28. Joseph Cossette, "Coquart, Claude-Godefroy," DCBO, www.biographi.ca; Trudel, *L'Église Canadienne*, 230–32.

29. Trudel, *L'Église Canadienne*, 232.

30. Ibid., 239; *Affaires de Canada*, 1/N2, 1/N2, 2, 1/N2, 4, AMUQ.

31. *Glimpses of the Monastery*, 288.

32. Ibid., 292; *Les Ursulines de Québec*, vol. 3, 360, AMUQ.

33. *Rapport de l'archiviste de la province de Québec (Québec City, QC: Proulx, 1921–1922)*; Louis Antoine de Bougainville, *Mémoire de Bougainville sur l'etat de la Nouvelle-France a l'epoque de la guerre de Sept ans*, (Montréal, CA: P. Margry, 1867); *Glimpses of the Monastery*, 292; Isaac Weld, *Travels Through the States of North America and the Provinces of Upper and Lower Canada During the Years 1795, 1796 and 1797*, vol. 1 (London, UK: John Stockdale, 1799), 390.

34. *Les Ursulines de Québec,* vol. 3, 360, AMUQ.

35. *The Boston Post-Boy,* July 6, 1761.

36. Mary Wheelwright's will, Maine Probate Records, vol. 1, PCRM; *Les Ursulines de Québec,* vol. 2, 103, AMUQ; Trudel, *L'Église Canadienne,* vol. 2, 263; "Copie d'une letter de Soeur Wheelwright de l'Enfant Jésus, Religieuse Ursuline de Québec," AMUQ.

37. Baker, *True Stories of New England Captives,* 66.

38. James Otis letter, Jan. 25, 1765, *Proceedings of the Massachusetts Historical Society,* 2nd ser., vol. 43 (1909–1910).

39. Trudel, *L'Église Canadienne,* 234; Morse memoir, Sept. 3, 1978, GKRM, MHS, carton 5; Coleman, *New England Captives,* vol. 1, 433. Since Mary Moody died in Wells in 1759, Joshua Moody may have inherited the portrait from his mother.

40. Baker, *True Stories of New England Captives,* 68.

41. Mrs. Esther Mitchell Morse to Edmund March Wheelwright, 29 March, 1892, 'Wheelwright Family Papers, 1779–1975,' carton 5, MS. N-199, MHS.

42. Op cit. MS. N-199, MHS.

43. *Les Ursulines de Québec,* vol. 3, 79, AMUQ; Coleman, *New England Captives,* vol. 1, 433.

44. Kirby, *The Golden Dog,* 661.

45. *Affaires du Canada,* AMUQ, 1/N2, 3.1/N2, 5, vol. 6, AMUQ.

46. General James Murray to Frederick Haldimand, the military governor at Trois-Rivières, HMC, MSS 21732.

47. *Glimpses of the Monastery,* 20.

48. Vicaires généraux, January 17, 1761, vol. 8, G. 1–12, AAQ, V. G, v-8, G. 1–12.

49. Frank Murray Greenwood and Beverly Boissery, *Uncertain Justice: Canadian Women and Capital Punishment, 1754–1953* (Toronto, ON: Dundurn Press, 2000), 40–53; Luc Lacourcière, "Le Triple destin de Marie-Josephte Corriveau," in *Cahiers des dix,* 33 (1968), 213–42.

50. WO, 71/46, 309–314, National Archives, London.

51. Mgr. Briand to Mére Marie de l'Enfant Jesus, Québec, July 18, 1770, 'Copies

des letters, vol. Iii, f. 331, in *Rapport de l'archiviste de la Province de Québec pour 1929–1930*, (Québec City, QC : Proulx, 1930)

CHAPTER 24: A TROUBLED PEACE

1. *Livre des entrées et décédées*, 1/G1, 1, 1.1, 1647–1783, AMUQ.

2. *Proceedings of the Chakara Club*, vol. 11 (Montréal, QC, 1947), 216.

3. *Les Ursulines de Québec*, vols. 3–4, 46–47, AMUQ.

4. *Affaires du Canada*, vol. 6, 1/N2,3 and 1/N2,5, AMUQ.

5. *Livre des entrées et décédes*, 1/G1, 1,1.1, 1647–1783, AMUQ ; Jan Noel, 'Beseiged but Connected: Survival Strategies at a Québec Convent,' CCHA *Historical Studies*, 67, (2001), 27–41.

6. *Livres des entrées et décédées*, AMUQ.

7. AAQ, 81, CD, SS, Ursulines, vol. 1, 344–45.

8. *Les Ursulines de Québec*, vols. 3 to 4, 46–47, AMUQ.

9. André Vachon, "Briand, Jean-Olivier," DCBO, www.biographi.ca; Noel, "Beseiged but Connected," 35. Decisions about convent procedures (including constitutions, expansions, size of dowry, and attire) rested with the French Crown rather than the bishop.

10. Vicaires généraux, January 17, 1761, vol. 8, G. 1–12, (AAQ).

11. Coleman, *New England Captives*, vol. 1, 434; Baker, *True Stories of New England Captives*, 66.

12. *Glimpses of the Monastery*, 309; *Les Ursulines de Québec*, vols. 3–4, 363, AMUQ.

13. *Glimpses of the Monastery*, 301.

14. SS Ursulines, Mère Marie-Antoinette Poulin de St. François to Mgr. Briand, February 21, 1772, vol. 1, CD 81, AAQ.

15. SS Ursulines, Mère Marie-Elizabeth Richard de St. Augustin to Bishop Briand, March 7, 1772, vol. 1, 15, CD 81, AAQ.

16. Ibid., 16.

17. Ibid., 17.

18. Ibid.

19. Baldwin, *I Leap over the Wall*, 82; *Glimpses of the Monastery*, 309.

20. AAQ, 81, CD SS *Ursulines* vol. 1, 20.

21. Ibid., 19.

22. Ibid., 20.

23. *Affaires du Canada*, vol. 6, 1/N2,3 and 1/N2,5, AMUQ.

24. Auguste Gossselin, *L'Église après la Conquête, Québec, 1911–1913* (Québec City, QC: Laflamme, 1916–1917), vol. 1, 259; AAQ, 81, CD, SS, *Ursulines,* vol. 1, 20.

25. Actés Capitulaires, AMUQ, 1/E4 1, 1, 1, AMUQ.

26. Coleman, *New England Captives*, vol. 1, 434.

27. A. G. Bradley, *Lord Dorchester* (London, UK: T. C. and E. C. Jack, 1907), 309.

28. *Glimpses of the Monastery*, 312.

29. Ibid., 313.

30. *Les Ursulines de Québec*, vols. 3–4, 59–61, AMUQ.

31. *Glimpses of the Monastery*, 313.

32. Ibid., 312.

33. Curtis Fahey, "Colonel Benedict Arnold," DCBO, www.biographi.ca.

34. *Les Ursulines de Québec*, vols. 3–4, 216–17, AMUQ.

35. Gosselin, *L'Église après la Conquête,* vol. 2, 57–58.

36. *Glimpses of the Monastery*, 304–305.

37. Monique Roy-Sole, "Trois-Rivières: A Tale of Tenacity," *Canadian Geographic* (Ap. 2009), 85.

38. P. Wheelwright, *The Wheelwrights of Maine,* 34; "Wheelwright Families in Maine," *The Bangor Historical Magazine* 7 (Jan. 1894–Jan. 1895), 77, 79.

39. James MacPherson Le Moine, *Picturesque Québec: A Sequel to Past and Present* (Montréal, QC: Dawson, 1882), 127.

40. *Glimpses of the Monastery*, 304.

41. Ibid., 296; *Les Ursulines de Québec*, vol. 3, 281, AMUQ.

42. *Glimpses of the Monastery*, 307.

43. *Actes des Assemblées capital,* July 18, 1778, AMUQ.

44. Bourque, *Twelve Thousand Years,* 208.

45. *Les Ursulines de Québec,* vols. 3–4, 364, 154, AMUQ.

46. Ibid., 403–404; *Annales du Monastère,* vol. 1, 331, AMUQ.

47. Coleman, *New England Captives,* vol. 1, 434.

EPILOGUE: LEGACY AND REPUTATIONS

1. Edwin Newton Wheelwright to Gerald M. Kelly, June 21, 1955, carton 2, GKRM, MHS.

2. James Otis to George Johnstone et al., *Proceedings of the Massachusetts Historical Society,* 2nd ser., vol. 43 (1909–1910), 204–207.

3. *Les Ursulines de Québec,* vols. 3–4, 252, AMUQ.

SELECTED BIBLIOGRAPHY

ARCHIVES AND MANUSCRIPT COLLECTIONS

Archives de l'Archidiocèse de Québec, Québec.

Archives of L'École de Ste. Geneviève, Paris. Wisconsin Historical Society, Madison.

Archives de Monastére des Ursulines de Québec, Québec.

Archives Nationales de France, Paris.

Fulham Papers. Lambeth Palace Library, London.

Gratz Collection. Historical Society of Pennsylvania, Philadelphia.

Haldimand Manuscript Collection. The British Library, London.

Library and Archives Canada, Ottawa.

Maine Historical Society, Portland.

Massachusetts Archives Collection. Massachusetts State Archives, Boston.

National Archives, London.

Province and Court Records of Maine. County of York, Alfriston, Maine.

Records of the First Church of Christ (Congregational). Historical Society of Wells and Ogunquit, Wells, Maine.

Society for the Propagation of the Gospel Papers. Lambeth Palace Library, London.

War Office Papers. National Archives, London.

Wheelwright Family Papers. Massachusetts Historical Society, Boston.

PUBLISHED PRIMARY SOURCES

Anon. "Relation du siege de Québec en 1759." In *Memoires sur le Canada: Études sur l'instruction publique chez les Canadiens-français,* ser. 1, vol. 4. Edited by D. P. Myrand. Québec City, QC: J. T. Brousseau, 1873.

Atkinson, Theodore. "The Diary of Honorable Theodore Atkinson, Commissioner, from the Governor of New Hampshire to Canada 1724–25." In *Register of the Society of Colonial Wars in the State of New Hampshire.* Boston, 1907.

Brooke, Frances Moore. *The History of Emily Montague.* Ottawa, ON: Graphic Publishers, 1931.

———. *The History of Emily Montague.* Edited by Mary Edwards. Montréal, QC: Centre for Editing Early Canadian Texts, McGill-Queen's University Press, 1985.

The Calendar of State Papers Colonial, vol. 1. London, UK: Public Record Office, 1860.

Cérémonial des vêtures et des professions pour les religieuses de la congrégation des Ursulines de Québec. Paris, 1860.

Elliott, John Huxtable. *Empires of the World: Britain and Spain in America, 1492–1830.* New Haven, CT: Yale University Press, 2006.

Gyles, John. *Memoirs of Odd Adventures, Strange Deliverances.* Boston, MA: Massachusetts Historical Society, 1936.

Hamilton, Edward P., ed. "Nathaniel Wheelwright's Canadian Journey, 1753–4." *The Bulletin of the Fort Ticonderoga Museum* 10, no. 4 (Feb. 1960): 259–96.

Holmes de St. Croix, Mère Josephine. *Glimpses of the Monastery: Scenes from the History of the Ursulines of Québec During Two Hundred Years.* Québec City, QC: L. J. Demers et Frère, 1897.

Johnson, Susannah Willard. *A Narrative of the Captivity of Mrs. Johnson*. Windsor, VT: Alden Spooner, 1807.

"A Journal of the Negotiation Between the Marquis de Vaudreuil, etc." *NewEngland Historical and Genealogical Register* 5 (1848): 21–42.

Journals of the House of Representatives of Massachusetts, 1752, 1753, 1754. Boston, MA: Massachusetts Historical Society, 1968.

Kelly, Sister St. Dominic, trans. *Marie of the Incarnation (1599–1672)*. Solesmes, France: Abbé St. Pierre, 1971.

Knox, Captain John. *An Historical Journal of the Campaigns in North-America, for the Years 1757, 1758, 1759, and 1760: Containing the Most Remarkable Occurrences of That Period, Particularily the Two Sieges of Québec, etc., etc.* 2 vols. Toronto, ON: The Champlain Society, 1914.

Lahontan, Nicholas Greudeville. *Dialogues de Monsieur le Baron de Lahontan et d'un sauvage dans l'Amérique*. London, UK: A. Amsterdam, 1704.

The Letterbook of Reverend Henry Caner, 1728–1778. Bristol, UK: Special Collections Department, Bristol University Library, Microform Academic Publishers, n.d.

"Lettre circulaire du P. Vincent Bigot le 10e septembre 1720." *Canada Letters*, vol. 15, no. 6. Gerald M. Kelly Research Materials, Massachusetts Historical Society, Boston.

Mather, Cotton. *A Modest Inquiry into the Grounds and Occasions of a Late Pamphlet Entitled "A Memorial of the Present Deplorable State of New-England."* London, UK: S. Phipps, 1707.

The New London Summary (Mar. 7, 1760).

Otis, James. "Diary of James Otis." *Proceedings of the Massashcusetts Historical Society*, 2nd ser., vol. 43 (1909–10).

Proceedings of the Chakara Club, vol. 11. Montréal, QC, 1947.

Rapport de l'archiviste de la province de Québec. Québec City, QC: Proulx, 1920–.

Rapport de l'archiviste de la province de Québec. Québec City, QC: Proulx, 1921–1922.

Rapport de l'archiviste de la province de Québec. Québec City, QC: Proulx, 1930.

Records of the First Church of Christ (Congregational), Wells, Maine. *Proceedings of the New England Historical and Genealogical Society*, vol. LXXV (Jan. 1921): 42–56.

Reminiscences of the Last Fifty Years, 1839–1889. Québec City, QC: L. J. Demers and Frère, 1897.

Society for the Propagation of the Gospel in Foreign Parts, Report, vol. 15. London, 1762.

Thomas, M. Halsey, ed. *The Diary of Samuel Sewall 1674–1729*, vol. 1. New York, NY: Farrar, Straus and Giroux, 1973.

Thwaites, Reuben Gold, ed. *The Jesuit Relations and Allied Documents: Travels and Explorations of the Jesuit Missionaries in New France, 1610–1791*. 73 vols. Cleveland, OH: Burrow Brothers, 1896–1901.

Trueman, Stuart, ed. *The Ordeal of John Gyles: Being an Account of His Odd Adventures, Strange Deliverances, etc., as a Slave of the Maliseets*. Toronto, ON: McClelland and Stewart, 1969.

Les Ursulines de Québec depuis leur établissement jusqu'à nos jours. Québec City, QC: Des Presses de C. Darveau, 1878; 4 vols. 1866 (vols. 3–4), 1878, (vols. 1–2).

Weld, Isaac. *Travels Through the States of North America and the Provinces of Upper and Lower Canada During the Years 1795, 1796 and 1797*, vol. 1. London, UK: John Stockdale, 1799.

Williams, John. *The Redeemed Captive: Returning to Zion*. Bedford, MA: Applewood Books, 1853.

PUBLISHED SECONDARY SOURCES

Anderson, Fred. *Crucible of War: The Seven Years' War and the Fate of Empire in British North America, 1754–1766*. New York, NY: Knopf, 2000.

Anderson, Karen. *Chain Her by One Foot: The Subjugation of Women in Seventeenth-Century New France*. London, UK: Routlege, 1991.

Armstrong, Karen. *Through the Narrow Gate: A Nun's Story*. London, UK: Flamingo, 1997.

Axtell, James. *Natives and Newcomers: The Cultural Origins of North America.* Oxford, UK: Oxford University Press, 2001.

Baker, C. Alice. *True Stories of New England Captives Carried to Canada During the Old French and Indian Wars.* Bowie, MD: Heritage Books, 1990.

Baldwin, Monica. *I Leap over the Wall: Contrasts and Impressions After 28 Years in a Convent.* New York, NY: Rinehart and Co., 1951.

Barnard, John. "The Autobiography of the Reverend John Barnard." *Collections of the Massachusetts Historical Society,* vol. 5, 3rd ser. (1836) , 177–243.

Bilodeau, Christopher J. "Policing Wabankis Missions in the Seventeenth Century." In *Ethnographies and Exchanges: Native Americans, Moravians, and Catholics in Early North America.* Edited by A. G. Roeber. University Park, PA: Pennsylvania State University Press, 2008.

Blair, Louisa. *The Anglos: The Hidden Face of Québec City.* Vol. 1, *1608–1850.* Québec City, QC: Commission de la capitale nationale du Québec, 2005.

Boucher, François. *2000 Years of Fashion: The History of Costume and Personal Adornment.* New York, NY: H. M. Abrams, 1965.

Bourne, Edward E. *History of Wells and Kennebunk, Maine.* Bowie, MD: Heritage Books, 2002.

Bourque, Bruce. *Twelve Thousand Years: American Indians in Maine.* Lincoln, NE: University of Nebraska Press, 2001.

Bradley, A. G. *Lord Dorchester.* London, UK: T. C. and E. C. Jack, 1907.

Bray, R. S. *Armies of Pestilence: The Effects of Pandemics in History.* Cambridge, UK: James Clarke and Co., 1996.

Burt, Alfred Leroy. *The Old Province of Québec.* Toronto, ON: Ryerson Press, 1933.

Calvert, Mary. *Black Robe on the Kennebec.* Monmouth, NJ: Monmouth Press, 1991.

Clark, Emily. *Masterless Mistresses: The New Orleans Ursulines and the Development of a New World Society, 1727–1834.* Chapel Hill, NC: University of North Carolina Press, 2007.

Coleman, Emma Lewis. *New England Captives Carried to Canada Between 1677 and 1760 During the French and Indian Wars.* 2 vols. Westminster, MD: Heritage Books, 2004.

Daviault, Pierre. Le Baron de Saint-Castin, chef Abenakis (Montréal, QC : Royal Society of Canada, 1939.

de Charlevoix, Pierre-François-Xavier, ed. *History and General Description of New France,* 2 vols. Translated by John Gilray Shea. Chicago, IL: Loyola University Press, 1962.

Dêlage, Denys. *Bitter Feast: Amerindians and Europeans in Northeastern North America, 1600–64.* Vancouver, BC: UBC Press, 1994.

Demos, John. *The Unredeemed Captive: A Family Story from Early America.* New York, NY: Knopf, 1994.

Doll, Peter. *Revolution, Religion and National Identity: Imperial Anglicanism in British North America.* London, UK: Associated University Press, 2000.

Douville, Raymond, and Jacques Casanova. *Daily Life in Early Canada.* 12 vols. London, UK: Allen and Unwin, 1968.

Earle, Alice Morse. *Home Life in the Colonial Days.* London, UK: Macmillan, 1898.

———. *The Sabbath in Puritan New England.* London, UK: Hodder and Stoughton, 1892.

Evangelisti, Silvia. *Nuns: A History of Convent Life.* Oxford, UK: Oxford University Press, 2007.

Foster, William Henry. *The Captor's Narrative: Catholic Women and Their Puritan Men on the Early American Frontier.* Ithaca, NY: Cornell University Press, 2003.

Frances, Sister Catherine. *The Convent School of French Origin in the United States 1727–1843.* Philadelphia, PA: Sisters of St. Joseph, 1936.

Francis, Convers. *The Life of Sebastian Rale.* Boston, MA: Little Brown, 1849.

Gosselin, Auguste. *L'Église après la Conquête, Québec,* vols. 1 and 2. Québec City, QC: Laflamme et Proulx, 1916–1917.

Gourdeau, Claire. *Les Délices de nos coeurs: Marie de l'Incarnation et ses pensionnaires amérindiennes, 1639–1672.* Sillery, France: Éditions du Septentrion, 1994.

Greenwood, Frank Murray, and Beverly Boissery. *Uncertain Justice: Canadian Women and Capital Punishment, 1754–1953.* Toronto, ON: Dundurn Press, 2000.

Haefeli, Evan, and Kevin Sweeney. *Captors and Captives: The 1704 French and Indian Raid on Deerfield.* Boston, MA: University of Massachusetts Press, 2003.

Hamilton, Edward P. "Robert Hewes and the Frenchman: A Case of Treason?" *American Antiquarian Society* (Oct. 1958): 195–210.

Heard, John, Jr. *John Wheelwright: 1592–1679.* Cambridge, MA: The Riverside Press, 1930.

Hubbard, Jeremiah, and Jonathan Greenleaf. "An Account of Wells." *Collections of the Maine Historical Society* 1 (1865): 336–92.

Johnson, Paul. *A History of the American People.* London, UK: HarperPerennial, 1997.

Kirby, William. *The Golden Dog: A Legend of Québec.* Montréal, QC: Lovell, Adam, Wesson, 1877.

Kuhns, Elizabeth. *The Habit: A History of the Clothing of Catholic Nuns.* New York, NY: Doubleday, 2003.

Lacourcière, Luc. "Le Triple destin de Marie-Josephte Corriveau." *Cahiers des dix,* 33 (1968): 213–42.

LaPlante, Eve. *American Jezebel: The Uncommon Life of Anne Hutchinson, the Woman Who Defied the Puritans.* San Francisco, CA: HarperSanFrancisco, 2004.

Le Moine, James MacPherson. *Maple Leaves: Canadian History and Québec Scenery.* Québec City, QC: Hunter, Rose and Co., 1865.

———. *Picturesque Québec: A Sequel to Past and Present.* Montréal, QC: Dawson, 1882.

Lenkin, Edward J. *Picture Rocks: American Indian Rock Art in the Northeast Woodlands.* Lebanon, NH: University Press of New England, 2002.

Little, Ann M. *Abraham in Arms: War and Gender in Colonial New England.* Philadelphia, PA: University of Pennsylvania Press, 2007.

Magnuson, Roger. *Éducation in New France*. Montréal, QC: McGill-Queen's University Press, 1992.

Marble, Allan Everett. *Surgeons, Smallpox and the Poor: A History of Medicine and Social Conditions in Nova Scotia, 1749–1799*. Montréal, QC: McGill University Press, 1993.

McBride, Bunny. *Women of the Dawn*. Lincoln, NE: University of Nebraska Press, 1999.

McMullen, Lorraine. *An Odd Attempt in a Woman: The Literary Life of Frances Brooke*. Vancouver, BC: University of British Columbia Press, 1983.

Miquelon, Dale. *New France, 1701–1744*. Toronto, ON: McClelland and Stewart, 1987.

Morgan, Henry J. *Sketches of Celebrated Canadians and Persons Connected with Canada*. Montréal, QC: R. Worthington, 1865.

Morrison, Kenneth M. *The Solidarity of Kin: Ethnohistory, Religious Studies and the Algonkian–French Religious Encounter*. New York, NY: State University of New York, 2002.

Neatby, Hilda. *Québec: The Revolutionary Age, 1760–1791*. Toronto, ON: McClelland and Stewart, 1966.

Noel, Jan. "Besieged but Connected: Survival Strategies at a Québec Convent." *Historical Studies* 65 (2001): 27–41.

———. "Women of the New France Noblesse." In *Women and Freedom in Early America*. Edited by Larry D. Eldridge. New York, NY: New York University Press, 1997.

Parkman, Francis. *A Half Century of Conflict*. Boston, MA: Little Brown and Company, 1893.

———. *Montcalm and Wolfe: The Riveting Story of the Heroes of the French and Indian War*. New York, NY: Random House, 1999.

Rapley, Elizabeth. *A Social History of the Cloister: Daily Life in the Teaching Monasteries of the Old Regime*. Montréal, QC: McGill Queen's University Press, 2001.

Reid, Claire G., and Micheline V. Demers. "Les Ursulines et la Musique." *Cap-aux-Diamants* (Summer 1989): 21–24.

Roy-Sole, Monique. "Trois-Rivières: A Tale of Tenacity." *Canadian Geographic* (Apr. 2009): 85.

Schultz, Nancy Lusignan. *Fire and Roses: The Burning of the Charlestown Convent, 1834.* New York, NY: The Free Press, 2000.

Schuyler, Reverend Henry. "The Apostle of the Abenakis." *The Catholic Historical Review*, ser. 1 (1910): 164–74.

Shelley, Hope Moody. *My Name Is Wells, I Am the Town: A History of the Town of Wells, Maine, on the Occasion of Its 350th Anniversary of Incorporation.* Wells, ME: Penobscot Press, 2002.

Sluhovsky, Moshe. "The Devil in the Convent." *The American Historical Review* 107, no. 5 (Dec. 2002): 1–52.

Sparks, Jared. *Lives of John Ribault, Sebastian Rale and William Palfrey.* Boston, MA: Charles C. Little and James Brown, 1845.

Speck, Frank G. *Penobscot Man: The Life History of a Forest Tribe in Maine.* Philadelphia, PA: University of Pennsylvania Press, 1940.

Taylor, Alan. *American Colonies: The Settling of North America.* London, UK: Penguin Books, 2001.

Trudel, Marcel. *L'Église Canadienne sous le régime militaire,* vol. 2, *1759–1764.* Québec City, QC: Les Presses de l'Université Laval, 1957.

Les Ursulines: 350 ans d'éducation au Québec. Québec City, QC: Ursulines de Québec, 1989.

Wheelwright, Edmund March. *A Frontier Family, Part 1.* Cambridge, MA: The Colonial Society of Massachusetts, 1894.

Wiesner, Frederick Bernays. *Civilians Under Military Justice: The British Practice Since 1689, Especially in North America.* Chicago, IL: University of Chicago Press, 1967.

Winship, Michael P. *The Times and Trials of Anne Hutchinson: Puritans Divided.* Lawrence, KS: University of Kansas Press, 2005.

Wiseman, Frederick Matthew. *The Voice of the Dawn: An Autohistory of the Abenaki Nation.* Hanover, NH: University of New England, 2001.

Austen, Barbara. "'Captured . . . Never Came Back': Social Networks Among New England Female Captives in Canada, 1689–1763." *New England/New France 1600–1850.* Annual Proceedings of the Dublin Seminar for New England Folklife, Boston, MA, July 15–16, 1989, 28–38.

Côte, Patrick. "Creation." Abenaki Museum, Odanak, QC, n.d.

Kelly, Gerald M. "Thy Hand Shall Lead Me: The Story of Esther Wheelwright." Gerald M. Kelly Research Materials, Massachusetts Historical Society, Boston.

Nash, Alice. "The Abiding Frontier: Family, Gender and Religion in Wabanakis History, 1600–1763." Ph.D. diss, Columbia University, 1997.

———. "Mary Accept This Wampum Forever: Gender and Wabanakis Catholicism." Annual Conference of the Institute of Early American History and Culture First, Ann Arbor, MI, June 4, 1995.

Wheelwright, Peter M. "A Frontier Family, Part 2: The Wheelwrights of Maine," unpublished manuscript, 2008.

ILLUSTRATION CREDITS

1. Artist and date unknown

2. Collections of Maine Historical Society, # 12486/1700. Reproduction rights reserved by Mason P. Smith

3. Collections of Maine Historical Society, # 12475/1745. Reproduction rights reserved by Mason P. Smith

4. Chris Cloutier, 1979. Historical Society of Wells and Ogunquit

5. Artist and date unknown. Archives de la Ville de Montréal, BM7, S2SS1

6. Hibbert N. Binney, c. 1791. History Collection, Nova Scotia Museum

7. Library and Archives Canada, NMC 000-4901

8. James Peachey, 1785. Library and Archives Canada, C-150742

9. Eugene Detromile, 1856. Collections of Maine Historical Society, # 7530

10. Richard Short, 1761. Library and Archives Canada, C-0003358

11. Richard Short, 1761. Library and Archives Canada, C-000354

12. Artist unknown, c. 1760. Archives de Monastére des Ursulines de Québec

13. Artist unknown, c. 1763. Bridgeman Art Library, with permission of the Massachusetts Historical Society

14. Attributed to John Singleton Copley, date unknown. Massachusetts Historical Society

15. Courtesy of the Archives du Monastére des Ursulines de Québec

16. Courtesy of the Archives du Monastére des Ursulines de Québec
17. Courtesy of the Archives du Monastére des Ursulines de Québec

Esther's funding, 98, 105–6, 116,
    128–29, 189
Esther's provisional baptism, 85
Esther's testimony to him, 40, 41,
    50–51, 56, 77
Esther's *vêture*, 112, 141, 142,
    144–46, 149, 189, 245
first Canadian mission, 74
ill-health, 105
Jesuit superior general of New
    France, 40, 74, 75, 105, 126
Marie-Anne Davis, 81, 82, 103
mission of, 74, 82, 97, 116
negotiations for Esther's release,
    83, 86
peace speeds up his recall to France,
    155
personality, 74, 81
plans for Esther's future, 78, 82, 87,
    102
procurator of the Canadian
    missions in France, 126, 149
rumour of Esther's child "with an
    Indian," 112–13, 184, 185
story presented to Esther, 64
successful conversion of several
    English girls, 81, 92
Bigot, François, 195
Billy, Marie Madelene, 208
Bilsby, Lincolnshire, 16
Blackpoint, Maine, 43
Bombazee Rips, 46, 73
Bombazeen (a sagamore), 168–69
Boston, Massachusetts, 7, 42
    asked for help after the Wells raid 51
    Esther's merchant brother John
        settles in, 120
    John Wheelwright exiled from, 16–17
    John Wheelwright flees from
        Lincolnshire to (1636), 11, 15, 16

John Wheelwright requests an
    armed guard, 34
Nathaniel's financial scandal, 267–68
Ned Wheelwright Boston's first city
    architect, 11
sends half a company of dragoons
    to Wells, 52
Wheelwrights become important
    merchants in, 182
Boston Fire Department, 11
Boston Police Station, 11
Botte, Catherine, 236
Bouat, Marguerite, 123
Boucherville, 124
Bourchemin, Margaret, 103–4
Bourges, France, 74
Bourne, Edward, 17, 20, 80, 180
Bowden, Richard, 271
Brand, Orso B., 225
Bray, R.S., 184
Break Neck Hill (Wells, Maine), 39
Briand, Bishop Jean-Olivier, 211, 214,
    229, 242, 250, 252–58
Briggs, Mrs. Lloyd Vernon (née
    Wheelwright), 226
Britain
    at war with France (seventeenth
        century), 19
    Battle of Québec, 207, 208, 211–15
    cattle and sheep as symbols of
        English colonialism, 38
    end of Queen Anne's War, 129, 155
    King George's War, 179, 187
    War of the Spanish Succession, 36
Brooke, Frances Moore, 231–35, 236, 256
    The History of Emily Montague,
        231–35, 259
Brooke, James, 236
Brooke, Reverend John, 219, 231,
    234–35, 236

de Berman, Claude-Antoine, 123
de Couagne, François-Marie, 195
de Glapion, Father Augustin-Louis, 243, 253
de la Colombière, Joseph, vicar general of Québec, 171
de la Fontaine, Marie-Josephte, 237
de la Peltrie, Madeleine, 98
de Muy, Charlotte, 176
de Muy, Nicolas Daneau, 176
de Muy de St. Helen, Mother Charlotte, 214–15
De Noyon, Jacques, 123
De Noyons, Dorothée (née Stebbins), 123, 126
de Ramezay, Catherine, 124–25, 176, 210
de Ramezay, Claude, 124–25
de Ramezay, Lieutenant Jean-Baptiste-Nicolas-Roche, 213
Dead River, 73
Deerfield, Massachusetts, 111, 112, 123, 128
Dêlage, Denys, 161–64
Demos, John, 111, 112, 183
   An Unredeemed Captive, 111
Denoiselle, M. (mayor of Trois-Rivieres), 193
des Roches de Ste. Angèle, Sister, 254
Deslandres, Dominique, 270–71
Dickens, Charles, 89
Dictionary of Canadian Biography, 110
Dodier, Louis, 242, 243
Dodier, Marie-Josephte, 242, 243
Downing, Joshua, 127
dowry (*dot*), 82, 103, 105, 116, 128–29, 140, 141, 219, 250, 268–69
du Fort, Madeline, 104

Dubreil de Pontbriand, Bishop Henri-Marie, 211, 214, 230
Dudley, Governor Joseph, 71, 81, 86, 107
   1703 raids, 42
   dispatches half a company of dragoons to Wells, 52
   Esther's father demands that Vaudreuil return his daughter, 78–79
   Lieutenant Williams's expedition to Québec, 126
   peace talks with Abenaki sachems in Casco (1702), 34, 38
   puts pressure on Vaudreuil to return captives, 85, 105
   reports of his planning an attack on Québec, 119–20
Duke, Timothy, Chester Herald, 269–70
Dummer, Reverend Shubael, 21
Duquesne, Marquis, 190–91, 199

Earle, Alice Morse, 57
Edgeremet (a sachem), 22
Elizabeth I, Queen, 33
Emery, Reverend Samuel, 24, 122–23
England, *see* Britain
English Civil War (1642–1651), 18
Esther, Queen, 145
Exeter, New Hampshire, 17

Farnsworth, Matthias III, 270
Feast of St. Ursula (October 21), 106
First Church of Christ (Congregational), 23, 29, 59
Fort Ticonderoga, 260
France
   at war with England (seventeenth century), 19